Praise for

Pouf is a masterfully written story of love overcoming all obstacles—even the obstacles of Alzheimer's. Heartwarming yet heartbreaking, vulnerable yet brave, Pouf will touch your soul and change your life as you walk this journey alongside Monica and her father.
~Angela Magnan Wiechmann

Pouf is an invaluable resource and guide for caregivers. It is a loving story that addresses the personal needs and emotions to help the reader understand the challenges of Alzheimer's.
~Ann Aubitz

A heartwarming and heart-wrenching account of a loving daughter and the arduous journey endured watching her father go through the cruel and invasive progression of the mind degenerative and plundering disease of Alzheimer's.

Her steadfast love, devotion and caring through this journey, together with her husband's unwavering support, show not only the depth of her love but additionally, how the person affected by Alzheimer's benefitted from that affection, bringing her father many moments of lucidity and happiness in his last years. You'll find yourself smiling and laughing as the author shares her experiences with her father and his colleagues. But, be ready to cry at the last chapter as the reality of "Pouf" shows its face.

Great reading for persons going through the same path!
~ Gracie Rayburn

Pouf

Renee —
I envie you so
much it's our
book club!
I'm glad you
enjoyed it. Niecie
Monica

A True Story about Love, Life, and Alzheimer's

Pouf

Monica Vierling Hall

Printed in the United States of America

First Edition

ISBN: 978-1-946195-79-1

Library of Congress Control Number: 2020912744

Cover Design & Interior Book Design: Ann Aubitz
Edited by: Angela Magnan Wiechmann

Published by FuzionPress
1250 E 115th Street, Burnsville, MN 55337

To God—my Holy Father, the Giver of Assignments
To all Alzheimer's hostages and their families

pouf (noun): a cloud or whiff of smoke, often caused by a sudden disappearance.

Pouf, he was gone.

Preface

An Assignment

In the beginning, I was given an assignment.

For years, I had merely puttered at writing. Strung interesting words together. Heard something that tickled my ear and quickly wrote it on a notecard before it fleetingly escaped me. I had no direction, yet I thought maybe someday something would pull together.

Then one night I had a dream. I was in a noisy classroom. A voice, which was clearly in charge, extricated itself from the others and boomed out forcefully, "Your assignment is to write!"

I bolted awake and found myself standing at attention in my mind.

It was God. How did I know, you ask? Your entire being recognizes God's Voice when you hear it. Your ears and heart just need to be open to hear Him.

After receiving the assignment, I began to write with more purpose. I knew I was writing a book, yet I was still unsure of my direction. I searched for a path I could more easily follow.

Meanwhile, my sweet, sweet dad took a fall and broke his hip. His already noticeable dementia nosedived, and he landed in Alzheimer's disease. He would never recover.

After his rehabilitation for his hip, he went directly into a memory care unit. There, we found that dementia and Alzheimer's play no favorites. We rubbed shoulders with schoolteachers, artists, a gynecologist, an aeronautical engineer, and a Raspberry Queen. Each person succumbed to the disease, with their brain disappearing.

It's a terrible thing to witness. It will drop you to your knees. Yet we also discovered an unexpected tenderness in our moments of connection with these residents, whom I will hold close to my heart for the rest of my life.

We visited Dad and the others three times a week, staying at least an hour each visit. I would hear delightful snatches of conversation during these visits, so I began to take notes on scraps I found at the bottom of my purse—old receipts, coupons, anything resembling paper.

Later, I shared some of these notes with my son Trent—words Grandpa had said that he might find amusing or even take comfort in. When Trent saw me rut through my purse to find a certain scrap of choice words, he bought me a small journal that would fit in my purse, so I could keep everything together. A record of sorts.

Time passed. Even though I was still taking notes in my journal at the care center, I stopped working on my book. I still didn't have a clear-cut direction. My mind would "write" throughout the day, but I struggled with how to put the pieces together.

One night, lying in bed, I found myself thinking about two separate ideas for my book.

I knew the core of my book would be the valuable time I spent with my dad at the memory care unit, where I captured the magic of his words. My journal was filling with snippets and pearls. Some were delightful and hilarious. Others were thought-provoking and poetic.

I also knew I wanted to intersperse that with flashbacks of my own childhood memories. I tried to figure out how I could possibly merge these very different aspects into one. In my finite capabilities, I was making a mess of it.

"I will guide you," the Voice said.

And He did.

Picking up where I had left off, I eagerly wrote. Pages after pages. Everything led by the Holy Spirit. I could not have done it alone.

This went on for a period. I was making headway. My writing became more focused. I still wondered about how to merge those two ideas. I believed the answer would come in time, but I wasn't seeing it happen soon enough. I lost the flow of the book but continued to take notes in my little journal at the memory center. I went on to fill three such journals.

And then my sweet dad passed away.

I lost all desire to write. It was too painful. Months went by with just a few half-hearted attempts.

In my youth, I had always been a dedicated, conscientious student, so I was quite distressed when I found myself immersed in a dream forty-five years later where I was cutting class, missing lectures, and not submitting my homework. Professors were frowning and whispering behind their hands to each other, casting disparaging looks in my direction. Classmates were tut-tutting and pointing.

Again, the Voice: "You are not doing your assignment."

I was startled awake.

God will do what it takes to get your attention. He got mine.

What you are about to read is what came out of that assignment. And the Voice did just as He said He would. He guided me in the merging of both my dad's daily living and my own growing-up years.

It is based on truth. Most, if not all, of the dialogue from the memory care unit is taken from my journals.

Prologue

This moment, I'm thinking how quiet it is. I can hear the birds twittering, the peeps of something younger, the caws of the lone crow circling above. I hate that crow.

Only if I strain my ears and concentrate, I hear what most people would hear immediately: the steady traffic roar that slides by the south side of our home. Trucks. A blast of a horn as an annoyed driver takes out his frustration. A distant siren. To others, these are intrusive sounds. I have learned to block them out.

This moment, I'm listening to the birds as they perform. I'm their audience.

Puff and Tigger, the two cats, have decided to join me. They're safe in the screened-in patio. At least the hawks won't snatch them, or they won't get flattened by the traffic that streams on the street to the west. My parents lost many dogs on that stretch of road.

Dogs and a son. Something they never did come to terms with—Stevie.

Stevie shows us his science project, explaining how the balloons lipped over the bottles expand with various gases that have formed inside the bottles. Proud. I take his picture with my camera.

A week later, I graduate. The three of us—Greg, Stevie, and I—are standing outside on the top step by the front door. Stevie reaches for the graduation cap perched on my head. I brush away his hand, too concerned about getting my hair messed up. Another picture is taken.

These are the last pictures to be taken of Stevie. His picture days are over.

How were we to know?

There's that crow, now strutting underneath the apple tree.

"Go find a friend," I mutter.

Table of Contents

Chapter One

And So It Begins

October 13, 2013

"Give me back my dad!" I hiss. The words come through barred teeth and are choked out of a pinched throat in the stranglehold of utter despair.

It is postsurgery, and we're at St. Gertrude's Health and Rehabilitation Center. I unconsciously mop at tears with my shaking hands—my heart is coursing down my face. The ground shifts beneath my feet. I want to keep my composure for Dad, who is seated in a wheelchair a mere four feet from me, a confused look on his tired, wrinkled face. I'm losing the battle. He looks so forlorn as he sits in that chair.

How did he get so small? It makes me cry all the more.

When I was a young girl, he was Daddy. And he seemed a giant. But he was never a big man. I felt so smug when I was taller than him when I reached five seven. What he didn't have in stature, he made up for in his wisdom and in his being as "Daddy." But now he looks so small, so frail, so lost.

Dad furrows an eyebrow, wondering what is causing his daughter so much distress. He is an innocent. He has no idea his dementia took a nosedive because of the anesthesia he received during his hip surgery. I will later learn that people with dementia or memory loss may experience further cognitive decline after a surgery with general anesthesia. The risks depend on the type of anesthesia used. It's an ugly, ugly side effect for which I wasn't prepared.

I avoid meeting Dad's eyes. I don't want him to see the shattered truth in mine. I turn my back to him to hide my face, knowing full well that my heaving shoulders are giving me away. I continually swipe at the stream of heartbreak running from my eyes.

Suddenly, I'm in a time warp. A slideshow with sixty years of memories flashes forward through not only my mind but also my entire being. My heart has catapulted; I am free-falling. Every thought is shoved out by the next as they tumble over one another.

Chapter Two

Get Back in Your Own Yard

It was 1959. I was four years old. Ours was an old brick house, the first house my great-grandparents lived in when they came over from the old country. The "homeplace," as we fondly referred to it years later.

It was built in the 1800s with no running water. We pumped our water from the well in the backyard. I liked how the water would gurgle and sputter as we kept pumping, then it would choke out its first trickle, working its way to a fervent gush.

Buckets of water spumed forth from that pump every Saturday because it was bath night. Mom wiped her brow after dozens of pumps. She would then heat each bucket on the stove, one after another. After a full day of dirty play, we were stripped of our filthy clothes and placed in an enormous metal tub filled with heated water in the middle of the old farmhouse kitchen. She would hand us a bar of soap. The cleanest of us would bathe first. The rest followed in the same water.

When pumping water on Sunday mornings, I'd stand back from the splash. I didn't want it to hit my patent leather shoes, which Mom had Vaselined the night before so they would shine for church.

Our brick farmhouse was on the left of a long gravel road that made a T at the end. There was a white two-story house on the right. That family had a half dozen kids, with half of them running around outside in diapers amidst the chickens that would peck their way into our yard until Dad sent them squawking.

"Get back in your own yard," Dad would mutter at the chickens as he turned back to the house, toying with a long piece of grass in his mouth.

When he was really irritated, he'd get a shotgun and shoot up in the air. The chickens would leap, flap their wings, squawk, and scurry with their short, spindly legs back to their own yard.

◆ ◆ ◆

Another memory tumbles forward.

The crunch and spit of gravel announced a car approaching along the long dusty road traveling south from town.

"Monica, look who's coming," Mom said as she continued stirring the gravy for the night's meal.

A smile burst deep inside. Standing on tippy toes, I hurriedly finished placing the silverware on the sides of each plate exactly as I had been shown many times before. Letting the wooden screen door slam behind me, I skipped to the side of the driveway and watched the dust billowing behind the car as it neared our home.

"Daddy! Daddy!" I waved as he got closer. Almost home. "Daddy!"

He smiled at me through his partially opened window as he let the car roll to a stop.

"That's my girl!" he said with his wink.

◆ ◆ ◆

I was five years old when we moved to town.

It was a new house in a neighborhood of ramblers. There were actual people and kids instead of chickens. We had running water. Fields separated our neighborhood from other neighborhoods, while banks of trees separated the farmers' fields.

It was a friendly neighborhood with lots of activity. Dads were out mowing lawns. Moms were out hanging laundry on the lines. Kids were out playing catch or riding bikes with laughter rippling the air.

I sat cross-legged on our gravel driveway, picking at small rocks—learned behavior from the chickens. With all my five-year-old might, I willed for someone to come by and ask me to be their friend.

I was painfully shy. I had never had playmates or much exposure to other kids my age. As much as I longed to be part of the group, I *needed* them to invite me.

I couldn't bring myself to be assertive and ask them if I could join in. What if they said no? I'd rather just sit there. I'd rather *die*. And whenever someone did stop to talk to me, I found myself so tongue-tied that all I could do was mutter my name and continue picking at the gravel.

Day by day, month by month, year by year, I eventually eased my way into the makings of the neighborhood. I went over to Candy Torberg's house, and we pretended we were Barbie and a friend going out on a date with Ken and a friend.

I also played marbles with the neighborhood kids. I used the same marbles Dad had used as a kid. Terry Hogan, the boy at the other end of our street, conned me out of a few prized purees—especially the shooters.

Sometimes after supper, Dad would hit the ball in the backyard, and my brothers and I would chase the ball down. One time, the ball clipped a newly planted sapling and sent its canopy sailing. All that was left was the stick trunk. Even Dad laughed. He had an amazing laugh. All was right with the world when you heard it.

We'd play Frozen Tag (other neighborhoods called it Freeze Tag, but it was Frozen Tag for us), Annie Annie Over, and Twelve O'Clock the Ghost Comes Out with all the neighborhood kids. There'd be a dozen of us on those dark, warm summer nights. It was safe. Parents knew where their children were.

Other times I would sit on the front step right after supper with a book perched on my lap. I'd read and read and read until the sun would set and the mosquitoes and june bugs would come out.

Every month, Mom would take me to Lavender Lady to get our hair cut. Ronnie Schesso, a police officer, also cut hair. I didn't like his haircuts.

I remember pinching back tears as I caught a glimpse of myself in the mirror after one of Ronnie's cuts. Mamie Eisenhower bangs. Again. I made a quick escape outside so the tears could freely fall.

Once home, I put on a triangular scarf and tied it with the two long ties under my chin.

"I am not taking this off until my hair grows!" I announced.

I let the door slam before running off to Nanny Mile's house to play on her swing set and in her sandbox.

I remember how I wanted a brown-haired Chatty Cathy but instead received a blond one from Santa.

And how Mom sewed so many beautiful dresses for me. She even hand-smocked the bodices.

And how Mom went on to make clothes for my Barbie, including a turquoise cable-knit bathrobe.

◆ ◆ ◆

There's a giant jump in the slideshow of memories.

I remember how I never learned discernment in my love relationships. (There should be a class on this.) Nothing had face value for me. For the losers,

I looked for something positive to hang on to. For the successful, I looked for their flaws. I was never swept off my feet by them. No matter how handsome or svelte.

I thought my choices consisted of those who liked me, not those whom I liked. If three boys (each with an undesirable character trait) liked me . . . well, those were my choices. Pick the best from the worst. (Not that they were *all* undesirable. Some were amazing. But then, I looked for their flaws.)

Somewhere, I should have been told the whole world was my choice. Whom did I, personally, want? Not just who wanted me. I should have been told to find someone like my dad, someone rock solid yet gentle. Caring. Loving. Selfless.

Shattered—A Mug and a Hip

Time warps again, sending me free-falling into other memories. Much more recent memories. From just a few weeks ago . . .

Early Fall 2013

Oreos were his favorite. He would eat a whole pack of them in a few days. He'd twist them apart, scrape the dark chocolate wafer clean with his two front teeth, look up at you, and grin. Then he'd dip each wafer in his coffee to soften it just a bit before popping it in his mouth.

Once, at a garage sale, I spotted a mug. It was white and tapered down to the base. It had a practical handle. Two inches from the top was a raised logo saying OREO in white letters set into a sky-blue oval.

I scooped it up and cradled it to my chest. (Why do we do this at garage sales? Do we fear someone else will snatch our "find" right out of our hands? Did I think someone else had a dad who loved Oreos?) Protecting the mug, I stood in line with my quarter.

It became known as "Dad's mug." Every time he'd come over for dinner, we'd reach into the cupboard for the mug, fill it with coffee, and hand it to him along with some milk in a creamer. He'd pour in a smidge of milk, bring his mouth close to the steaming brew, then blow, flapping his lips. We'd laugh. His eyebrow would lift as he'd look our way. It was the same performance and the same audience appeal for years.

After one of Dad's last visits to our house, someone opened the kitchen cupboard where Dad's mug sat atop of a tower of other mugs. Dad's mug teetered, fell to the floor, and shattered.

Shards slipped into unreachable corners.

◆ ◆ ◆

Not long later, Trent called one morning to alert us that Dad wasn't answering his phone.

"Mom," Trent said, "I think you need to walk over there to check things out."

My heart stopped.

"Halsey, come with me—please," I begged my husband.

We walked to Dad's house, right next to ours, dreading what we might find. As we entered through the garage door, we heard moaning from the kitchen. We found Dad lying on the floor, twisted in an unnatural way, near the kitchen sink. Baxter, his dog, hung back.

Halsey and I were quick to realize that the two of us could not manage Dad by ourselves, so we called Trent. The three of us were able to lift Dad without adding unnecessary weight-bearing on his one side. We carefully got him in the car.

Why didn't we call the ambulance? I have no idea.

To the emergency room we went. We soon found out he had broken his hip. They scheduled an open reduction surgery, a procedure to fix a severe bone fracture or break.

The surgery itself went fine. They put three screws into his hip and were able to fasten things together. The hip will heal.

But his mind will never recover.

Determined to Escape

October 14, 2013

We're back at St. Gert's, where Dad was sent after his surgery. We're discussing how he'll receive physical and occupational therapy in preparation for, presumably, his transition back to living at home.

But he doesn't seem to remember much about anything. Not even the fact that he has a home. *Home* has been obliterated from his memory.

Also, conversations with him have radically changed. Before the surgery, there were paragraphs, stories, exchanges. They didn't always make sense, but at least we had them. Now we have snippets. No story. Just phrases.

In time, that will become OK—we'll take whatever we can get.

We visit Dad every day at the rehab center, searching for any fragment of conversation that gives us hope. Something, anything to grab and clasp with all our might. Never to let go.

I make notes.

October 16, 2013

Dad lost his balance and fell today on his way to the bathroom. The staff at St. Gert's didn't see it happen because his room has walls facing the central common room.

His vitals are fine. They will follow up with an X-ray and CT.

They are moving him to room 2207, which has glass windows, so the staff can see when he tries to get up on his own. Hopefully this will curtail another fall.

Despite the fall, he does have some good humor. I've taken to writing down the nuggets that warm my heart. Snatches of words that show that Dad is still "in there." His sense of humor, his tenderness, his mischievousness, his strength—I grab it all.

◆ ◆ ◆

Us: "How do you feel, Dad?"
Dad: "Nothing hurts anymore. A good laugh feels good."

◆ ◆ ◆

Staff members tell us that Dad tried to escape twice. I'm reminded of the promise he wrenched from me a year ago . . .

"Monica," he said, "promise me you'll never put me in a nursing home. *Promise* me. Because I will escape," he warned. "If I have one piece of muscle and just a bit of brain, I *will* escape."

He then proceeded to tell me how I had a great-aunt who had been put into a nursing home. She didn't want to be there. So she escaped in the middle of the night in the dead of winter, barefoot and clad in only her nightie. Dad was proud of this story—as if it epitomized the strength of his German family.

"But Dad," I said, "didn't she catch pneumonia that night and eventually die from it?"

He let this comment pass, choosing instead to punctuate the point that it was in his genes to escape.

And now I see it is.

◆ ◆ ◆

It's time to eat lunch.

"OK, Dad—it's time to eat."

"I forgot how," he says.

We reach over to help him. At the same time, a nice-looking nurse comes over to get him ready for physical therapy.

"No," he tells us. "*She'll* help me."

◆ ◆ ◆

He's bothered by the IV tube.

"I have a pinch in my arm."

"Yes, you have a needle sticking in your arm," the nurse responds.

"A *noodle?*"

◆ ◆ ◆

The social worker comes to visit. "I bet you don't want to be here," she says.

Dad says, "I ain't got anything against you people."

◆ ◆ ◆

"I ain't gonna drink anymore—and I never drank that much to begin with," Dad says. "Very little, actually."

He's right. Maybe he'd have a can of beer after mowing the lawn, but really nothing aside from that.

Of course, there are stories of his drinking escapades back when he was a "young buck" sixty-some years ago.

Still, I find it odd that thoughts of drinking would even pull their way up as we sit here now with him at St. Gert's.

◆ ◆ ◆

Bob, the Eucharistic minister who serves shut-ins and the incapacitated, comes to administer Communion.

He reminds Dad that Dad fixed his antique clock two years ago.

"Yep, now it doesn't work anymore," Bob teases.

"Oh?" Dad's concerned. He stands fully behind his clock-repair work.

It's nice to see he's still conscientious about that. A little shred of hope, and I make a note of it.

Then Bob starts telling humorous stories. One about his schnauzer.

"Yeah, he's a mean little bastard," Bob says. "Took him in for a haircut, and he got real nasty. But the little dog forgets quickly. Not like my wife. Takes her two weeks to forget."

We chuckle.

Bob asks Dad, "Would you like Communion this morning?"

"I think I was good enough to have it," Dad replies.

Bob then asks, kiddingly, "Do you have money? We'll take up a collection." He winks at us.

In earnest, Dad starts digging for his wallet, being the good Catholic he is. He's wearing a hospital gown. There are no pockets.

◆ ◆ ◆

Later in the evening, Dad motions toward all the tubes and wires he's hooked up to.

"I'd sooner be home," he says. "I'm done with these 'toys.'"

It's his first mention of home since his fall.

◆ ◆ ◆

"I don't want any part of those snowmobiles," Dad suddenly says. "I'm not a young kid anymore."

It's out of the blue, relating to nothing.

Chapter Five

I Can No Longer Run

October 19, 2013

It's 2:00 a.m. I'm startled awake. Not by any sound. Not by the cats. Not by Halsey snoring.

No, I am awakened by the noise within myself.

Twists and turns and swirls of thoughts strangle their way around one another. Then an actual frenzy gathers. The thoughts become one solid knot. They wake me with a start.

Dad! What happened? What caused this plummet? Where do we go from here?

WHERE DID MY DAD GO? I WANT MY DAD BACK!

In the peripheral of all these chaotic, piercing thoughts is a low-frequency hum. Words to a song. I feel the song's words in my subconscious, echoing in a chamber behind the tangled knot of my racing dream-mind.

I sense a subtle comfort from the song, but I can't yet grab hold of it. My angst is the star performer of a play gone horribly wrong, while the song itself is only a backstage hand.

The words to the song continue to whisper in my mind, weaving peacefully amidst the shouted, harried thoughts that insist on taking center stage. The words tumble like clothes in a dryer in a distant room. White noise.

Then they grow louder. Soon they're audible. Then they crescendo. Each word is now distinguishable. The dryer is starting to rock. A string of words. And then whole verses.

"Love . . . Thy Will Be Done" by Martika punches my despair to the ground until the song itself becomes the victor of acceptance.

I can no longer hide
I can no longer run
No longer can I resist Your guiding light
That gives me the power to keep up the fight

. . .

Even when there's no peace outside my window
There's peace inside
And that's why I no longer run
Love . . . Thy will be done.

My subconscious hands me the harsh truth: I can no longer hide. I can no longer run from the effects of the anesthesia.

Dad has Alzheimer's.

Telltale Signs Not So Telling in the Moment

2010–2013

The signs were there—I can see that now. So many of them. But they insipidly entered our life in small degrees, unnoticeable to us.

Once we stand back and view the signs in totality, however, we now have to ask ourselves, "What were we thinking? How could we *not* see?"

◆ ◆ ◆

I remember a trip Halsey, Dad, and I made to Golden Valley to meet with the attorney to work on Dad's estate plan. Dad knew exactly what he wanted to do with his estate. That wasn't the issue. But Dad's driving was. Not only the driving itself but also his tendency to get lost.

We drove to Dad's house so he could follow us to the attorney's office. After the meeting, though, Halsey and I told Dad that we wouldn't be driving back to Shakopee with him.

We told him to follow us onto Highway 55 East and then onto 169 South. From there, however, Dad needed to stay on 169 all the way to Shakopee, while Halsey and I needed to take the 394 East exit into Minneapolis. We had plans to run an errand before going downtown for the Timberwolves game.

"Do *not* follow us when we exit," I emphasized. "Keep going straight, staying on 169 South, Dad," I restated. I couldn't repeat it enough. "We'll be exiting, but do *not* follow us. Keep going straight on 169 South. You know the way, don't you, Dad?"

He looked at me, searching whether I believed he could do it. I wasn't too sure.

"I'll tell you what," I said. "Before we make our exit, I'll stick my arm out the window and point forward, so you remember to stay on 169. Remember— *keep going straight* at that point. Just look for my arm. Will that help?"

He nodded.

Still unsure, I went over the plan one more time.

Then we headed out. We kept checking the rearview mirror to make sure we hadn't lost Dad. It was so far, so good. He was right behind us as we made it onto 55, then onto 169. The exits for 394 were approaching. Halsey and I needed the second exit. I waited with the window open, wanting to time my arm gesture just right.

But then . . . I couldn't believe what I was seeing in the rearview side mirror. Dad suddenly took the first exit—the ramp for 394 West! I'd been so worried about him following us onto 394 East. This was even worse.

Off he went in his red Mustang like a Ping-Pong ball ricocheting off the blunt edge of a table. As we approached our own exit, I spun my neck to watch Dad's car until it shrunk into a red dot and then finally into nothing. It was out of our hands. Even if we tried to loop back onto 169 South, he would be too far ahead of us, heading into Minnetonka, Wayzata, who knows.

My mouth dropped open as my heart sank. How would he get home? *Would* he get home? Halsey and I helplessly looked at each other and simultaneously crossed ourselves.

Jesus, please watch over Dad as he flounders into parts unknown. Please protect him and lead him home safely.

He made it home hours later, but we were never to hear his adventure story.

◆ ◆ ◆

We often invited Dad to dinner. It was a short fifteen-minute drive from Shakopee to our home in Chaska. There were just a few turns, including one roundabout. Usually, he had no problem.

But as time went by, we started getting reports from the neighbors that Dad no longer knew how to properly yield on the roundabout. Apparently, he was taking the roundabout without a glance in any direction, even when other drivers blared their horns. He had no clue they were honking at *him*.

The neighbors were concerned, and rightly so. "Monica, we just thought you should know," they said.

After hearing this, Halsey came up with the plan to always pick up Dad for dinner and bring him back home afterward. But getting Dad on board with this plan would be a sensitive matter. Dad had two prides at stake here. First, the inborn pride of a German—something you don't want to step on. And then the pride of someone trying to "hide" dementia.

"I'll tell you what," Halsey began over the phone with Dad. "Why don't I come and pick you up? We can have our own little talk in the car. Plus, Monica wants me out of the way while she's cooking."

Perfect. That kept him off the road in our community—though we still had the issue of him driving around his own town. Each day, a new opportunity for disaster was waiting to happen.

◆ ◆ ◆

Little Baxter, Dad's Boston terrier, needed to go to the vet. (Side note: I'm sure it had *nothing* to do with what Dad concocted for Baxter's meals. He thought he'd take the dog nuggets up a notch with squirts of mustard. After a few weeks of that, his creativity skyrocketed. He tried mixing a little ice cream with the nuggets. Maybe with a splash of twenty-year-old Worcestershire sauce he found in the kitchen cabinet, left over from when Mom was still living. When we'd visit Dad, Baxter would implore us with his eyes bulging, "Help me! Please!")

Anyway, the vet.

Dad put Baxter in the car and set off. Three hours later, I was at work when he called me to say he couldn't find the clinic.

It was, literally, less than a half mile from his house.

He'd been driving around lost all morning. I could hear his distress, his words pinched with held-back tears.

Poor Dad.

◆ ◆ ◆

As the weeks passed, Dad's judgment in driving failed on every score. The last ride we took with him behind the wheel was another trip to Golden Valley for estate planning. I was sitting in the back seat while Halsey sat in front with Dad.

When Dad was the lone car on a straight road with no stop signs, we were in pretty good shape. But that was rarely the case.

Even lane changes were disastrous. As soon as he decided to change lanes, he'd just do it. No checking his mirrors—not even a cursory glance. No turn of the head. No signaling. Nothing. He'd just change his lane.

It was the same with merging onto the freeway from the on-ramp. From my back-seat perch, I saw the oncoming traffic and shockingly realized that not a single driver would have the notion that this Mustang would just merge right on in without a second glance.

I couldn't handle it a second longer. I threw myself down and hunkered low with my face planted in the car seat, gagging on the cigarette smoke smell saturating the fabric.

Meanwhile, in the front passenger seat, Halsey had to white-knuckle the dashboard. "Whoa, let's take it easy here," he said.

But Dad had no idea he was doing anything wrong.

After the attorney meeting, Halsey asked Dad if he'd mind being the passenger while Halsey drove the Mustang back to Dad's house. Halsey said he wanted to feel the way a Ford drove. Dad, a Ford retiree, liked that idea, especially because all Halsey ever drove were Chevrolets.

Dad had two cars: the Mustang and a Ford sedan. He mostly drove the sedan around town for everyday trips. The Mustang, though, was for special trips and for show. There was a lot of horsepower under that hood. And given Dad's current tendencies behind the wheel, it was maybe more than he could handle. We had to get the Mustang keys from him. We'd still have the sedan to worry about, but one car at a time.

When I relayed Dad's car escapades to Trent, he had a great solution. He spent Wednesday nights at Dad's house, playing darts in the downstairs game room. Trent said he could easily snag the Mustang's keys the next Wednesday. He said if Dad mentioned not being able to find his keys, it would be simple enough to say, "Really, Grandpa? Did you check everywhere? I'm sure they'll show up," then move on to another topic.

That's just the way it went down. Dad, Trent, Halsey, and I were standing in Dad's kitchen a few days later.

"Now here's something else I can't find . . ." Dad started. "My keys."

"I thought you just drove to get hot dogs last night," I commented, referring to the sedan.

Dad had been eating hot dogs every day for about two years. No exaggeration. It was a steady daily diet, unless he ate dinner at our house or we took him out.

"Not those keys. The keys for my Mustang. I wanted to take it out for a spin this afternoon. But do you think I could find the damn things?"

"Oh, Grandpa—I'm sure they'll show up," Trent reassured. "Remember how you couldn't find your glasses the other night, when they were on your head?"

"Oh, Christ. I'm going nuts. Is that right?" Dad laughed.

Just like that, we skirted the issue. Dad would never drive the Mustang again. It went quite well. In comparison, my friends had horror stories of the battles they'd fought when taking keys away from their aging parents.

The next night, Trent said that while we were discussing the missing keys at Dad's house, he heard his grandma's heavenly whisper from behind his shoulder, "Thank you."

◆ ◆ ◆

Dad could never remember how to turn on his TV or change the channel. We had to spend forty-five minutes over the phone trying to walk him through it.

I finally went over to his house in Shakopee, drew a diagram of his remote, and took it back home to Chaska with me as a visual aid for myself. That way, I could exactly describe to him what button to look for and where it was on the remote, without having to make the trip to Shakopee to turn on his television.

That plan didn't work. Ultimately, we did end up driving the twelve miles over to his house to turn on the TV and set the channel for him. Dad could no longer follow step-by-step instructions.

We couldn't hide from it any longer. It was apparent Dad needed help. Quite honestly, we all needed help.

We went online and took a look at a few dementia tests. We soft-pedaled suggestions for him to see a doctor.

Finally, Trent was able to strike a deal with him. "Grandpa, if you check out fine, we'll drop it."

Dad did not check out fine. He was put on medication. But the problem was, he couldn't be counted on to remember to take it twice a day. Trent volunteered to make the "Time to take your pill!" call each morning, and we made the call each night.

A few weeks went by. Dad doesn't find it strange at all to confide in me that occasionally he and Mom passed each other on the stairway in the house.

"We don't talk," he said. "Just nod to each other and keep going."

That was interesting. Mom had died seventeen years earlier.

◆ ◆ ◆

Dad hadn't been feeling well. Some chills and a headache. I called one evening to check in on him.

The first thing he said was, "I think there's some goddamn bugs in the logs next to the fireplace."

"Oh?"

"Now I'm all bit up!"

Dad lay on the floor every night to watch TV, a habit I picked up myself. I wasn't convinced that he had been bitten by any "bugs," so I pressed for more details.

"Did you actually see bugs? Did you inspect the woodpile?"

"I moved the whole damn woodpile back outside where it came from."

"Oh. Did you vacuum the carpet?"

"Yes, but it didn't help. I'm not kidding, Monica. My back is all bit up."

None of this added up. I was dog-tired after a long day at the office, and I knew morning would come sooner than I wanted, but I had to figure out what was happening. "Why don't I come over and take a look at your back?" I offered.

"No. I could be contagious. I don't want you coming over."

"Dad, I'll just slip in quickly."

"No."

Case closed. I dropped it, and we let the conversation dip into other areas.

A few days passed, and I followed up again.

"How are the bug bites these days?"

"I can't get rid of them." I could hear desperation in his choked voice. "I went to the hardware store and got some bug spray. Doused the carpet with it, took my shirt off, and just grounded my back into the carpet, trying to get rid of that damn itch."

"Dad, that doesn't sound good. Did it work?"

"No," came the mutter. "Monica, it's driving me nuts."

Picturing Dad inch-worming across the old '80's orange shag with his bare, rubbed-raw back was too much. "I'm coming over."

"The hell you are. The door is locked. I won't let you in. I can't have anyone else get this. I just can't get rid of those goddamn bugs."

I tried a different route. "Have you actually *seen* any of those bugs yet, Dad?"

"Not a one."

"So maybe it's not bugs. Maybe you should go to the doctor."

"I'm not going to any damn doctor for bug bites."

I called the next afternoon. "Dad, how are you today?"

"I went to the doctor."

"Oh? What did he say?"

He muttered something I couldn't catch.

"What?" I asked. "I didn't hear that."

"Shingles," he repeated. "I've never heard of any such thing. The doctor wouldn't even let the nurse in. Called her to the doorway and asked her to look from there. 'Now here's a case of shingles,' he says to her. Puts me on display like some sort of goddamn show horse."

◆ ◆ ◆

One of the three lights on Dad's garage was flickering. He tried replacing the bulb, but the flickering continued. He was very sure *we* had something to do with his problem, seeing as we were now living right next to him in Shakopee.

Dad's house was a brown split-level built in the '70's. Mom and Dad chose to build it next to my dad's parents' old farmhouse, where Dad had grown up. He told stories about how he and his older brother, Lawrence, would have frost on their bedroom walls up in the second story.

Building the new house next to the farmhouse was a great situation. It allowed my parents to wander over and check on Grandma and Grandpa as they became less able to care for themselves. That went on for fifteen years. After both of my grandparents passed away, my parents rented the farmhouse out.

After thirty years of renters, I suggested to Halsey that *we* should purchase the farmhouse, renovate it, and move in. Then we could be next door to Dad and care for him, as he had cared for his parents. Plus, we would be living in my grandparents' home, where my dad grew up! It felt like one huge hug.

After two and a half years of renovations, we were able to do just that.

Not long after we moved in, Dad showed Halsey the flickering light on his garage, then tried to explain why we were to blame for it—and more.

"You know what's causing this? Look over there," Dad said to Halsey. He pointed to my office window. There was a soft, steady glow from my hibernating computer. "What you've got going on over there is becoming my problem."

"What problem is that?" Halsey asked.

"Well, this flickering. Not to mention, I'm paying for your electricity."

Halsey paused. "You know," he slowly answered, "I think that light on Monica's computer just stays on. Besides, it has nothing to do with this flickering light or your electricity bill. They're two separate households."

But Dad was angry. He was convinced that the electricity we used for our home impacted his flickering garage light. He was also dumbfounded that Halsey couldn't understand his point.

"Can't you see that over there?" Dad asked, wagging his finger at my computer light again, as if it explained everything.

Halsey shuffled and stammered, "Yeah. Yeah, I can."

He didn't want to argue. He didn't want the controversy—and he didn't want to blow Dad's cover-up that nothing was wrong in his way of thinking.

"Well, you're costing me money," Dad continued.

After a while, Halsey left, subtly shaking his head. This dementia business was new to us. We didn't yet realize that there is *no* arguing. We had yet to learn the art of just going with what was. You can't make your point by showing rationale. You can't make sense out of nonsense. If you're going to relate to the heart of your loved one with dementia, it's best to just nod your head and move on to another topic.

To appease the situation, I threw a towel over my monitor at night so the light wouldn't trigger another outburst. All that did, though, was cost me a new monitor because it caused a burn on the top of the screen.

◆ ◆ ◆

It was 2:15 in the afternoon. I called Dad to tell him I'd stop over at 4:30, and we could go to dinner together. I suggested that he take a bath, shave, and put on some clean clothes. It was time, after all. I'm sure he had worn the same clothes for at least ten days.

At 4:00, I looked out my window across the way. Dad was outside. Yep, he had a different set of clothes on. That was good. He leveled his "Ford: Built Tough" cap. He had a broom in his hands. He must have decided to sweep his driveway. OK. Good.

Five minutes later, I looked out the window again. Dad was now sweeping the grass.

It was four days before he fell . . .

From Home to Hip Surgery to Rehab

After Dad's surgery, we visit him as often as we can at St. Gert's rehab center. At every visit, we think, again, how easy it should have been to see the signs of dementia. We have no excuse to not have recognized them.

October 20, 2013

We're sitting at a table in the main living area. We're talking about my grandpa and how he always named his dogs Bubby.

Dad says, "I think I know how he got that name, but I already forgot."

◆ ◆ ◆

We're talking about Dad's belongings, and he comments, "I wouldn't miss it if they did take something—don't tell anyone this."

◆ ◆ ◆

As we're leaving, he says, "I'd like to go home anytime. But this restaurant does have good food."

I'm sure this "restaurant" does seem nice to him, after his two-year regime of Ho Hos in the morning and two hotdogs with mustard for dinner. And mustard for Baxter's nuggets.

October 21, 2013

Dad has been given some red socks with white rubber grips on the soles. They catch his eye occasionally. He wiggles his toes, admiring them.

"You like the red socks, huh, Dad?" I ask.

Smiling, he says, "And they like me."

Making conversation, I ask Dad about his childhood. "Who was your best friend?"

"I hate to say it, but Donny Ward," Dad answers. "He had humpy, bumpy eyes. I felt sorry for him. My dad didn't like him. I hung around with Donny, but my dad didn't appreciate it, and I know that. His eyes crisscrossed. I don't know how he did it, but he did."

Humpy, bumpy eyes? I enjoy these words. He and I both laugh.

I find it odd that Donny Ward is the name that surfaces as his best friend. I've heard Donny's name mentioned maybe only three times over the last fifty-some years. He must have been a good friend from his childhood.

October 23, 2013

We're given a rundown on Dad at a brief meeting with the doctor, the activities director, and the occupational therapist. I take notes as fast as I can.

"Good news," Dr. Stockman begins.

He goes on to explain that he has Dad on a nebulizer three times a day. Right now, nebulizers are best, he says. But hopefully, they'll be able to change to inhalers. He also has Dad on 1000 mg of Tylenol three times a day.

Dr. Stockman has had Dad on the antidepressant Fluoxetine as well, but he will switch that today. It can cause confusion and anxiety as side effects. It's also the number two or number three cause of falls. Dr. Stockman recommends 50 mg of Zoloft.

He's also made a note to bump up in two weeks Dad's Namenda, which treats dementia and Alzheimer's. It will increase to 10 mg per day. Dr. Stockman wants us to have Dad's primary physician up the prescription, but he, himself, will do it now.

Also, in three to four months, we are to ask Dad's primary physician to add Razadyne, starting at 4 mg two times a day with a gradual increase. Also known by its generic name, Galantamine, this drug is used to treat dementia related to Alzheimer's. It's not a cure, but it may improve some symptoms and functions.

Blood work looks good. Dad is now on oxygen.

October 24, 2013

We get another update on Dad. Some of the information is exactly the same as yesterday. Some of it is new. Once again, I scribble notes, trying to take it all down.

He's on two liters of oxygen. He's at 94 percent—and 90 percent is normal. He's at only 88–89 percent when taken off the oxygen.

He has a DuoNeb three times a day.

Takes Tylenol three times a day.

Takes a Boost supplement.

They have made the change to Zoloft.

Still on Namenda.

Baby aspirin 81 mg daily.

There's 25 mg Seroquel as needed (usually two times a day) for agitation.

Dad is "impulsive, sleeping well at night, incontinent."

A seventy-two-hour bladder assessment will start Saturday.

Sam, the activities director, tells us how in the afternoons, he gathers those who are interested and leads the group to work on a crossword puzzle together. He says Dad sits and observes.

Dad was never one to do crosswords on his own, so I'm OK with him just observing. In fact, I'm surprised that he would even observe.

Sam also tells us that Dad listens in during newspaper readings.

He's eating well at meals. But he has lost two pounds, from 115 to 113. Hence, one can of Boost a day.

Hayley, the occupational therapist, works with self-care, safety, dressing, and grooming. She shares that Dad is very well physically. He does his own grooming with standby assistance. He doesn't sequence, though, and he needs a lot of queuing cognitively. When doing tasks, he reverts back to long-term memory rather than short-term. He needs lots of verbal reminders.

We're cheered to hear that he's "always very pleasant and wants to please" and by the fact that he's "very cooperative and hard working."

But then Sam continues: "On the other hand, his follow-through . . . well, he seems to be very confused. He's lost so much of his power."

Alarmingly, we find out that out of the eleven questions on the safety assessment, Dad got zero right. He also took the Saint Louis University Mental Status—or SLUMS—assessment for people suspected to have dementia or Alzheimer's. It's a seven-minute test administered and scored by a clinician. We're told that an individual needs nineteen correct answers to avoid a "dementia" rating. Dad got two correct.

My heart is crying. *How can this be? This is my dad! How has it come to this?*

Dad has also undergone physical therapy testing. On the first day he was tested, he could walk one hundred feet using a contact guard and no assistance. Now, only four days later, he needs a front-wheel walker to go that same distance. *Really?*

He was also given a Tinetti test to assess his balance—essentially, his risk of falling. Dad scored at "high risk."

They've found that the oxygen tubing is a big hindrance to his balance and movement. When nudged, he loses his balance and goes around in a circle. He's also unstable with his eyes closed. His gait is OK. His balance has gone down, but I'm hearing that they think it will improve.

Their biggest concern, however, is his judgment as he struggles to move about. He seems challenged in this environment and doesn't always make the best decisions as he navigates his way.

Imagining myself in his shoes, I look around the rehab center. Would it be a challenge for me to move in this environment? I don't think so. Yet somehow it's a challenge for Dad. I wonder if it would be a challenge for him to maneuver in his own home, where he lived for the last forty years. Is it the newness of the rehab center that's affecting his judgment? Or is it the newness of how his brain now works?

The goal: to see him more independent, without a walker. They will work with him for another couple of weeks.

And then what? I wonder.

◆ ◆ ◆

After the meeting with the staff, we stay to visit with Dad. Halsey shares a story, then waits for Dad's reaction. When there is none, Halsey leans toward me and says as an aside, "I don't think your dad heard that."

Dad nods. "I think he did," he says.

◆ ◆ ◆

Later that day, Trent joins Halsey and me for a visit with Dad. Over the past number of years, Trent and Dad have delighted each other with ongoing jabs at Obama. Trent knows he can get a rise out of Dad if he brings up Obama's name.

"So, how's that Obama treating you, Grandpa?" Trent says.

We are pleased with Dad's reaction. His eyes light up in recognition of where Trent is going. He shakes his head, and both he and Trent share a roll of the eyes.

After a moment, I quietly comment on the side to Trent: "That was neat how you slipped in Obama."

Dad winks. "He gets slipped in often."

I'm delighted. Dad is tracking the conversation so well that he picked up on my aside. These exchanges encourage me—I can see Dad popping back into the world.

But then Dad points to his head. "The battery wore out. Well, I did put a new battery in when Mom passed away, but that must have worn out too."

November 2, 2013

Dad is stressed and confused, so a staffer at St. Gert's calls to ask if I can help settle him down. When I first enter the room, I can see by Dad's posture that he feels cornered. He holds himself tight as if in a protective mode against the strangeness of his whole situation.

I can only think, maybe he had a flash of his home life? Of Baxter? Of his television room? Of his Ho Hos and two hotdogs with mustard? Whatever flash it was, it obviously did not meet up with his reality of being at St. Gert's rehab center.

As soon I sidle up to him at his table, he turns and fixes his eyes on me. I can see, as though through a View-Master, his eyes change from panic to recognition to relief. I feel as though I have grounded him.

After a bit of small talk, I say, "You're my dad. You're my favorite person."

"I know this," he answers. "I'm in favor of all this, one hundred percent."

"That's my dad," I say.

"That's my girl."

◆ ◆ ◆

Later in our visit, Dad looks around. "There's a lot of old people here," he remarks.

He's seventy-nine. They're all about his age.

◆◆◆

He starts talking about mud chips—something about them being used for bartering. I try to make sense out of this, pulling from whatever I know of Dad's history . . . but *mud chips?* Eventually, his rambling ends, and I never come to an understanding.

I realize he has now popped out.

◆◆◆

Pulling on his neck, he says, "I have an itch."

Then he suddenly makes a head motion pointing to the woman next to him, indicating that he doesn't want her to hear this.

◆◆◆

I see he's beginning to relax a bit. He seems less agitated now. But I decide to have dinner with him—just to keep him calm.

I have Chinese. Dad chooses a cheeseburger and goes on to comment on how good it is. I'm surprised—he hates cheese.

Along with the burger, they've also given him a small portion of peas. He discreetly slides them and lines them up single file like soldiers behind an empty sauce dish on his plate. I see he still remembers that he doesn't like peas.

I open my fortune cookie. "Keep your idealism practical."

Point taken.

At St. Gert's, there's a woman named Martha with once-upon-a-time-beautiful blue eyes. These days, her eyes are wet and sad. Her mouth droops on one side. Yet her nails are finely polished.

Despite all, we do what we can to keep up appearances. To feel better about ourselves.

Dad looks across the table at a man named Bruce, who somewhat resembles Halsey. Dad mistakes Bruce for Halsey and starts making eyes at him in fun.

When I tell him it's not Halsey, Dad laughs.

Fifteen minutes later, Bruce walks by.

"Here comes 'Halsey,'" Dad says with a twinkle in his eye.

He knows full well now it's not Halsey. He's cracking jokes. This is good.

◆ ◆ ◆

Dad hasn't been home since his fall just short of three weeks ago. Trent has brought Baxter home to his own house to care for him.

I mention to Dad that Baxter's been a good boy.

Dad responds with, "I'm a good boy too."

"Yes, you are," I assure him.

November 3, 2013

As a nurse passes by, she addresses one of the residents: "How ya doin'?"

"Pretty good," the resident responds.

"Me too," the nurse answers.

Dad whispers to me, "I think they're both lying."

November 4, 2013

I decide to play a little with Dad. "Are you ticklish?" I ask. I test to see if he is, first tickling him on his rib cage and then his feet.

His answer: "Our family was ticklish on the running board of their feet."

November 6, 2013

Dad has fallen again, landing on his hand, which has caused quite a bit of swelling.

Halsey's remedy for an injury is to ice it, so he helps Dad ice his hand.

"You're a tough guy," Halsey tells him.

"Oh, I wouldn't say that," Dad replies.

Halsey continues to rub ice over and over the swollen portion.

"You don't have to rub yourself to death," Dad says.

◆ ◆ ◆

Out of the blue, Dad says, "I can't win. Not like I want to win."

◆ ◆ ◆

After three weeks, they have done as much as they can with rehab therapy at St. Gert's. Dad needs to move on.

But to where?

We consider an assisted-living arrangement. There are four main factors to consider when contemplating assisted living for a loved one: safety (the highest priority), health issues (being able to perform personal-care functions), behavior changes (forgetfulness, confusion, sundowning, aggression, to name a few), and the burden placed on the caregiver and extended family.

We're forced to accept that Dad is not going home. And he is not going into assisted living.

He will go directly into a memory care unit.

Chapter Eight

A Tiny Messenger of Change: The Turning of Another Page

November 8, 2013

We've moved Dad to McKenna Crossing, a senior-living community. The brochure says it was "created from the shared vision of Shepherd of the Lake Lutheran Church and Presbyterian Homes and Services—two non-profit organizations dedicated to serving individuals through faith-based ministry." We are not Lutherans, but we are faith based.

This facility offers independent living, assisted living, and, the final stop, the memory care unit. We made the big leap, going right to the memory care unit, aka the Arbor.

After any move, individuals with dementia often have relapses; we see it firsthand today, on day one. Nothing but a mash of words and fragments of thought that seems to be nonsense. His thoughts are untethered.

We call this plummet "the new normal."

◆◆◆

61982*

Bzzzzzzzz.

Click.

After you enter the security code and pass through the main entrance, you have a choice of two hallways—one going straight and one turning right. Both hallways are flanked by residents' rooms. Dad's room is down the hall that goes straight ahead.

This same hallway lands in a small gathering room called the Sun Room. It has a couple of comfortable sofa chairs and a small sofa with tables on either side. It's a nice, intimate gathering spot.

The other hallway ends with an activity room with a long table in the middle. Bins of ribbon and other craft items line three of the room's walls, and the fourth wall has bins containing locks and other "guy" things the men can toy with.

Back at the point where the two hallways begin is the area I call the Commons. It's a large open area with about a dozen four-by-four tables. This is where all the residents eat, have coffee and snacks, and generally congregate for the better part of the day. Compared to the Sun Room, there's a lot of hubbub here.

We learn, as time goes by, that the residents tend to have their "preferred" tables. Sometimes two tables are joined together to accommodate larger groups. This might happen when the recreation coordinator oversees a project or maybe when the women are having their nails polished.

In the immediate corner of the Commons is the station where meals are plated, coffee and tea are made, and packaged Oreos and Fig Newtons are stored in cupboards. Staff also has a small office tucked behind this station, where they can log in the information on each resident.

Cutting across diagonally from this staff station is a small den with a television and easy chairs. Here, residents can watch movies and football games. As any den would have, there's also a shelving area that houses books and knickknacks.

◆ ◆ ◆

Halsey and I are sitting at a table in the Commons with Dad.

Upon seeing one of the staff members walk by, Dad says, "She lives down the street. There's a black hole. It's kind of sticky, but it still tastes good." Without much of a pause in between, he says, "I wonder how these people like the dogs running around here. I don't want animals running around stoves and chains and black whistles. I don't know the name of that street. I have Oklahoma in mind."

It's a total mishmash.

◆ ◆ ◆

The ramblings continue.

"Downstairs mirror for the professor," he says.

Trying somehow to work into these ramblings, I ask, "Where is the mirror, Dad?"

"Not far away from Junkman, where I put his tools in my basement."

Who is the professor? What downstairs mirror is he referring to? And "Junkman"?

◆ ◆ ◆

"I did mail some cards out—three of them."

He looks down at his hands.

"I have workingman's hands. Dirt I worked in—the old Model T. And I'm washing my house too—going into the kitchen."

Watching him inspect his hands as he rambles, I am transported to a fuggy warmth in my mind. I reflect on Dad's hands . . .

Strong and capable. Blue-collar hands. Calloused from years of use. Fixing. Repairing. Creating.

- ◆ Carpentry work. Building. Improving. Sanding. Grinding. Planing.
- ◆ Bodywork on cars. Welding. Soldering. Painting. Buffing.
- ◆ Engine and motor work on cars. Tinkering. Wrenching.
- ◆ Engine and motor work on small appliances. Twisting. Tightening. Lubricating.
- ◆ Yard work and lawn care. Hoeing. Raking. Planting.

"Look at her," Dad would say to us, rubbing Mom's arm with his hand as she passed with dinner platters to set on the table. "I'd marry her all over again."

"Honey, don't," she'd say. "Get those hot hands off me." But I could tell she was pleased.

Dad's hands were what men's hands were supposed to look like. Da Vinci could have drawn none finer. Not smooth and soft, but rugged. Not fleshy and stubby, but sturdy. I loved his hands.

When I first started dating in high school, hands could end a potential relationship before it even got off the ground. Everything else might be just fine with the new date, even with a few minor hiccups. But in the end, if I couldn't get past the hands, the relationship would never get off the ground. Seems rather petty, now. Maybe just another "flaw" to have me move on.

◆ ◆ ◆

Dad nods in the direction of a passerby.

"He looks familiar. His glasses and windshields."

◆ ◆ ◆

"Hell of a nice-dressed movie," he says. "But I didn't want to lose anything, so I turned the key, and it was gone."

◆ ◆ ◆

Dad continues, and we try our best to follow.

"It was all his own doing. He had paintings on the wall in the hen coop. A few things too heavy on the wall. A little flower about this size." He indicates a quarter size with his pointer and thumb. "That flower is bigger and brighter," he adds, looking at a checkerboard.

There are no flowers. No pictures of flowers. No vase of flowers. Nobody's wearing a flowered blouse. Nothing. Yet "flower" has found favor with him.

◆ ◆ ◆

"Four-wheel Galaxie on a trunk. I'm sure he carved it off or something."

◆ ◆ ◆

"I'm just a little skinflint," he says.

A skinflint?

Yes, Dad has always been thrifty and frugal, but *skinflint* sounds like he's selling himself short. I've never even heard him use the word, let alone use it to describe himself.

If I were to describe him, I would say he was the one who played checkers with us when we were kids.

He would hit the ball in the backyard for us to learn how to field and catch.

He would play hide-and-seek with us while Mom made dinner. Sometimes he would lift us up and set us on the top shelf in the bedroom closet, tucking us in between Mom's Sunday hats and gloves.

He taught me how to shoot marbles so I was a force to be reckoned with when I joined the Marble Team in school.

He taught me how to ride the turquoise Thunderbird bicycle I received for my First Communion. It even had cream-colored saddlebags strapped over the bucker in back. (We called it a bucker because that's where someone could hop on and buck a ride.)

He took me to work with him when his company had Ford Day Camp. He showed me how he had only a few precious seconds to set screws and make other adjustments and fittings on a car before it passed his station via the assembly line. Then the next car would slip in, and he'd have to do the procedure all over again. And again. And again. All day long. Working eight-to-ten-hour shifts. Sometimes time and a half. Sometimes double time.

After fourteen years, he moved into the parts department. He memorized hundreds of twelve-digit or longer numbers, knowing what part each number represented when he heard it yelled up the line.

Thirty years as a Ford employee. And he continued to be a Ford man to the end of his days. Or at least until he remembered he had a car.

After dinner, he'd read the paper, then he'd lie on the living room carpet on his stomach. I would sit on his lower back and scratch it. He was in heaven. I knew it because of the goose pimples that would appear.

I would write words on his back with my pointer fingernail, and he would guess them letter by letter. A giant capital *D*. Short pause after he guessed. A huge capital *O*. Wait for his guess. And end with an even bigger capital *G*. After he guessed the word *dog*, I would "erase" the word with a quick rub of my hand, smoothing out the scratch marks. Then I'd begin a new word.

He also found time to play with his friends. Bumper pool games, Ping-Pong, horseshoes, shuffleboard, RC airplane flying, slot car racing, snowmobiling, darts. They were all done with gusto. Whatever activity, he immersed himself into it entirely. And he was enjoyed by all. You lived to hear him laugh. It was the best.

After retiring from Ford, he apprenticed under Eldon Bishop and learned to repair antique clocks. He could repair them all. When parts became near impossible to come by, he resorted to making his own. Bushings, for example— miniature screws the size of dust. If you breathed too hard through your nose, you blew the bushing away. He did clock repair for a solid twenty years.

He was also a fixture at the Canterbury Car Wash. Customers could rely on him to answer any question or fix any problem as it arose.

In whatever aspect your path crossed my dad's, you were always guaranteed a "listener." No one gave you their undivided attention as he did. You felt special.

And again, his laugh would be a happy punctuation to the conversation that would warm you the rest of the day.

Just a little skinflint?

He was so much more.

Chapter Nine

Meet the Residents

Do Not Ask Me to Remember

Do not ask me to remember,
Don't try to make me understand,
Let me rest and know you're with me,
Kiss my cheek and hold my hand.
I'm confused beyond your concept,
I am sad and sick and lost.
All I know is that I need you
To be with me at all cost.
Do not lose your patience with me,
Do not scold or curse or cry.
I can't help the way I'm acting,
Can't be different though I try.
Just remember that I need you,
That the best of me is gone,
Please don't fail to stand beside me,
Love me 'til my life is done.
—Owen Darnell

61982*
Bzzzzzzzz.
Click.

We do it twice a week. We put in the security code, the lock clicks, and we know we have ten seconds to pass through before the alarm goes off.

November 12, 2013

Dad is seated at a table in the Commons. He seems "popped in" today—very cognizant. "I don't know how long they're going to keep me. I want to go home," he states.

But then he pops out.

"I still don't know what to do about my car in the ditch."

There is no car in the ditch, but he's concerned. Actually, ever since St. Gert's, he's claimed that he has two cars "in the ditch."

We reassure him that we're taking care of the cars, that he needn't worry. We're finding that cars in a ditch is a recurring theme for a number of men in the Arbor.

We're also finding that we need to meet Dad where he is—whether what he's saying is truth or not. This is true for all Alzheimer's patients. Arguing or trying to point out reason does no one any good. Instead, you smile and nod. You reassure them that you're taking care of things.

Don't try to force them into your world. Instead, join them in theirs.

◆ ◆ ◆

It's so apparent tonight that my dad is a gentleman. Everyone has just finished eating dinner. A woman is to my dad's right. She's very, very confused. I ask her her name, and even that won't come to her. She can't remember.

As Halsey, Dad, and I talk, I occasionally glance over at this woman and smile. I try to engage her with eye contact, since conversing is out of the question.

After a while, Halsey gets up to go retrieve something. So, then it's just Dad, this woman, and me. The woman gets agitated and very anxious. Dad leans toward her and asks if everything is OK. She's fidgeting with her glasses, so Dad very gently asks if there's a problem with them.

After a number of kind attempts on his part to help her, she finally sputters, "No! I just don't like them."

Dad responds with, "Oh. Well. I can't help you with that. Everyone has their own likes." And he smiles warmly at her.

Later, I call my oldest son, Chad, to share this with him. Chad has a son, Freedom. I'm struck with the similarity of gentleness that Dad, Chad, and Freedom seem to share.

December 1, 2013

As soon as we open the door, and before we cross the threshold, we take off our Shoes of Normalcy. Only then do we enter the gentle World of Dementia. Here, Shoes of Normalcy are not needed. Here, the residents are soft souls. Here, everyone looks up as we enter, each person thinking we are their own personal visitors.

And that is what we have become. We have come to know some of the residents, and we always share extra moments with seven of them.

Charlie, Ann, Joyce, Bob, Shirley, Winnie, and Jerome.

◆◆◆

Charlie is a very proud Alzheimer's patient. He has stature, with his tall, slim physique. His white hair sometimes sticks up in places, just like my grandpa's used to. I imagine he was a professional of some sort when his mind was all together. I didn't know him then—when he was one with his mind. I only know him now.

I always make a point to say, "Charlie, how's it going?"

Charlie always responds the same way: with a neat dip of his head, a nod in greeting. A small half-smile appears on his face.

◆◆◆

Ann is a frail little old lady with a small back hump. She's unstable on her feet, and her eyes dart to the left and right, looking around cautiously. She's happy when I ask how her day's going.

She walks the halls, using the railing as her life support. One time when I was visiting, she went down. I quickly came up behind her to pick her up, just a little bird.

"Oh, thank you! Thank you! You're such a nice girl." Her eyes lit up.

I felt blessed by her.

◆◆◆

Joyce is crabby. She has platinum hair, she sports sturdy eyewear, and she carries all her notes and cards in the tray in front of her walker. She pushes along, cranky and stiff legged. She'll show her treasures to you, but if you don't respond in a fitting manner, she'll chew your head off without a backward glance.

I pretend I don't notice this. On any other day, in any other setting, I probably wouldn't take the time or make the effort to engage with someone who bites the way she does. Here, however, I smile. Like my mom always said, "You'll attract more bees with honey than with vinegar."

I try to spread a lot of honey with Joyce. I remind myself of her age. I remind myself of where she is. It softens me, and it seems to soften her, as well. Eventually, she forgets whatever got her dander up, and then I'm her friend. For today.

Tomorrow, she'll forget she liked me today, and I'll have to start all over again.

◆◆◆

Bob is a big man. Cushy. A Pillsbury Doughboy. Most often, he's wearing his overwashed yellow Iowa sweatshirt.

His white hair is always in need of a haircut. Where is his family? Isn't there someone to arrange haircuts for him?

He tilts his head at just the right angle to look at me through the bottom third of his glasses. His hair fringes over the tops of his ears. My fingers just itch to tuck his hair behind his ears.

"Bob, how's it going?"

"Yep."

◆◆◆

Shirley is a feisty ninety-three-year-old with a colorful tongue. I often wonder what she's doing in this facility. She's sharp and has a quick wit. I wonder if she has dementia or if she's just willfully eccentric.

Shirley's joy is to obsess over and seemingly sniff out relationships. If I'm talking to Ben, the staff worker, Shirley will quip from across the room: "Hey, over there—is that your new boyfriend?" Or if another staff person is helping a resident: "Are you two married?"

There's got to be a story there. Maybe someday I'll find out.

◆◆◆

Winnie makes me smile. She's in a wheelchair and is not mobile at all. But she still proudly preens each time she gets her hair done.

"Winnie!" I say. "You look so beautiful! Did you get your hair done today?"

"Oh, yes. Yes, I did. You look beautiful too."

"Why, thank you, Winnie!"

Her eyes twinkle.

I lightly squeeze her hand.

◆ ◆ ◆

Finally, there's Jerome. Jerome is my very favorite.

He's my dad.

Chapter Ten

Lorraine, Followed by Mayhem

December 4, 2013

I walk into the Commons, all set to greet Dad for another nice visit. But my steps come to a screeching halt and my mouth drops open.

My sweet, forever-loyal-to-Mom's-memory-even-seventeen-years-after-her-death dad is holding hands with one of the residents! It's a shock. I don't know who this woman is.

It's not that I have a problem with their handholding itself. I see it as a tender exchange. It's comforting to know Dad has someone who cares about him.

The problem, rather, is that I feel so intrusive. It's as though I walked into a bedroom unannounced and encountered something I shouldn't have. I am shocked, speechless. Not knowing what to do with myself, I keep walking straight ahead, eyes averted, as I make my way down the hallway to his room to sign in.

I don't know what to do with my thoughts. I want to spin this encounter into a good thing. *Think kindly of the woman. She appears nonthreatening. She's just in need of some attention. She's simply offering affection. She has an angelic profile. Probably a very nice old lady. When I come back to the Commons, the handholding thing surely will have ended.*

But no. They're still at it.

I want a name for this Dad-snatching woman. Come to find out it's Lorraine.

And now, I'm remembering. Lorraine . . . wasn't she the one who sidled over to Charlie the night before and rested her pretty little eighty-two-year-old head on his shoulder while they were sitting side by side on the couch watching TV? Pretty sure Charlie never knew how that happened. One moment he's sitting by himself, minding his own business—and then, out of the blue, a harlot has her head on his shoulder. Unaware Charlie.

I sit down and begin conversing with Dad. Lorraine desperately clutches at his hands. His da Vinci hands. He tries to pull away—kindly. But Lorraine will have nothing doing with that. She frantically grabs on like a snow crab.

Finally, Dad says, "Not so hard. I might still need them."

◆ ◆ ◆

We're talking about Baxter.

"I think I should get four of them, so I can have him on all sides of me," Dad says.

I think to myself, *How astute that he knows it would take four, one for each direction.*

◆ ◆ ◆

There's a female resident here who's often in the back of the Commons, near the TV, calling for help. She doesn't need help. It's just what she always calls out. Always. It gets monotonous and annoying.

Sure enough, she starts in.

"Help! Help!"

Colorful-tongued Shirley responds with, "Oh, go to sleep."

Thirty minutes later: "Help! Help!"

Shirley says, in her brusque manner, "I'll help put you to sleep."

◆ ◆ ◆

It's nearing the "sundown hour," and the crowd is restless for dinner. Sundown hour is the point in the late afternoon when the residents start to fade and their memory slips further away, ready to tuck in for the night. It's when most residents' cognitive skills decline.

The witching hour, I have come to think of it.

Shirley sits at a separate table directly across from Dad's table as I visit. She slides comments over our way occasionally, begging for attention.

She raps on the table. I recognize it's the cadence of "Shave and a haircut."

There's an answering rap from an adjacent table: "Two bits." I hear the words loud and clear in my mind, although it's only rapping on the table.

Again, Shirley raps, "Shave and a haircut."

Someone else raps, "Two bits."

The residents love it! Each has a gleeful smirk plastered on his or her face.

Before we know it, there's another round of rapping from Shirley along with answering raps.

Now, boldly, others decide to take the lead. They drum the "Shave and a haircut" rhythm on the table.

Five answering raps: "Two bits."

Abraham, a staff member from Kenya, is becoming unglued and ready to snap. "OK, now. That's enough," he says.

I watch as Shirley puffs out her chest. She enjoys stirring the pot and getting reactions.

And so mayhem ensues.

She pounces on the bedlam and rallies the room with another "Shave and a haircut" rap, this time louder. She's in her element. And loving it.

More rapping answers her: "Two bits."

The whole room is on board. The noise level is mounting, tipping the scale for a room full of Alzheimer's and dementia residents. It's a scene from *One Flew Over the Cuckoo's Nest.* "Crazy" has come home to roost.

Abraham is beside himself, trying to keep his composure. "OK! OK! That's enough. Let's get ready for dinner."

I look over at Dad. He's not rapping, but a big grin is pasted on his face. He's a great audience.

Chapter Eleven

Poetry and Dad's Crying Eyes

Dad's been in the memory care unit for about two months. Over the winter and into spring, we ease into a rhythm of visiting three times a week, usually in the Commons.

January 10, 2014

Halsey greets Dad at his table. "Jerome, you look like a million."

Dad winks. "Oh, my God! Sell me. I'll share it with you.

◆ ◆ ◆

"I love my life," Dad says. "It's perfect. I *feel* perfect. Except the words are up too far, and they just don't come down to come out."

He gestures to his head, motions down his neck, and ends with his mouth.

I come away with two things. First thing: he loves his life! What more can I hope for?

He doesn't know, though, my inner turmoil about putting him in a home and breaking my promise to him. A staff person from a different facility helped me to come to grips with this.

"Monica," she said, "you kept your promise. You did everything you could for him, as only one person can. He now requires a team. A nurse, a nutritionist, an OT, a PT, and so on. You were a good daughter."

He requires a team.

I need to often remind myself of this to get past my Catholic guilt.

Second thing: sadly, he's aware of his struggle to bring forth words. That's just plain heartbreaking to me. It would be much easier if he didn't know that he didn't know. But he does.

I make a note to myself to always reassure him that I "know" what he's trying to say.

Hand-clutching Lorraine is talking to the baby doll she carries around. "Now, now. There, there." She pokes the doll's eyes, over and over again with each word.

Another resident gets fed up and demands that Lorraine stop poking the baby's eyes.

Lorraine continues. "Now, now. There, there."

Poke. Poke.

Finally, the indignant resident does an about-face. "That's it. I'm going to headquarters!"

She stomps off.

I'm left wondering where "headquarters" is.

◆ ◆ ◆

As Halsey and I get ready to leave, Dad ends our visit by saying, "I have to say, I love you. That's a big word, but I don't lie. I love both of you."

He points to his eyes, which start tearing up.

"And these don't lie."

He finishes by saying, "I'll be at your side forever."

Oh my. Is that not the best?

January 13, 2014

We have a care conference today. In attendance is Kevin, the recreation director; Mary, a staff member in the Arbor; and Brenda, the nurse. They give us an update on Dad's progress, and we have an opportunity to join in the discussion.

Dad is a wanderer, they tell us.

Very conversational.

Is able to identify his belongings.

Participates in activities.

Laughs at ball catch.

Tosses the ball very gently.

Is in the Commons a lot.

Very gentlemanlike.

Reassuring to his peers.

Is high functioning in his dementia.

Is incontinent.

We hear most of this with happy ears, with the exception of his being incontinent.

The next care conference will be in six months, but we could request one sooner, if we'd like.

January 19, 2014

Dad greets us as we come through the doors.

"When I see you two—BOOM! My whole body falls in love. I see you, and it shocks me. Two beauties."

January 26, 2014

We learn again that he does know that he doesn't know.

"My memory," he says. "Something in there . . . turns it off and throws it out."

It breaks my heart.

◆ ◆ ◆

We tell Dad we will be taking a road trip to Florida.

"Be safe on your trip," he says. "You're not young birds, y'know."

Halsey responds with, "Oh, I don't know, Jerome. We're in pretty good shape."

"Well, you may know what's on the inside, but I see the outside."

Funny, Dad.

◆ ◆ ◆

Dinner is being served.

"How's the salad, Dad?" I ask.

"It tastes like it doesn't have any freedom."

With fewer connecting points between thoughts and speech, his words aren't confined by boundaries. They're given wings of their own. Words that at first sound nonsensical take on new life. They spew forth and create beautiful magic. Beautiful cadence. Beautiful poetry.

But you have to open your mind and get out of the small framework of "normal." Sometimes I can't figure out the meaning of his words. I can't fill in the gaps of those connecting points. But when I do—my soul soars, and I marvel at the beauty of the words.

So, let me think: the salad doesn't have any freedom . . .

Ah! Of course it doesn't. It's nothing out of the ordinary. It's just a plain old salad. It's boring. There's no life to it. It lacks the freedom to be the incredible salad it truly should be.

Even when I don't understand the poetry, Dad's words have a wonderful twist that brings much imagery to mind. My eyes are often soft as his words spill through my being. My Dad bathes in the warmth of my eyes and I can see that he feels understood.

We're building a connection that will forever resonate in both of us.

February 9, 2014

We're sitting at Dad's table in the Commons. He wags his finger at Halsey and me.

"These two people here, I want them to live forever! I don't want to lose either one of you."

February 11, 2014

"Dad, I just love you," I say.

"That's all I need," he replies.

February 22, 2014

"I like both of you," he says. "Halsey I might like to kick around a little bit." He winks and smiles big.

Again, he takes his finger and wags it at both of us.

"These two people mean the most to me. Very helpful and kind. They're my charms. We have a great conversation. Just like body and soul."

February 25, 2014

We come to sit at Dad's table.

"How do you always find me?" he asks. "I'm glad that you do—but it's always a shock. But a good one."

◆ ◆ ◆

Dad laughs at something he's said.

"I have fun with myself."

◆ ◆ ◆

A woman keeps looking at him.

"She probably likes what she sees," he says. "But I doubt it."

◆ ◆ ◆

"I'm a good boy, and I know it."

March 9, 2014

Dad tells us something, and I'm trying to follow, but it's difficult to understand. Upon seeing the furrow of my brows, he thinks whatever he said was offensive. He tries to apologize.

"I hit it by accident," he says, "but then I rewound it."

March 19, 2014

I see Dad, shoulders slumped, at his table. It's on my heart to say a small prayer aloud, so I do. I intend the prayer for Dad, but I don't want him to wonder why I'm praying specifically for him.

So I say, "Jesus, look after Dad, Halsey, and my kids."

"I have tears in my eyes right now," Dad says, hearing this. "They even want to fall down. You're good people, and I love you. I need to tell you more often."

◆ ◆ ◆

He's stringing thoughts together.

"Grandpa had about six calves. Family is small, but they mean a hell of a lot to me." To me, he adds, "You're on top of the list."

March 22, 2014

As poetic as I find many of Dad's words, sometimes he says and does things that are simply hilarious. This totally fills me with joy, knowing that this poetic, funny man belongs to me. My dad.

Trent is visiting Dad with us today.

"My teeth don't feel right," Dad says.

"You don't have your teeth in, Grandpa," Trent responds.

This is true. Or at least partially true. Dad is wearing only his top set of dentures.

Dad flips out his top teeth, then reaches into his shirt pocket and pulls out his lowers, like magic. Now we have a set of dentures, uppers and lowers, sitting on an otherwise empty dining room table.

Nice. I snap a picture to record the moment.

◆ ◆ ◆

Charlie is sitting at our table. He's about the same age as Dad.

With a nod toward Charlie, Dad comments to us, "That's one of the ol' timers."

◆ ◆ ◆

Charlie has an exchange with Trent. "Did you ever serve?"

"Nope."

Charlie asks Dad, "Did you ever serve?"

"No."

Charlie points to himself. "Three years, nine months, three days."

Dad raises an eyebrow. "Really?!"

A few moments later, it's repeated.

Charlie says to Trent, "Did you ever serve?"

"Nope."

Charlie asks Dad, "Did you ever serve?"

"No."

Charlie points to himself. "Three years, nine months, three days."

Dad raises an eyebrow. "Really?!"

March 23, 2014

"Dad, guess who I saw today? Stan Brinkman."

"Is he still up and down?" Dad replies.

I assume he means, "Is he still around?" But "up and down" works too.

◆ ◆ ◆

Then, out splashes a comment from Dad, and I just want to tape it to my heart so I don't forget it.

"I wish I could put you under my arm and hold you there forever," he says. "I do have great feelings even when you're not there."

◆ ◆ ◆

"My mind . . . I put the wrong words to it and then spit it out anyway."

◆ ◆ ◆

We've given Dad a stuffed puppy. It's not a Boston terrier, but at least it's a puppy. He's always had dogs as pets. From a little boy on, he's loved his dogs.

He starts talking to his little puppy.

Shirley, the killjoy, says, "He's not alive, you know."

Without missing a beat, Dad says, "He *is* alive."

Gwen, a former elementary school teacher, might as well have kicked Shirley under the table. "Never mind," she tuts to Shirley.

◆ ◆ ◆

Dad starts talking to Ted, who's also at our table. Ted is in la-la land 95 percent of the time. He bobs his head with his boxy glasses and grins as he looks toward the ceiling.

Dad suddenly realizes he's talking to Ted and has mistaken him for Halsey. "Oops!" He points to Ted. "I meant to talk to Halsey. I went crazy there for a while."

◆ ◆ ◆

Shirley still wants to continue with the stuffed animal conversation. "Would you like to trade him for a wife?" she asks.

"No! Heavens, no!" Dad replies.

March 27, 2014

The folks from Optage come for their monthly visit. Optage is the home and community services division of Presbyterian Homes & Services. They provide house calls, care management, hospice, and other services to the residents. Their mission is "to enrich the lives of older adults through services and communities that reflect the love of God."

Dad's pulse is good (67). Amount of oxygen in lungs is very good (93/100). Blood pressure is perfect (128/68).

As his blood pressure is taken, Dad mutters, "I kind of have skinny arms."

"We'll have to give you more cookies," the nurse says.

"If it's the right kind, I'd like it."

There's a tiny bit of swelling at his ankles, which is typical. Dependent edema. His socks leave indentations.

The nurse tells Dad to take a deep breath.

"I forgot how to do it," he says. He then figures it out and takes a breath.

There's a little bit of noise in his lungs at the end of his breathing cycles. The nurse tells me it's rhonchi, which are low-pitched rattling sounds in the lungs. Normal for a smoker. The nebulizer will keep the inflammation in his lungs under control.

We conclude by having Dad do an "Up and Go" test. Dad is asked to stand up and go walk down the hallway.

Dad got up and went.

April 3, 2014

I notice Dad is busy with a staff member at his table, so I go into his room at the end of the hallway to sign in. When I get back to the table in the Commons, I mention to Dad that I saw his puppy on his bed.

"Well, that little shit," he says. "I'm going to cut Mom loose, and she can buy as many as she wants."

He then says, "I know I feel a lot more freedom now that you and Halsey are looking after things. I don't want to break up the farmlands. I'd like to keep it as a partnership."

Halsey and I look at each other. Dad remembers he has farmland and a partnership! It's amazing what memories and thoughts can pop in and out, how he can go from poetic to a spot-on statement.

"That Halsey. He's my boy." He winks as he says this. "When I see you two, I just melt."

◆◆◆

Making conversation, I ask Dad, "If you could have anything you wanted to eat right now, what would it be?"

Without missing a beat: "Hot dogs."

We bust out laughing.

April 10, 2014

"Here, here. Now, now." This comes from Lorraine. She flutters from table to table with the mantra, "Here, here. Now, now."

Shirley: "Could you leave? You're bothering us."

Lorraine: "You old bag."

Lorraine sidles over to Halsey and starts rubbing his back. I can see the hairs on Halsey's back rising. He is uncomfortable with Lorraine's advances. Finally, Lorraine leaves.

Shirley asks Halsey, "Were you flattered by all that?" Before he can answer, she turns her attention to Dad and the mixed vegetables on his plate. "Are you going to eat that? It looks suspicious."

"Oh, yeah," Dad says. "I'll eat it because I know what it is."

"What is it?" Shirley asks.

"I don't know."

They share a laugh.

◆◆◆

Since Shirley's always talking about marriage, and turnabout is fair play, Dad asks her, "Are *you* married?"

"I have to go home to find out if he's still there," she says. "I haven't been home for a while."

A while? Like, years.

◆◆◆

I say to Dad, "You're so cute."

"I know. I like to be cute."

Lorraine is back to touching Halsey all over. He looks at me in pain.

"It might be time," he says, gesturing with his head toward the door.

Once Halsey finally manages to pry himself loose, he walks around the table and stands on the other side of Dad to say goodbye.

Shirley looks at Dad and says, "Save him."

Chapter Twelve

Kamikaze Blackbirds

Time spent with Dad transports me into the Other World. Each time we visit, the transition gets much quicker and easier. Which is good—as long as I can make my way back to my own world.

Walking helps. I plant my feet back on the ground. I have open space. I slow myself down and walk to nature.

On my morning walk, I admire the small lake to my right. Surrounding the edge, the tall grasses wave in the gentle breeze. I observe four drakes floating in a circle, congregating just like retired men in a coffee shop on a weekday morning. Three ducks barefoot ski as they come in for a landing to join them.

Meanwhile, a cacophony of titters and trills, warbles and whistles, screeches and squawks interrupts my thoughts as I approach an upcoming bend. Red-winged blackbirds are making their presence known in the whispering leaves of the cottonwood tree ahead. I sense they're about to have an altercation—with me.

This same spot has become a war zone on previous walks. I've tried the nice approach many times, uttering reassurances that I'm on their side, that I'm not going to harm their nest.

"I'm not even sure where your nest *is*, exactly," I quietly reassure them.

Well, I'm done with the nice approach. They're not buying it, anyway.

The little kamikaze bastards swan-dive at me in pairs.

I put my head down and tuck my chin against my chest to avoid having my eyes pecked out. Keeping my stride, I quickly untie the sleeves of my sweatshirt from around my waist. Keeping one sleeve in my hand, I masterfully helicopter the garment over my head, trying to make my way past the terrorists. I windmill my arms as I round the bend, staving off the pilots dive-bombing me.

Trying to recapture my calm, I take a few deep breaths, inhaling the scent of fabric softener sheets wafting through the air from a nearby home. I focus on and appreciate the familiar household scent. It softens the moment. I can fold up the blackbird disruption, flip it over my shoulder, then continue my solitary respite of a sunny early-morning walk.

An oblivious bunny nibbles at the tired grass blades near a discarded plastic Mountain Dew bottle. We haven't had any rain lately, and the area's watershed is bone dry.

I retie the arms of my sweatshirt around my waist and come upon the culvert that passes under the road. It houses a small puddle that didn't have enough push to make it into the small lake behind me, where the ducks lounged.

A frog ensemble lies hidden in the weeds by the dormant water. Cicadas call from the roadside. I'm not fond of the sight of either creature, but the music of both makes me smile. Steady and harmonic.

My walk is composed of four segments. Mentally, I make note of what segment I'm on as a measure of my progress. I've just finished the first segment.

As I cross the road, I begin the second segment. I always see the Dog here. He's in his position at the corner of his house; he lets out his daily single bark. Doing his job as guard dog. When the Dog notices my glance in his direction, he nods with a flop of his tail.

This second segment has a litany of human activity. The beauty of the walking trail is marred by scraps of a colorful Doritos bag and a brown plastic Cub grocery bag shredded in bits by the early-morning lawn crew. More traces of shredding are farther up the trail.

I pass the pink bike with training wheels and a single sock, both of which have been abandoned and forgotten for six days now. I reflect on how society has become a generation that finds most things disposable.

I remember how we were not allowed to come home unless we brought all our belongings with us.

"Where are your baseball gloves?" Dad would ask my brothers.

"Monica, where are your sandals? Go get them," Mom would say to me.

I continue on my walk. And now, a bike seat. How is it possible to ride a bike and not know your seat fell off?

It's funny how memories are suddenly triggered. I remember the time I rode my bike to grade school but then walked home at the end of the day, forgetting the bike. Mom asked me where my bike was. *Oh no.* Back to school I trudged to collect it and ride it back home. It was over a mile each way. It was a good lesson, and I didn't forget the bike again.

Walking, steering clear of puddles created by the lawn sprinklers. Walking, keeping my senses alive. Feeling the crisp breeze as I clear the wooded area and am now on the path where nothing holds the wind back. Feeling the sun as it cups my face and warms it in its hands.

Walking. The smells, sounds, visions are contradictions. Some are man-made; others are God-made. I am a product of both. Prayers of thanksgiving being sent upward for the beautiful day.

Walking. Without the distraction of a headset, I can listen to my own memories, capturing Girl Scout tunes of the past. I can listen to my own prayers. There's power and beauty in silence. It gives room for God. It's real.

On my way back, I reflect on Dad's words three months ago, back in January: *The words are up too far, and they just don't come down to come out.* Are there things up there that he can no longer impart to me? Thoughts? Memories? Advice? I can't imagine the horror of that. Trapped by circumstances.

I'm hit by the many things in my own mind that I want to relay to my boys and their families. What if I'm not given that opportunity?

I start mentally tallying them:

- When you can't control what's happening, challenge yourself to control how you respond to what's happening. That's where your power is.
- Most people do not listen with the intent to understand; they listen with the intent to reply. Listen to understand. Very important with your wives and children.
- Do not judge others.
- Enjoy your families.
- Cultivate silence. Invite the Holy Spirit to guide you.
- Nature is good for perspective.

I need to make a point to tell them. Soon, while I'm still able.

Chapter Thirteen

Receding Gums and Memory

April 14, 2014

We've scheduled a dentist appointment. Dad hasn't been keeping his dentures in. Ben, Dad's primary daytime-care provider, says the dentures are rubbing sores on Dad's gums.

Halsey and I agree to meet at the dental office. Halsey picks up Dad from the Arbor, then drops Dad off at the dental office door while he goes to park the car. I'm already inside, waiting.

Dad spots me at the revolving door and greets me with, "Oh, my sweet little heart."

Just hearing these words, this "sweet little heart" catapults and does cartwheels!

Absolutely nothing can be accomplished at this dental visit for two reasons. First, if your connectors in your brain don't connect, then you can't explain where the dentures are rubbing, where they're too tight. In turn, your dentist can't home in on what to correct. Second, even if Dad could express his discomfort, there's little the dentist could do anyway. Dad's lower gums have all but disappeared, so his dentures pretty much just float.

It's unproductive.

The three of us go back to McKenna and settle in the Commons. Twice, without me prompting it, Dad says, "Oh, I love you!"

We never really mentioned love as we were growing up. In fact, I remember Dad very clearly stating, "I *love* my wife. I *like* my children." Love was evidently reserved for marriages. We got it. I didn't feel shortchanged. I knew the love was there all around.

But this current normal of Dad's life is all-new, unchartered territory. I quickly grab the now-said words and tuck them safely inside. I find it interesting that as much as he struggles to find words, he still fully understands and conveys love. Statements of love are spot-on, instead of being replaced with the "poetry" of his confusing logic.

◆ ◆ ◆

That same day, we have another Optage visit in the Commons.

"If I were home," Dad tells the nurse, "I think there would be more laughter in me."

This is rare—an acknowledgment of his *not* being at home. After his hip replacement, he seemed to have forgotten many things. His forgetting wasn't always bad. He forgot he had a home, which meant he didn't struggle as we put him in a care facility. He forgot he smoked. He forgot he didn't eat vegetables. He forgot he hated pizza.

"They feed you well here and give you coffee?" the nurse asks him.

"And keep me clean," Dad answers.

"Do you ever feel sad, Jerome?"

"Sometimes I complain about myself. I'm surprised it doesn't stick to the wall." He nods in my direction and winks. "I'd rather live with Monica. We know each other."

This makes me sad. It's taken me a long time to come to grips that Dad's care requires a team. One person, or even two, cannot do it.

The good news is that once Dad says something, it immediately exits his mind. He won't be dwelling on it.

I hope.

I try to refocus on his assessment.

Blood pressure is 138/78. ("Good.")

Pulse is 52. ("Don't worry unless it's low 40s.")

Oxygen is 93. ("Really good reading, but need to continue the inhaler, given the COPD.")

Respiration is 18 when sitting; 22 when he first sits down.

He's been on Zoloft for some time. ("Should continue for sadness.")

Might discontinue Namenda, which is used for dementia for the Alzheimer's type. ("It does help to slow progression, when started very early on. He's past that now. Not effective at this point.")

He's past that now. The words kill me. It seems like we just went down a notch on the Alzheimer's scale. I feel like Dad's presence is being chipped away.

Continue with his inhaler. ("Ordered a thirty-day supply just yesterday with three refills from Walgreens.")

As the assessment ends, Dad says, "I'm real pleased with everything. I enjoy my family, and they enjoy me."

"He's very stable," the nurse tells us. "I think we can go to every other month, so no visit next month."

April 20, 2014

It's Easter!

The restaurant downstairs offers buffets for the holidays, so residents can have a special dinner with family. We signed up ahead of time to guarantee a time and table.

We take Dad downstairs for the Easter buffet. They have it nicely decorated to give it a spring feeling.

Dad spots a waitress. "She's like a little ant running around. I love my own family. I don't need any ants."

◆ ◆ ◆

"I can't ask for it better than I have right now." He points to me and Halsey.

◆ ◆ ◆

"I've been doing some singing too," he says. "And I *like* it!"

Dad never sings.

He starts to say something else but comes up empty.

"My mind isn't realizing anything," he says.

April 25, 2014

"Here, here. Now, now."

Lorraine's coming from across the room in the Commons. She spots Mary, a staff member who's there regularly. They more than likely see each other every day.

"What's your name?" Lorraine asks.

"Mary, Mary, quite contrary," Mary responds.

"Oh, I think I know you," Lorraine says.

Then off she putters.

"Here, here. Now, now."

April 30, 2014

Ann, with the small back hump, has been sitting with us in the Sun Room. She gets up and heads down the hallway. Suddenly, she folds to her knees.

I push back my chair and rush to pick her up. Halsey has trouble getting up and down from a chair, so he's not making any move to help out.

"You're strong!" she says as I help her steady herself. "Who's that man with you?"

"Oh, that's my husband."

"He's a smart man to marry you."

"I like to think so." I smile. I'll have to be sure and tell Halsey this one.

May 4, 2014

We're visiting Dad in the Commons while he's still eating breakfast—cereal, fresh-cut fruit, and a sweet roll. He slides the pineapple and other pieces of fruit he doesn't want any part of into his empty cereal bowl. Dad was never one for fruit. Or vegetables. Or anything healthy, really.

"Are you going to eat that, Dad?" I ask.

"Doesn't look too good. That's why it's in there, and it'll stay there."

◆ ◆ ◆

He takes in the sight of Halsey and me.

"I'd like to put the two of you together, make you kiss, and take the credit for it."

May 8, 2014

"Trent was a great help and buddy to me," Dad says. "And then bingo—he's not here."

Actually, Trent hasn't visited in a while. Mariah's in Mexico, so Trent's been single-parenting this week. I'm surprised Dad's even aware of someone missing a visit.

◆ ◆ ◆

"Our family was so big it broke apart," Dad says, shaking his sad face.

Our family really wasn't big. But I understand why he says "it broke apart." With my younger brother having been killed, and Mom dying at such a young age, I imagine he sees our family as almost nonexistent. Plus, we don't gather together as a whole family anymore. It's just separate visits from individuals.

I feel the same way, I want to tell him.

For me, it happened when Mom died—almost twenty years ago. She had always pulled us together with her weekly Sunday beef roast dinners and festive holiday dessert parties. Those holidays included all the extended family too—aunts, uncles, cousins. From both sides of the family. Did Mom hold our family together? Or was it just a different time?

At any rate, I silently agree with him. Yes, our family "broke apart."

◆ ◆ ◆

Of all the residents at the Arbor, Ted has the most-advanced stage of Alzheimer's. Ted, with his sturdy box glasses.

Dad is becoming a good friend of Ted today. Is this a measurement of Dad's further memory loss—does he relate to Ted the most? Or is he just displaying his kindness by including Ted in conversations?

"He knows," Dad says of Ted. "We think alike. I can't bring out what it is. It gets locked up."

Words. Dad's words are locked up. Maybe he realizes the same holds true for Ted.

Maybe Dad really does relate to Ted.

Dad is a prisoner in his own body. So is Ted.

May 15, 2014

"I wasn't thinking," he says. "I never think anymore. It's all guesswork."

He knows.

May 21, 2014

"Monica, when you smile, it's like you've got a nice long area of teeth." He smiles at me. "And that's a good thing."

He punctuates it with a wink.

June 4, 2014

"You two." He points to Halsey and me. "You're the best piece of medicine I can get here."

June 9, 2014

We're at the orthopedic surgeon's office. The surgeon notices Dad limping, so he wants to take another look at his hip. Dad has been asked to stand with his back tight against the wall for a hip X-ray.

"I have a muffin back here," he says as he presses his butt to the wall.

He wears a Depend undergarment.

June 11, 2014

Someone's stomach rumbles at a nearby table.

"I don't think that's *my* machinery that's bubbling right now," Dad remarks.

June 12, 2014

The hip X-ray showed that Dad's hip bone has shifted, and the screw ends are now rubbing against bone. It explains the limp. Dad didn't have the words to say he was in pain whenever he moves.

All three screws need to be removed. The surgery is scheduled for today. Right now, we're on the way to patient registration.

My biggest concern is that the stress of the surgery and/or the anesthesia might cause his Alzheimer's to further plummet.

We visit with Dad after surgery. He will not need an extended stay at the hospital. We're happy we'll soon be able to get him back to life as he knows it.

As he lies in the hospital bed, a part of me wants to test the waters, to see if his Alzheimer's has been affected with this surgery. I want to know, yet I don't.

We try to bring up some lighthearted memories for him, but he doesn't remember playing pool or Ping-Pong. Doesn't even know what the games are. I see his eyes searching for the memory but coming up empty.

This may not be evidence that the surgery has worsened his Alzheimer's. When I'm honest with myself, I realize it's just the way pieces of his memory have been disappearing.

I pat his arm reassuringly.

"Oh, Monica," he says in response. "You are my favorite in every way."

◆ ◆ ◆

A nurse comes into the room to check on Dad, and she gives us more details about when he'll be released to head back to the Arbor.

"You're doing good, Jerome," Halsey says after the nurse leaves.

"Thanks. I guess. If I am doing good, I don't know it."

◆ ◆ ◆

"Whenever I see you and Halsey walk in together," Dad says, "it does something to me. I don't know what it is, but I just feel great."

We haven't "walked in." We're still sitting in Dad's hospital room, chatting.

I've noticed that when Dad comes up empty with what to say, he often reverts to complimenting us. He might not remember what Ping-Pong is, but he remembers the feelings he has when he sees his family. On top of heartwarming words, his moist eyes convey his love.

◆ ◆ ◆

"I'm all done at the car wash now. They were good to me, I'll have to say."

He's been done at Canterbury Car Wash for a couple of years, actually. When he could no longer keep track of his time and add his hours from week to week, the frustration became too much for him.

June 29, 2014

Dad is back in the swing of things at the Arbor. We're visiting with him in the Commons. The staff is setting up for dinner at the surrounding tables. They'll set our table last, so as not to interrupt our conversation.

Dad notices that our table is still empty of plates and silverware.

"No juice. No connection. They need to collect the rainwater."

Interesting. Is that why he thinks nothing is set up yet—the rainwater? But what does that mean?

Once his dinner is served, Dad takes a forkful and says, "It just puts sparkles on my tongue."

July 3, 2014

The last few weeks have been stressful for us all. It's been stressful for Dad because his mind has no idea that he even had surgery two weeks ago, yet his body is still on the mend, and that affects his mind in ways he can't possibly understand. And it's been stressful for us in that we are still *looking* for any signs of regression as a result of the surgery.

And then he says, "I get lost in my doings. I don't know why I do what I do."

Be careful of what you look for.

Chapter Fourteen

Walking Reverie

Another early morning walk. It's a means to untangle and iron out thoughts.

I'm still traumatized from last night's escapade with the cats. Tigger was on my right, and Puff was on my left—both vying for my pillow. Puff moved in a way that startled Tigger. Tigger sprang up, using my face for traction. It startled Puff, and the floor lamp went flying.

As soon as Tigger ran over my face, I knew it was not good. There was blood. I could feel it but didn't know from where. I ran to the bathroom sink and allowed the water to pour over my mouth with the blood draining out. Halsey came with some ice cubes.

Somehow Tigger's back claw punctured my top lip from the *inside*. Now it's all swollen and hurts when I move it. I look like a Botox job gone bad. I couldn't even drink my green tea this morning—it just ran down my chin.

We're supposed to go to dinner with friends tonight. Great.

Maybe this walk will help me feel better.

As I near the corner by the cottonwoods, I take note that the fledglings must have fledged. No longer am I being targeted by the red-winged blackbirds—though I have a stick ready, in the case of an unsuspected attack.

In my hurry to get away from the danger zone, I trip over a root heaving through the asphalt of the walking trail. I startle the ducks lounging in the tall grasses at the edge of the pond. The sun shimmers on the ripples they leave behind as they quack and glide their way to the other side of the pond. The movement steers the muck and algae slime to the edges. Frogs are amidst the muck.

I continue with my thoughts of what I'd like to impart to my kids . . .

- Take time to be. You don't have to do. Just be.
- When your frustrations mount and you're overwhelmed, do one of three things:

- o   Leave the room.
- o   Take a bath.
- o   Make soup.
- ♦   You'll have bad times. But they always wake you up to the good times you weren't paying attention to.
- ♦   Being "family" does not give you permission to trample on one another's feelings.
- ♦   We're all too impressed with ourselves.
- ♦   Don't believe everything you *think*. Listen to the voice of truth. It will tell you a different story.
- ♦   Forgive. And forgive again.
- ♦   Don't let your cats sleep near your face at night.

A bunny runs ahead of me to hide in the bushes. His long leaps remind me of an epic LeBron James move when his feet left the ground while loping down the court. Suspended timelessly in the air, he turned his head and cheeked a grin at the crowd, all before slam-dunking for a two-point lead. The bunny had the same move, sans the grin.

I find myself avoiding cracks. Even though it's a hiccup in the smooth rhythm of my stride, I plant my feet between the cracks threaded with tufts of grass. *Step on a crack, break your mother's back.* When I come upon a stretch where there are more cracks than asphalt, I set aside the childhood superstition.

I'm surrounded by sound. Mingling with the nearby bird prattle is the rustle of cottonwoods. I wonder again about people who choose to wear headphones as they walk or jog. They choose man-made sounds when they could listen to the majestic orchestra God created with all the birds and insects and frogs in perfect harmony.

Are people also afraid of listening to themselves? I like listening to my thoughts. I wish I could just hit a "record" button in my brain, then play it all back later. I lose something in the translation when I try to retrieve thoughts from my head and make them come out my mouth when speaking or through my fingertips when writing.

Kind of like Dad saying, "What's in my head doesn't come down so it can come out."

There's a far-off howling of a train and a rumbling of cars on the rails. An airplane drones overhead.

The nature songs are interrupted.

Chapter Fifteen

Heart Connections

July 7, 2014

While walking helps me get close to nature's heart, my visits to the Arbor keep me close to my dad's heart. Even though his words often leave him, his heart remains with us.

Halsey and I are back in the Commons at our table.

"There's no Mom or anything," Dad muses. "There's not much of anything except the two of you."

◆ ◆ ◆

Almost twenty years ago, I wondered what was going through my mom's mind when she was in a three-week coma just prior to dying. Today, I wonder what goes through my dad's mind in the absence of connecting points. Is it like a connect-the-dots children's workbook—but without the dots?

He says, "I am kind of wobbly. I forget. I have to pick it up on my forehead before I forget."

And that's exactly what I imagine. *Where's that next dot?*

◆ ◆ ◆

"I think the two of you should get married again," Dad tells us.

Actually, this means he's pretty connected today. He remembers Halsey and I are married. That's encouraging.

"How's Lawrence doing?" he asks.

Even better! Today he remembers he has a brother.

We use both of these remarks as a launchpad to further our conversation. Some days Halsey and I find ourselves grasping at anything to talk about with Dad, just to have conversation. We pick random thoughts out of the air, hoping that they strike a chord with him.

But today he's giving us the tools! We can tease out and build on what's he's handing us. We can talk about marriage—not only Halsey's and mine, but also his and Mom's. We can even delve into Dad's memories about Lawrence and his wife, Connie.

As we talk, we see a slight upward tilt of Dad's head. I believe he feels some confidence in being a key player in the conversation. He initiated the conversation!

Score!

◆ ◆ ◆

"You know me and how much my skin stretches," he says.

I do?

Maybe Dad's not being literal here. Maybe he's talking about stretching in the sense of how much leeway he's willing to give.

In many ways, Dad was firm, and his word was always the bottom line. Yet if you could present your point without arguing with him, he'd stretch and melt your way. Just a bit.

Could that be what he's trying to say? *His skin stretches?*

◆ ◆ ◆

Dad glances over at Halsey. "That Halsey. I could kiss him sometimes, but then I'm afraid he wouldn't let loose."

We all laugh. Inside, I'm so touched by the warmth Dad obviously feels for Halsey. He has allowed Halsey into his heart and trusts him completely. Halsey is part of this family as truly as if he had been born into it.

◆ ◆ ◆

"Trent helps me with the firewood," Dad says. "He's always very good. He doesn't sass or anything."

Yep. I can see that.

Trent did more than throw darts with Dad on Wednesday nights. If Dad needed any help whatsoever, Trent would jump right in. Sometimes they wouldn't even get a game of darts in because they were too busy trying to get an engine started or whatever else had come up that night.

Often, kids whine and complain when their parents ask for help. But being a grandson is different.

Theirs was a special relationship.

◆ ◆ ◆

"That's my girl. And that's my boy." He points to Halsey. "I don't have to fake anything with Halsey. We get along fine."

And there you have it. Halsey is one of the family.

July 13, 2014

Dad looks at the stuffed puppy on his lap. "If something happens to him, I'd like to go with him," he says.

With that, my thoughts tumble to earlier memories of my own, of wanting to go with a field mouse . . .

Chapter Sixteen

The Convalescent Mouse and Making Dandelion Necklaces

Summer 1968

"Monica, get outside and get some fresh air," Mom insisted. "You can't lie around reading all day. The sun is shining. Go make some use of it."

I didn't want fresh air. I was getting all the fresh air I needed as I read the different adventures of the Bobbsey Twins. Still, I shuffled out the door, shoulders drooping, head hanging down.

I found myself smack-dab in the middle of my brothers' imaginary war zone with their neighborhood friends. They were running for their lives, wearing camouflaged helmets, looking over their shoulders, and firing their plastic machine guns. Bodies were thrown down in front of me as one after another were "hit." They grabbed their stomachs, groaned in pain, and rolled over and over into a ditch, where they flopped down. Dead.

This war would last all summer, and at the end of each night, they would be filthy. Dirty and dusty from head to foot. When they removed their helmets, their hair would be sweaty and matted down with dust. The whites of their eyes would bug out from the dark of the filth.

With a whisk broom, Mom would pound out their clothes—with the boys still in them. She'd then steer each boy downstairs to the laundry tub to hose them down. "You aren't fit to use the bathtub," she'd say. (We had indoor plumbing by then.)

I was so glad to be a girl.

After dodging the boys' war bullets, I wondered what I should do with all this fresh air. I plopped myself down in the middle of a big circle of dandelions, sat cross-legged, and started daydreaming.

I absentmindedly plucked dandelions. When you sniff them close, they leave a yellow kiss on your nose. I imagined I was a nymph fairy in the forest, where no other human existed. I was "the savior of all injured animals." I was Saint Francis. A little girl version.

After all, when told to get some fresh air a couple of weeks ago, wasn't I the savior of a field mouse with little black seed-bead eyes? The poor little thing had been limping its way down the alley on the other side from the cornfield. I could see that his back leg had been crushed.

The mouse had no chance to escape as I quietly circled him and slowly eased myself down. I imagined he saw me as a giant ready to pummel him. I tried to reassure him with coos as I gently picked him up, cupping him in my small hands. With one finger, I stroked him softly, tenderly.

Surprising myself, I found a few tears in the corners of my eyes and tried to pinch them back. Pulling myself together, I made my way back to our house, gingerly carrying the invalid mouse.

"Mom! Mommy! We need to h-h-help him," I hiccupped, my heart in a knot. "Can we fix him?"

Together, Mom and I fashioned a little hospital out of a shoebox with bits of grass, where the mouse could convalesce. I was instructed to feed him and give him water regularly. Mom said there were no assurances that he would make it, but maybe with a little TLC, he could get stronger and then be released.

He died two days later.

I wanted to go with him.

Sitting there in the circle of dandelions, I pinched off a few more stems and said a little prayer for the mouse. Before long, I had a dozen dandelions surrounding me.

I'll make a necklace, I thought to myself.

I attached them by tying one stem in a knot high up near the flower of another. I kept going until all the dandelions were strung together like a Hawaiian lei. I slipped it on, trying not to get it hung up on my pigtails.

I pirouetted around and around in a small circle with my arms outstretched. I wanted to send a part of myself out to the universe to meet up with the field mouse.

I looked up to see my mother standing by the kitchen window doing dishes. With a half-smile on her face, she watched me in my make-believe world.

In the background, I could hear my brothers in another imaginary world of warfare.

Chapter Seventeen

When You've Got Something Missing, You Really Miss It

July 10, 2014

It's been nearly a month since Dad's second hip surgery. We're visiting in the Commons, as usual.

"Dad, you look like a million," I tell him.

"I feel like a million when I've got you two. If you ever need help, let me know. I'll do my best. Even if it's picking noses."

❖ ❖ ❖

"My mind doesn't work as well as it used to," Dad says. "I don't push it either. I let it wear itself out."

This fills my mind with competing questions. *Does this mean he accepts this Alzheimer's for what it is? Or is he depressed? Just giving up?*

But then he says, "I sure enjoy this here. I think the most pleasing thing I could have is this right here—being with my children."

July 15, 2014

"Monica, if you can keep that smile, it would be a lot of power for us."

He said "smile." He hasn't used that word for a while. Usually, he refers to my "teeth."

We're told the staff will be adding oxycodone for his pain.

July 20, 2014

"If I was single," Dad says, looking at Halsey and me, "I'd get married to both of you. You're both so beautiful."

Aw, shucks. You can't love anyone more than that—enough to want to marry both of us! I glance at Halsey and see the warmth for Dad in his eyes too.

We're getting used to the illogic of the Alzheimer's comments. Instead, we just listen to the beauty of the bare bones.

July 24, 2014

"That's my girl. She's so good looking. Yeah, I could waltz with her. Now I feel really good thinking about her."

Waltzing—I would love that!

I'm not so sure Dad ever waltzed before, but the image tickles me. Snatches of "The Tennessee Waltz" sneak a peak in my mind. Dad used to play it on his accordion.

◆◆◆

We take Dad for another follow-up visit with Dr. Olson, the orthopedic surgeon.

Dr. Olson greets Dad and asks how his hip is doing.

Dad answers with, "When you've got something missing, you really miss it."

Isn't that the truth? Also, interesting how he knows something is missing.

Dr. Olson advises that we *not* put him on oxycodone. Or if needed, a very limited dose—at the most, 5 mg once a day. He recommends we manage his mental status with physical movement.

Because Dad has been complaining of pain, Dr. Olson wants us to check to see if there's been a change in his activities at the memory care unit. Maybe this would account for the pain.

"We want to manage his pain so that he can function, yet his mental status will be better if he moves than if he takes oxycodone. For example, a walker is better than a wheelchair. Do not limit him to a wheelchair," Dr. Olson emphasizes.

◆◆◆

We drive back to the memory care unit after our visit with Dr. Olson. Dad's riding shotgun while I sit in back. His nose is running.

"I need a rag or something," he says. "Tears are coming out of my nose."

I almost snort, and he joins in laughing.

"I have to laugh at myself, so I guess I'm enjoying it," he says. After a pause, he adds, "It's too bad—I should have had Monica sit on my lap up here."

Apparently, he feels guilty that I'm sitting in back.

July 29, 2014

Dad appears to be confused. Probably because of the oxycodone—even this small amount.

Dr. Olson was right.

◆◆◆

"I think I would like things different," Dad says. "But at the same time—what?"

I would like things to be different too. But I, unlike Dad, *do* know what.

I would love to see Dad back home. I envision him nonchalantly meandering over for a visit on our front porch. We'd sit side by side on the Adirondack chairs, watching the traffic go by in front of our house. Sharing laughs and memories. Commenting on the dandelions creeping into the grass.

Yes, I would like things to be different too.

My dream got snatched from me when he fell and broke his hip. I've come to accept what I cannot change. I slap a smile on my face and in my heart. I shake my thoughts of what could have been and instead make the most of what is.

◆◆◆

It's time for another Optage visit.

Blood pressure: 118/70.

Pulse: 60.

Oxygen: 89.

Lungs sound clear.

The Optage nurse finishes with her exam by saying, "I do notice some confusion and paranoia. We'll stop the oxycodone."

August 4, 2014

"I know there's a lot of news out there, but you and Halsey are my top dogs," Dad says.

I love that he's aware, to some extent, that life is going on around him. He might even realize that something's going on outside of the Commons, out in the huge world beyond his windows.

What I'm feeling, though, is that he doesn't really *care* what's going on out there. Halsey and I are his "top dogs."

In his world, we're all that matters.

◆ ◆ ◆

"I try to play in the cylinder mode," he says. "And I don't sit by the same person."

I grapple with the second part of his comment, but I think I've translated the first part.

"Cylinder mode" seems like an odd concept at first. But then, knowing my dad and his years at Ford Motor Company, it's really not that surprising. The number of cylinders is an important factor in the overall performance of an engine. I'm assuming, then, that Dad is equating himself with an engine.

So interesting how far you have to delve into someone else's being to come up with their logic—if there is logic. And in this case, I find that there is!

◆ ◆ ◆

"I like my girl," he says. "And if I have to carry her home, I will. And this guy." He nods in Halsey's direction. "I love him as much as I ever did. And I love my dogs. No civet cats, though. I just like your company so much. I just want to be with you."

◆ ◆ ◆

Dad's shoes have become a safety issue. The staff has mentioned that they're having problems with him wanting to play with the laces. More often than not, his shoes are untied because he's constantly fiddling with them. I'm pretty sure he doesn't even know what they are—just something dangling from his shoes, which piques his curiosity.

So, we make an outing of it and take Dad to get a new pair that won't require laces.

We chat in the car on the way to the shoe store. Dad has one condition for the new shoes: "Just so they're not women's shoes. But then," he adds, "there's not a person in a hundred who would know who I was."

He continues talking as we drive along.

"I think a lot, and I love my parents a lot. Even the ones that are gone."

They've both been gone for close to forty years.

It's a hot day, making it stuffy in the car.

Dad comments with, "The heat is warm."

After our trip to the shoe store, we return to the Arbor and continue our visit in the Commons.

"I like my lifestyle," Dad begins. "But I don't like what happened to my family. Not only my parents, but my animal family."

Dad has always had dogs in his life. A few come to mind.

When we were young, there was a mutt named Blackie. I'm guessing this dog just roamed over to our farmhouse and decided to stay.

When my parents intentionally picked out dogs, they chose Boston terriers. The first Boston was a mix named Butch. Butch didn't care for anyone in uniform, so the mailman was a good target.

Our front door had three windows spaced equally apart, going down the center of the door. Each window was a square—about fourteen inches. I can't tell you how many times Butch smashed right through the lowest window, which was at just the right height to allow him to see someone coming to the door. If he didn't like what he saw, he'd race from the side door in the kitchen to the front door in the living room. Back and forth. Back and forth. He'd race until he worked himself up into a fever pitch, and then CRASH! Right through the lowest front door window. We'd have the vet stitch him up, but Butch didn't learn. It was a repeat performance.

After ten years or so with Butch, he passed away. My parents then sought out purebreds. Buster, Pepper, Corky, and Baxter. All Bostons. All Dad's "animal family."

♦♦♦

Dad shakes his head as he looks at me, then he turns to Halsey. "You've got something there," he tells Halsey. "Don't turn her loose."

Before we can respond, he's on to a new point.

"They have words for guys like me. And if you need to throw me in the river, go ahead."

Looks like we're starting to throw people in the river.

"I don't like how I lost my family, but I like the ones I have now," he continues. "I might sound like a braggart, but I like the ones who are left."

Who are the lost ones he's remembering? Stevie? Mom? His parents?

"I feel a hundred dollars better now that I have you two."

◆ ◆ ◆

Dad brings Trent up.

"He's my favorite, too, but don't tell him that. He's no dumb boy. He knows what he's doing, and he's good."

I have to chuckle. I wonder if he's remembering how they participated in dart competitions in various local bars. Dad didn't care for the bar clientele, but you have to go to the venue where the activity is hosted. I think Dad and Trent lent each other a sense of protection from the bar crowd.

We hear a car with a loud muffler pass by.

"I don't know who that is," Dad says. "It could be Chad or Trent." He's thinking of both of my boys now. "I don't know which one."

◆ ◆ ◆

"I don't know if I should tell you this, but I will," Dad begins.

I'm curious what "secret" he's going to let me in on.

"I clean up this place," he says. "And the sooner I get it done, the sooner I can go home. I'm in the middle of housecleaning. It's getting hotter and hotter. And I told them we had to get it done before the snow flies . . ."

It's August. The snow won't be flying for a while.

After Mom died, Dad didn't do much housecleaning. He managed to put things away after he used them, so there was that. But nothing else, really. No dusting, no vacuuming.

I managed to clean his bathrooms on occasion, but I was working full-time and struggling to keep my own house clean. I suggested he get a housecleaner, but he didn't like that idea.

"Monica, I only trust you," he said.

Well, that laid a lot of guilt on me.

Quite frankly, Dad's house needed a power cleaning. One Saturday, I recruited my two sons and their families to dive in for the entire day. Ten of us, plus Dad. The men did yardwork, trimming trees and so on. The women headed inside. The younger kids mainly played.

I probably should have managed the cleaning in a different manner. It would have been better to just hit the high spots and keep moving through the whole house. Instead, I had visions of bringing the house back to its former pristine state—reminiscent of the days of Mom.

Consequently, we finished only one room. We spent the entire day cleaning the family room, where Dad spent most of his time. (And just a reminder: this was the room where Dad grinded his back into the carpet to rid himself of the itch from his shingles.)

There was a lot of smoke residue. Dad would lay in front of the fireplace and blow his cigarette smoke up the chimney. Of course, though, the smoke still circled all around the room. It permeated everything with its smell and left its film on anything wood—including the bookcase, which housed hundreds of books. Each book had to be wiped down. Some of the smoke film was so thick that we weren't sure if it was worth our time even trying to get it off.

"Jerome isn't playing games," Dad continues, breaking me from my memories. "He's just telling them the way it is. If they get rough with me, I can kick them in the butt too . . ."

He reconsiders this last statement.

"No, I doubt that!"

And he laughs his very special laugh.

◆ ◆ ◆

We move into discussing politics. We ask if he knows who the president is.

"I have to think about this. No, I don't really have to."

We can still rib him about Obama.

◆ ◆ ◆

Reminiscing, I ask, "Dad, do you remember how Halsey broke a shovel planting trees for you?"

"*My* shovel," Halsey points out.

Dad grins. "Tough luck."

August 8, 2014

"I'll never change, and I never want to," Dad says.

That's the German in us. Stubborn.

I smile inside—and maybe even a bit outwardly.

◆ ◆ ◆

"I feel bad for not seeing my parents. I have tears now, and they bite."

He points to his eyes.

◆ ◆ ◆

"I'm just a hundred percent happier person when I can look and talk to my daughter," Dad says. "Monica, there aren't enough words for me to tell you how I feel about you."

He must have felt himself sliding into sadness—and wants to break the slide. I'm relieved that he makes the transition himself.

◆ ◆ ◆

But then, he reverts to thinking about those who have passed on. We share a short memory about Mom.

"Even talking about it, I get damp."

Again, pointing to his eyes.

◆ ◆ ◆

There's always a bit of sadness when we get up to leave. It's like when you get ready to leave your house, and you turn back around to see your pets looking at you, imploring with their eyes to not leave them behind. You almost can't do it.

As I get up to leave today, Dad looks at me.

"I'll do my best to stay with you," he says.

It's all I can do to not just sit down and spend another few moments with him, to treasure his words. He'll do his best to stay with me.

What a gift!

Chapter Eighteen

Mom's Greatest Lesson

It appears that reminiscing about cleaning Dad's house with my whole family and the feeling of "we're in this together" just barely scratched the itch of my memories. I have more memories fighting to get in now . . . memories of how much cleaning Mom did in her short life . . .

◆ ◆ ◆

We could read Mom's anger from the rising of her hackles. I'm sure it's because we saw the back of her head almost every night at suppertime, when she had to mop up the milk one of us invariably spilled. She would be on her hands and knees, sputtering the whole time.

"It would be nice if just once I could enjoy my meal while it was hot!"

The area she wiped always seemed to grow in circumference. It might have started as a four-inch splotch of milk, but before we knew it, we were all lifting our feet so she could get under us with her scrub rag.

We'd sneak a peek down at her and see the steam circling her head. Quickly, we'd avert our eyes back to our plates and try to eat. Each bite was hard to chew and even more difficult to swallow. We were choking on guilt.

"Eat it while it's hot. I certainly won't be able to," came from under the table.

We'd sneak a look at each other and feel terrible. We'd done it again.

After scrubbing under the whole table, she'd start to resurface to join us, but then she'd freeze, spying more milk splatters on the table legs and walls. She'd get a clean pail of water and rinse her rag, squeezing it tight to wring out the milk.

"All over. It's even on the walls!" she said as she began wiping again.

"Glor," Dad would say. "Come and eat."

But all we'd see is just more of the back of her head.

Twenty minutes later, she'd get up from the floor and rejoin us, her face pinched.

We tried not to spill our milk. But the harder we tried, the more assured we were that it would happen.

◆◆◆

Mom worked hard outside the home too. Not a lot of moms did back then. Maybe it was because she was younger than most of the other moms. She was only seventeen when I was born, just a young girl herself.

She started working in the nursery at the hospital—the night shift, from eleven to seven in the morning. She took care of all the newborns. We enjoyed hearing stories about the preemies.

Mom would come home in the morning and get us sent off to school before going to bed herself. She would tie on her pink eye mask before lying down in her bedroom, shades pulled to block out the bright morning sun.

During the school year, she would get some good sleep without two fighting kids in the house. Sleep was trickier when we were on break for Christmas, Easter, or summer.

I remember being in charge during breaks when I was eight years old. It was my responsibility to make sure Greg, my six-year-old brother, and I were good. It's hard to believe that Mom was only twenty-five years old, herself, at this time.

It's impossible not to fight when all your brother wants to do is annoy you. I was always happy to read in my bedroom, but he'd want to wrestle with the dog or shoot rubber bands at me. I'd go chase him down, and, sure enough, something would go crashing.

We'd freeze.

Mom would spin out of her room, eye mask in hand. With tired eyes, she'd ask why we couldn't be good. Just for once. Then she'd trudge back to bed with shoulders hunched, feet dragging. (Maybe this was why she had us tack on to our nightly prayers, "Help Monica and Greg be real good kids. Good night, Jesus.")

We were instructed not to wake Mom until one o'clock. It was my job to make lunch. I knew I could use any leftovers in the refrigerator. I always hoped there was leftover gravy.

I'd butter some bread while the gravy heated in a small skillet—on low with a cover so it didn't splatter all over the stove, as Mom instructed. Then I'd spoon the gravy over the bread.

Voilà! Gravy bread!

Sometimes I'd open a can of Van Camp's beans and heat them up with hot dogs from the night before. After lunch, I'd carefully spoon our leftovers into a Tupperware container. On a slip of paper, I'd write "porken beans" in my best eight-year-old handwriting and tape it to the snapped-on lid before putting it in the fridge.

At one, and after cleaning up the kitchen, I'd tiptoe into Mom's room and gently touch her shoulder.

"Mom, it's one o'clock."

She'd stretch and thank me.

I would tiptoe back out.

By one thirty, Mom would be ready to start another day.

◆ ◆ ◆

Mom somehow found a way to work the night shift full-time *and* keep our house more pristine than some homemakers' houses. She had a strict cleaning schedule that she adhered to religiously. My aunt and many others asked her to share that schedule.

Weekly cleaning—dust-mopping, vacuuming, dusting, and cleaning the bathrooms—happened every Saturday. Beyond that, she had a monthly rotation for deep cleaning.

◆ **January—bedrooms:** Everything hanging on the walls was taken down. All curtains were hung on the clothesline to air out. The ceiling, walls, and corners were attacked by the wall duster. Anything glass (fixtures, knickknacks, trinkets) was washed and dried. Furniture was polished. Anything metal got buffed.

◆ **February—bedroom closets and drawers:** These were all emptied. Clothes were hung outside on the line to air out. Clothes no longer serviceable were put in a pile to donate. Drawers were vacuumed out and sprinkled with powder. Drawer liners were replaced. Then everything was put back and away, neat and orderly.

◆ **March—kitchen:** All cabinets were emptied. Every dish and glassware that wasn't regularly used was washed to free it from the cloudiness that occurs over time. The cabinets themselves were also washed before the dishes would be returned. All silver was polished to a sheen. All pantry food items were wiped down. Items with expired dates were tossed. Cabinet doors were wiped down and dried. Food smudges around the cabinet knobs and crumbs on the shelves were eliminated. Wallpaper was wiped down and light fixtures washed.

- ♦ **April—windows:** All windows and screens throughout the house were sudsed up with ammonia water and dried with a cotton dishtowel (to eliminate lint on the windows). She made sure to clean out the dirt embedded in the inner tracks of the screen windows and in the corners.
- ♦ **May—wooden floors:** All wooden floors were waxed by hand and then buffed with a floor buffer. (For the next two months, you'd go flying if you rounded the corner too fast in your stockinged feet. Even the dogs couldn't stand upright. Dad got a kick out of that—unless it was he who was sent flying.)

The list continued for the remaining months. But May was as far as I could get during my first years of marriage, with two small children. I ultimately decided the schedule was not for me.

Instead, I hung a plaque on my kitchen wall that read: "My house is clean enough to be healthy, but dirty enough to be happy." End of story.

Mom gave her head a little shake. A sad shake, I think.

♦♦♦

Of course, Mom taught me much more than her cleaning schedule.

She taught me how people would see my smile before they noticed my too-short bangs. "A smile shows confidence," she said.

She taught me how to pray. I can still see her holding her rosary before Mass, praying each bead, giving the evil-eye in our direction when Greg and I poked each other as we knelt.

She taught me how to show hospitality. How to not just set a table but make it sing! How to find a recipe, wear an apron, prepare a meal, and greet guests with a smile and an air that suggested I didn't just spend the last week making sure every single detail was perfect.

I know it was to her credit that I snagged the honor of being named Betty Crocker Homemaker of Tomorrow for my high school and received a commendation from Congressman Ancher Nelsen. I also received a Betty Crocker stick pin that still sits after all these years in the bottom of one of my jewelry box drawers. It's a symbol of the life skills Mom passed on to me.

(Never mind the fact that I had to go through two divorces before getting it right the third time. Ha! I wonder what Betty Crocker would say about *that!*)

She introduced me to the library and revealed the magical world of books, teaching me to dream big.

She taught me how to nurture—even little field mice. (She hated mice—but she saw through her disgust to enkindle tenderness in me.)

She showed me how to respect others and their belongings.

The one thing I didn't learn or inherit from her was an interest in local politics and community involvement. Mom retired after eighteen years of nursing at St. Francis Regional Medical Center and twelve years of successful management of the Sundance Medical Clinics. She then played an active role in the community, getting elected to three four-year-term offices as well as serving on numerous committees and task forces.

Mom gave me so much of herself. But her greatest lesson came unexpectedly.

◆◆◆

It was Halloween 1995. My sons were seventeen and fifteen, so they were out and about with their school friends.

Not wanting to give up my second-favorite holiday just because my boys were too grown up, I continued with my practice of being in costume as I handed out treats. I transformed into a mummy using strips of white bedsheets winding around my body. As the finishing touches to scare the neighborhood kids, I strategically hung cobwebs with black plastic spiders from corners of doorways, and eerie music played in the background.

Then the phone rang. Mom was being taken by ambulance to Abbott Northwestern.

Heart in throat, I turned out all the lights, demummified myself, and got in the car.

Brain tumor. The most aggressive kind.

"We got as much of the cancer as we could," the surgeons said.

After the surgery, our family tried to carry on with life as best as we could. But life was surely different, due to Mom's side effects from the scheduled radiation and the chemo treatments.

Christmas was uncomfortable. Mom put on a false front of Christmas cheer, but I could read through it. Every gift that was exchanged had an element of "this might be the *last* gift."

After about three months of what seemed like "pretend living," Mom was admitted at Mayo Clinic.

◆ ◆ ◆

It was February 1996. Mom had been in a coma for over two weeks at Mayo Clinic.

I was at her side, rambling on about this, that, and the other. All the things on my to-do list.

"The windows are filthy," I said. "I can't wait until April to get them washed. And I still have Christmas things to put away. The cats keep shedding fur. I need to dust-mop. Again. Why do they have to *shed so much*? And what they don't shed, they yank out of each other when they fight. I'm so behind on laundry. Not even to mention the bedroom closets and drawers that I should be doing this month."

I thought she would be proud that her daughter was finally adhering to some sort of cleaning schedule. But as I rattled on, Mom's forehead became tight, wrinkled, and pained.

I paused. And then it dawned on me.

"It's not about all that we have to *do*, is it, Mom?"

Her forehead started to relax. I watched it. The peace spread.

I paused again. I tried to read her. *If it's not about doing, what is it about?* Then finally, *Ah!*

"It's about the people."

She lifted her eyebrows in affirmation.

Without uttering a single word, she gave me the most important lesson in my life. *It's about the people.* I tucked that lesson inside me, taped it in a forever place of my being.

Less than a week later, she left us. Fifty-seven years old.

Chapter Nineteen

Don't Pee-Pee on Me

Hard to believe we've been doing these routine visits for nine months already. They've been like clockwork. The Commons has become our "home" with Dad.

August 10, 2014

I think Dad must be having a good day. He's full of smiles and has a twinkle about him. He shares an episode out of who knows where.

"I had one guy who kicked me while I was taking a leak. And I sprayed him." He laughs. "And then I took off!"

He looks to us for a reaction. We give him the thumbs-up he wants.

◆ ◆ ◆

Dinner is over, so staff members are trying to clear the tables as we sit and chat with Dad. Ours is the last to clean up—I can sense we're in their way. Kind of like when you're the last people still sitting in a restaurant, and your waitress discreetly gets you to leave by sweeping all around your table but not under it.

So, rather than make the staff steer around us, I decide it'll be easier if we just move to an already-cleared table.

"Let's go, Dad," I say.

"I don't have anything in my pants," he replies.

Maybe he misunderstood. Perhaps he thinks I want to take him to the bathroom . . .?

For fun, I decide to address his claim that there's nothing in his pants. "You have your butt," I answer.

"That ran away too," he says.

Along with his mind, I think. *Does he realize that too?*

◆ ◆ ◆

"I feel just as strong as any nut in here," he says.

All I can do is just smile and shake my head. "Oh, Dad—I love you!"

"Totally in *my* mind, you're with me all the time," he replies. "I gotta put you ahead of all of them."

◆ ◆ ◆

Dad's trying to tell a story but coming up short. I try to help him along, but for some reason, that doesn't go over well. I only end up interrupting him.

"When you live alone, everything is supposed to come toward you, but it don't." He says this matter-of-factly, not angrily.

I'm wondering if maybe he's referring to being interrupted. Over the years, that's one thing that could always get him upset. If he felt you cut him off midsentence, he'd let you know.

I assumed he felt it was rude to interrupt. Now, I'm reassessing this. Maybe he got irritated because the interruption caused him to lose track of his thoughts. Could it be that his memory issues started even earlier than we originally thought?

I rethink his remark now. When you "live alone," you certainly don't have anyone interrupting you. That means everything can "come toward you."

But these days, the words just aren't coming toward Dad—with or without interruption.

◆ ◆ ◆

Someone sneezes, startling him.

"Jesus Christ! I hope she doesn't have bullets in there!"

◆ ◆ ◆

"I do feed all the cattle. I haven't missed one yet. I do respect the bulls. I will run a little faster with them."

To my knowledge, Dad's growing-up years on the farm did not include cattle. Or bulls. They had chickens and maybe a hog or two.

I just can't grasp what he's thinking about. Maybe when he was young and chumming with his cousin Leo, they pestered the bulls. I wouldn't doubt that.

◆ ◆ ◆

"That Monica. I love her. How can I not?" He pats my arm. "No one's going to steal you from me. I'll jump in the ocean for you."

◆◆◆

Dad ponders some deep thoughts.

"Life changes. People disappear. Everyone's doing the best they can. I'm not eliminating Monica either. Or Greg, your brother. And that Trent treats me very good. I have to say that time and time and time again."

◆◆◆

It's time for us to end the visit.

"Well, Dad," I say, "we're going to head out."

"I'll follow you out to the car," he says.

It's a nice thought, and it's what we all usually do for guests. Maybe it's a Minnesotan thing. You say your goodbyes at the table, get up, walk to the door together, then visit some more. You say goodbye again, then head out to the car together, talking all the way. Then everyone stands by the car and visits some more. The guests finally get in their car, only to roll down the window and say, "Good night. Thank you for the nice time!"

Much as we'd like to continue with this practice today with Dad, he can't leave the building. So he goes as far as he can by following us to the door.

I back my way to the door, open it, and say, "Great seeing you, Dad." I toe-nudge him so he doesn't escape, then I stop myself. Shoot! This is what you do with your pets!

As Dad turns to head back to his table, he looks at me lovingly once more, then winks at Halsey. "I don't want anything to happen to her," he says over his shoulder.

August 14, 2014

Dad is ruminating today.

"I don't know what I'm going to do with Monica," he says. "I should keep her here at home with me. Oh, but now I'm just thinking of myself. I love you more and more each time. Look at you. I'll call you a wife even though you're not. You're one great daughter."

A wife? I have to admit my ears creep out when these words first hit the airwaves. But it doesn't take but a second to get over it. This is Dad, doing his best with his disconnected words to let me know how important I am to him.

And then, he adds, "I'm signed up at the Ford plant again. I put in my recommendations."

He retired in the '80s after thirty years.

◆ ◆ ◆

"When I see Monica, I could run for the woods," he says.

"You're going to run away from me, Dad?" I tease.

"No. I'm going to take you with."

I smile. "You touch my heart, Dad."

"I do? Does it click louder, then?"

I shoot a glance to see if he's cracking a joke. He's not.

He's dead serious.

◆ ◆ ◆

Dad's always been very particular about how or where meals are prepared. He especially doesn't like it when people don't wash their hands before they cook.

So, it's great humor when he says, "Monica could have her cats and dogs bring food over, and I would eat it."

◆ ◆ ◆

Back in 1969, Dad bought a brand-new candy apple red Mustang, which he polished weekly. He had it through the early '70s. Then Mom smashed it.

Apparently, she spotted me walking home from school while she was driving. She got caught up watching me as I stopped to pet a loose dog in the street. She must have been daydreaming and ran the stop sign at that intersection. I looked up when I heard the crash.

Dad is thinking about that Mustang now.

"I don't know if Greg has that car or not," he says. "If he does, it would be broken up."

Greg had a history of car accidents as a teenager, especially after Stevie died.

"Poor Mom. Poor me too!" he continues.

Mom was not hurt in the accident—thank goodness. But the car was totaled.

August 19, 2014
Today is a sad day for Dad. I rarely see this. I try to cheer him up. He says he feels OK physically. Instead, it's his "feelings."

"I don't want to be with these people," he says. "They're killers."

Did he have a run-in with someone? Joyce? Did someone ask him to do something he didn't want to do?

I'm frustrated. I know there must be a story here, but he just doesn't know how to tell it.

◆ ◆ ◆

Knowing how important dogs have always been to Dad, I searched online a few days ago and found a stuffed Boston terrier for him. I had already given him the one stuffed puppy, but I thought he might have an even closer connection with a Boston.

I present the stuffed Boston to him from behind my back.

His face lights up. "You're reading me, Monica. He's just what I need."

We sit and watch TV together. With the stuffed Boston on his lap.

◆ ◆ ◆

"Dad, would you like to go visit your brother, Lawrence, sometime? He called last night."

I'm thinking maybe we could make a field trip of it and have the two brothers reunite.

"I don't think so," Dad says. "I think I would die in whatever car I'm in. The people who got me in here are actually the ones who killed me. The whole pack of them. They're mean. If I had to, I'd go to a nursing home. I want no part of these nuts."

Dad's agitated again. Hearing this disjointed reply, I'm rethinking whether it would be a good idea—for either brother—to get together.

And I'm still wondering who these "mean" people are and how they've "killed" him. Again, has he had an altercation with one of the other residents? I know Joyce can be brutal. But who knows what happened? And Dad is still not able to tell me.

Trying to distract him, I point to the patio door. "Look at all the action going on outside."

"I got my activity, and it's right here." He wags his finger at me. "Too young, Monica. I don't feel I'm ready for this yet."

I'm left wondering if a piece of him realizes that this is not his home or his real life. Maybe he realizes this is a "next stage" in an older person's life—one he's not ready for.

I believe there's more going on inside of him, and he's frustrated that he can't convey it. Sometimes it seems he lives in another world in his head.

Sometimes I wish I lived there with him.

◆◆◆

He starts talking to and petting his puppy. Then he talks about his mother.

"She liked her goldfish and her cats. And in a different way, she liked her cattle. She even milked them."

◆◆◆

He says he thinks he fell this morning. Doesn't know if he hit his head.

"It all started this morning," he says. "Wish and hope you could take my place. I don't know what I want to say. The guy in here is a roughneck."

I don't like what I'm hearing. In fact, I'm alarmed. I can't believe he's referring to the staff. Could this "roughneck" be another resident? It all leaves me feeling protective. Maybe my earlier concern is valid—he realizes that the Arbor really isn't "home."

"You're my greatest person, and I ain't saying this properly," he tells me. "I sure like my people and pets. No chickens, though."

Maybe, on some level, he knows the people at the Arbor—the staff and residents—are not "his" people. Maybe he's caught a glimpse of the reality of his situation. I just don't know.

I switch gears. I tell him I'm pulling together a garage sale.

"I want you to have my parents' stuff," he says.

Then he turns to his stuffed Boston on his lap.

"I don't want to hurt *you*, either. If you have to pee-pee, don't pee-pee on me."

August 24, 2014

"I just admire your whole family," he says to me. "Whether it's cats or dogs or whatever. Even Halsey."

Ha! Even *Halsey.*

August 28, 2014

Re: Biting an Oreo cookie: "My cookie is bending my teeth."

August 31, 2014

Dad looks back and forth between me and Halsey.

"This Halsey guy and you. You two. I can't add anything. You're both perfect. I've got my two children here. I feel I'm on top of the hill. Monica, I love you so much I could take you over my lap and give you a lickin'."

◆ ◆ ◆

"I have to move away," he says. "But I want my children to know that I enjoy them."

What is he saying—he has to "move away"?

"I like my children," he continues. "And I'm going to keep liking them."

◆ ◆ ◆

"It's always a mystery to do innocent stuff because the government won't let it be done the way you want."

Now isn't *that* profound?

Dad does not like to be misunderstood, and to be criticized on top of it would be the frosting on his cake. Somewhere along the line, he must have been chastised for doing something he felt was right.

It's a riddle, though. I don't think it was the "government" specifically. He doesn't think that broadly anymore. Could "government" just mean the people in charge here at the Arbor? I know he had a really rough day with the "roughnecks" and the "mean people." Did he internalize that day? Store it away and allow it to fester?

Do thoughts fester in an Alzheimer's mind?

I remember one of the residents stomping off when Lorraine was poking at her doll's eyes. This resident was taking it to "headquarters." Is Dad's "government" the same as that resident's "headquarters"?

I feel like I'm untangling a pendant chain that's all knotted in a ball, trying to find the right loop to take the chain end through to remove the kinks.

Sometimes when I try to follow Dad's thoughts, I feel like I'm left with a lot of kinks.

◆◆◆

He's reminiscing about his schoolteachers.

"I didn't like them, but I kept my mouth shut. If not, I'd be doubly punished—by the schoolteachers and my parents."

I smile inside as I recall Dad telling us about the time he first spotted Mom. She was in fourth grade with pigtails and freckles, onstage for a play. He was a farm boy in the eighth grade and in the audience. He stored away her cuteness until she grew up.

Dad attended St. Mark's School in the '40s. It brings back my own memories of attending the same school back in the '60s.

Penance, Pagan Babies, and Peashooters

It was 1963. We were in second grade at St. Mark's School. In order to receive the Sacrament of Holy Communion, we first had to receive the sacrament of penance. Every one of us has a dark and a light. The shadow is what we take into confession.

Sister Irene had us line up two by two to go outside and walk to the church, which was just up a small hill. Sister led the way, with the rest of us trailing behind. We entered through the side door.

Girls had to wear something on their heads. We had little beanies, but Linda Schrupp always forgot hers. So, she would toss a hankie on top of her head. Sometimes it was a used hankie.

We followed Sister as she went down the side aisle and ushered us into the pews, grabbing the wayward boys who always managed to push or poke at Linda. Once in our pews and kneeling, we were to bow our heads and make the sign of the cross, followed by saying the Act of Contrition quietly to ourselves. We had practiced for weeks in class, so we knew the words by heart.

As I knelt facing the altar, I looked up to the apex of the sacristy. My eyes lingered on the crucifix with Christ hanging for my sins. The longer I looked, the smaller I felt.

I began to feel the weight of my sins that He shouldered for me. All those times I fought with my brother. All those times I woke up Mom with our bickering.

I began to feel so horrible and responsible for Christ's death that I could feel tears biting in the corners of my eyes. Then my eyes welled up, and before long, I was quietly sniffling.

Kids around me were snickering and elbowing, whispering in ears, looking back at me, pointing. I could feel the tears bubbling up. I stood to take flight out of the church. Sister Irene rescued me as I stumbled out of the pew. She escorted me down the aisle, taking me out the side door, into the fresh air.

I don't remember how she comforted me at that moment. All I know is that my first confession impacted me greatly. I have not been able to go to confession since without a piece of me falling apart inside.

◆ ◆ ◆

The boys called them "the crows"—the nuns, in their black habits with bands of white across their foreheads and over their shoulders. Their headdresses tucked all hair away from sight. All were very stern and severe, in keeping with their appearance.

Tap, tap, RAP! The pointer struck the map. The force caused the pull-down map to snap up, taking the United States away with it.

Laughter. It sent the nuns over the top.

More rapping.

"Quiet!"

Laughter subsided into snickering.

◆ ◆ ◆

Peggy Richardson raised her hand. "May I please go to the bathroom?"

"Wait."

Peggy squirmed in her chair directly across the aisle from me. The squirming increased. Then, to my horror, I witnessed a puddle forming under her chair. Red crept from her face, down her neck, and into her maroon school uniform.

I wanted to die of embarrassment with her. I don't think anyone else saw it.

◆ ◆ ◆

Sirens could be heard outside the old brick building's windows, which were thankfully opened to the fresh air. (So unlike today's school classrooms, with their permanently sealed windows and no chance of air—or escape.)

"Boys and girls, you hear the sirens. We need to say an ejaculation." Ejaculations are small prayers said spontaneously throughout the day.

We dropped our pencils into the slots on our wooden desktops. We dropped our heads as well and quietly chanted three-word ejaculations.

"Come, Lord Jesus."

"Jesus, hear us."

"Lord have mercy."

◆ ◆ ◆

There were always tin coffee cans on the windowsill, one in each classroom. That was where we put our spare pennies for the pagan babies.

And where were these pagan babies? We were never told.

◆ ◆ ◆

The boy behind Becky Morgan would take his crayons and color the ends of her long hair, which lay on his desk.

My mom never allowed me to have long hair. Seeing Becky's hair being transformed under that crayon, I was kind of glad.

◆ ◆ ◆

"Here's the church. Here's the steeple. Open the doors, and see all the people." My fingers moved and weaved and wiggled.

"Show me! Show me! I want to do that," Patty begged.

"OK." I started to instruct, going through the motions again. "So, instead of clasping your hands with your palms together, put the backs of your hands together with your fingers pointing toward your chest, and lace your fingers, like this."

Patty tried it.

"Keep your fingers laced," I coached. "Now, bring your palms together. Your fingers are inside your 'church.'"

I looked from my hands to hers to make sure she was following instructions. She was.

"Your two thumbs need to stand straight up—those are the church doors. Now, spring your pointer fingers up and touch the two fingertips together. That's the steeple."

"Like this?"

"Yup. That's great! Now, open from the wrist, and wiggle all your fingers inside."

"And those are the people, right?"

"Let's do it together," I said. I begin the rhyme. "Here's the church. Here's the steeple. Open the doors, and see all the people."

A few more girls slipped over to see what was going on.

"Show us too!"

Sister Irene blew her whistle. Recess was over.

After lining up single file, we snaked our way back into the school and into our classroom, where we all sat at our assigned desks.

◆ ◆ ◆

Sister Irene always said to be sure to sit on the left side of our desk chairs so there would be room for our guardian angels to sit on our right—just next to us, for our protection.

The desks and chairs were screwed into wooden runners, one on each side, like skis or railroad tracks. Each morning, all five rows were filled with students, each sitting on the left side, head down, getting ready for the morning prayer. Thirty-eight young voices, reciting:

Angel of God
My Guardian dear
To Whom God's love
Commits me here
Ever this day
Be at my side
To light and guard
To rule and guide.
Amen

◆ ◆ ◆

Sister Irene was so pretty and gentle. Her goodness just spilled out from her.

Even if your eyes happened to stray to the student's paper next to you, she did not embarrass you. She would clear her throat, causing you to look up and see her left eyebrow quirk. You knew right away that you needed to keep your eyes on your own paper.

I could practically see a halo over Sister Irene's head. You couldn't say that about all the nuns, as we found out by the time we completed eighth grade in the parochial school system.

Let's see. There was Sister Anita Marie for first grade and Sister Irene for second. Third grade—who was that? I'm drawing a blank.

Not all the teachers were nuns. There was Mrs. Mahoney for fourth and Mrs. Klehr for fifth grade. Then it was Sister Marion for sixth and three different teachers, not all nuns, for seventh grade. (Each had too short of tenure, so my memory doesn't pull their names out.) Finally, it was Mrs. Maureen for eighth grade

Oh, and Sister Mary Roy. Where did she fall in? Was she one of the nuns from seventh grade? Maybe part of eighth?

◆ ◆ ◆

By seventh grade, we had moved from childhood to adolescence, so we girls no longer needed to wear the standard one-piece maroon jumper with the white blouse with a Peter Pan collar underneath. Now our uniforms consisted of skirts. Red-and-blue-plaid skirts. Still with the white blouse. We also had navy blue cardigans for the winter months. And navy blue knee-highs.

There was a rule about the length of skirts. They had to reach down to the middle of the knee—not graze the top of the knee and certainly not end midthigh.

Most of the girls wanted none of that. This was the late '60s. Twiggy and miniskirts were "groovy" and "far out." As soon as we got into the school building and away from our mothers' eyes, we quickly turned over our waistbands, hiking our skirts up a solid two inches.

We wouldn't get away with it for long, though, due to the discerning eyes of Sister Mary Roy. (OK, yes. She was the math teacher in seventh grade. It's all pulling together now.)

"Girls," she would demand. "In the hall."

We'd all march out into the hallway and line up single file.

"Kneel down."

We'd do as we were told.

Sister Mary Roy would make her way, one by one, down the line to the last girl. She'd scrutinize each one of us to make sure our skirts touched the floor. If not, she would measure with the ruler she always carried, tutting the entire time.

(Of course, she had a ruler—she was the math teacher!) She would tell each girl just how much hem her mom would have to let out of her skirt.

"And I want this done *tonight*. You are not coming into the classroom with skirts so short. It's a disgrace. *Hmph.*"

Hemming wasn't necessary. The next day, we'd all come with our waistbands unrolled so that our skirts were at the proper length.

Eventually, over the weeks, our waistbands would get rolled back up. And sure enough, we'd be taken back out to the hallway and told to kneel.

◆◆◆

So, about those three teachers in seventh grade . . .

The first teacher was a nun ready to retire—and vulnerable.

We held our school programs in the lunchroom. She would stand in front, holding the microphone close to her mouth. With some "encouragement" from the students, she would start whistling a tune. The boys would cheer her on, and she would be so proud of herself that she would start another tune.

They weren't applauding her; they were making fun of her.

I was tempted to laugh along with the others, but the best I could manage was a lopsided grin. (Like my dad, I make a good audience. I'm not always proud of that. This was one of those times.) But in the end, it was more important for me to be a good student, so I would quickly wipe the grin off my face.

That nun was eventually sent to the infirmary.

◆◆◆

Next up was a nun from Guatemala. She was a tiny thing.

I have to admit: she put forth a good effort. But the students did their best to derail her.

The boys would take BBs and wrap them with a single cap from the Fourth of July cap strips used for cap guns. Once everyone was armed, they would ping the BBs off the blackboard while the nun tried to get our attention to listen to Don Miguel on TV for our Spanish lesson.

"*Buenos dias, amigos,*" came the greeting from the TV set.

"*Buenos dias, Don Miguel.*"

Ping! Ping! Off the blackboard. *Ping! Ping! PING!* One after the other.

"Stop that," she'd say. "I said, stop that!"

Ping! Ping! Ping!

She couldn't catch who was catapulting those little BBs because it was all so fast.

That wasn't all. BIC pens were emptied of their ink cartridges and end caps, then loaded with wrapped BBs. All the boys had to do was put the pens up to their mouths and blow quickly. Homemade peashooters.

Each day ended the same way for the Guatemalan nun: everyone would stack their books on the left side of their desktop. At the appointed time of 2:55 p.m., we'd all look for the signal from Tom Monnens.

After a nod of his head, we would nonchalantly stretch our arms and—whoops!—bump our books, sending them crashing to the floor at the same time.

She would jump up and down in rage. "Stop that! Stop that!" The sweat would pool around the white coif of her headdress, and her black veil would flutter around her as she jumped.

It was pure torment. We sent her back to Guatemala within two months.

◆ ◆ ◆

Our third teacher was a layperson. I can still see her serious "librarian" face with glasses but cannot recall her name. She had a Polish-sounding last name. Something-ski, I think.

She survived the rest of the year, but it was painful for her.

◆ ◆ ◆

Oh. Now I remember my third-grade teacher's name.
Mrs. Heimkes.

Happy Crying Eyes

With each visit, I fervently try to capture the nuggets and the love drops as they sprinkle out of Dad's mouth. I often have no context about what he's saying. The words free-fall. Sometimes all I can do is transcribe them in my journal.

September 7, 2014
Again, we're sitting at our table in the Commons. Halsey and I watch as staff distribute cookies and coffee to various residents.

"My eyes could run out right now, roll to the floor, and poop out the backside," Dad says.

♦ ♦ ♦

"You're a good girl. You'll be a powerful lady when you grow up."

Dad says this to Ann, who's actually older than him.

September 11, 2014
"Somebody's got to keep me going," he states. "And I don't think it's going to be me."

Funny, Dad. I feel that way myself.

September 14, 2014
Dad's having dinner with Ted and Bob.

Ted never talks. He listens to music in his head. Once in a while he conducts an orchestra with a sweeping movement of his arm. Sometimes the ones who hide are the ones who want most to be found. It's the loneliest thing in the world, waiting to be found.

Bob merely looks up every so often and peers through his bifocals.

Dad comments on his relationship with the two of them: "We have a lot of fun, and no one's going to go to hell because of it."

September 17, 2014
"I don't know if this life will go on until I'm dead, or what."

◆ ◆ ◆

"You're so nice. You're the best," he tells me. "I wish Greg were better, but he's OK."

Greg had made some poor choices over the years. He and Dad had locked horns on more than a few occasions.

"I love you as far as I can go," he says.

◆ ◆ ◆

Dad has a bit of a struggle lifting a heavier coffee mug.

"Dad, where's your arm muscle?" I ask.

"I don't know where I put it."

September 22, 2014
"I think I died before I was on the bottom rung."

What makes him say this? Does he feel there was so much more he wanted to do with his life? That he was only just beginning when this happened?

◆ ◆ ◆

He's biting a hard Oreo. "My teeth like to bend over."

This strikes me as funny. He's said Oreos "bend" his teeth on more than one occasion.

September 24, 2014
"I gotta laugh at my own self," he says. "And I can get away with it too."

◆ ◆ ◆

"That Monica. I'd take her anywhere." To Halsey, he jabs, "I'd throw you out and keep her."

He wears a shit-eating grin.

"I like my pair here," he says, now pointing to Halsey and me. "I like my friend—and my buddy." He pats Halsey's knee. "I don't want to hurt you or her, or I'd want to go to my grave too."

◆ ◆ ◆

Two young women walk in.

"There's one for me and one for Halsey." He winks.

What? I almost spew my coffee through my nose.

"I like puppies, and I like dogs," Dad continues. "And I like girls too. But I stay further away."

Good plan.

"And that's my boy, Halsey. I wouldn't give him away. He's cuter than hell. Look at his smile."

October 2, 2014
"I'm just a little old man who doesn't know nuthin'."

◆ ◆ ◆

Joyce is hitting on my dad—wanting to go out to dinner. Whoa! This is a whole different Joyce than the one we've come to know. She is practically *purring* at Dad. Usually, she greets people with a ram of her walker.

"I'm so sorry, but I couldn't find a restaurant," she says.

"No need to apologize," he replies. "I'll try to be nicer to you."

Joyce persists. "Well, if you can make it, we can go down to my apartment. It's been two weeks since we talked about it."

Just what, exactly, does she think they "talked about"? I guarantee you—my dad had no part of such a conversation.

"I'll do better," Dad insists. "More, I really can't do. I don't want to make enemies."

I know my dad—he's feeling backed into a corner.

◆ ◆ ◆

Now a staff member is talking to Lorraine. "The Vikings play the Packers tonight. Who do you want to win?"

Lorraine doesn't feign any interest. "I don't give a damn."

October 5, 2014

Halsey and I join in as the residents tackle the problems of the world.

Bob, our Iowa fan, seems to have landed on the solution, though he doesn't verbalize it. "If they let us in," he says, a follow-up remark that makes sense to only him.

"Who?" I question. "The world?"

We're making up comments as we go along. This makes entirely no sense to us, either. Just an exchange in a crazy conversation.

"The whole human race," Dad answers.

It makes sense to him, I guess.

◆ ◆ ◆

We've started giving Dad a shoulder massage just before we leave to go home. I remember how much he loved getting them when we were kids, growing up.

"That's my children," he says. "You can squeeze me. You can love me."

October 7, 2014

"I think Greg is getting a little closer too," Dad says.

I do know from the visitor log that Greg always comes with one or more of his three boys. That makes me feel good.

I'm relieved to see Dad is coming to terms with Greg. Maybe in this new normal, he's forgotten the complicated and challenging relationship they've had over the years.

I hope that's the case.

◆ ◆ ◆

"I didn't feed the chickens," he says, "but they look like they're around."

◆ ◆ ◆

"I wonder how your mom is peddling around. I don't want to criticize her."

And he wouldn't ever criticize her. He was content as long as she didn't drag him along with her on outings or anything that would take him away from home. When she did drag him out, he'd complain that everything he owned was back home—his dogs, his TV, his bed.

"The only belongings I have with me now are my wife and my watch!" he'd say.

How many times did I hear that?

◆◆◆

"I like my family," Dad states. "Can't put them in a pile and hope for the best."

He mentions his family often. I've come to realize that family— even the word *family* itself—is Dad's tether to a world that is becoming vapor, slipping through his fingertips. He needs us. He needs *family*. He remembers what is important.

"What else do I know?" he says. "Can't be very much."

◆◆◆

"I got a bag sitting by the door. Could be Lawrence's. But my ma doesn't have one. And Monica, you do too much. You wash the eggs. Those chickens do produce a lot of eggs. If I let loose, then it's all mine. If I cooked two chickens in my life, I never went over that mark."

Chickens again. That's the only thing I can pull out of this. I don't "wash the eggs." And he wouldn't know the first thing about cooking *a* chicken, let alone *two* of them. Ha!

◆◆◆

Shirley (to Ted): "And who *are* you?"
> Ted: (Pulls on his shirt tag.)
> Bob: "He's searching for his nametag."
> Shirley (still to Ted): "Who *are* you? Did you forget who you are?"
> Dad: "That happens."

October 12, 2014
Dad pauses in conversation.

"I can't remember what I was going to say. I think the dog might know more about it than me. I'm losing more than I'm gaining." And then, to me, he adds, "You're slipping away from me."

Oh, Dad—never!

October 16, 2014

Dad coughs. "That's not cigarettes. It's carbon monoxide."

Ha! He remembers he smoked!

◆ ◆ ◆

"Greg's coming around," Dad says. "He's trying. We don't have any arguments." He looks to me. "And that Monica. There's no one more pretty. That's how I feel about it. There don't have to be words. I see you. I feel you. And I know you're with me."

Wow. Those words sound straight from a love sonnet. Yet Dad is not a poetic man and never was. Dad is and was many things, a jack-of-all-trades. His thoughts are linear.

But so much of what pours forth these days has the flair of poetry in motion. It's almost as though being unable to connect dots has lifted boundaries for him, allowing words to creatively pour out. It's beautiful!

◆ ◆ ◆

"I like my pets. First of all, I like my children. And that Monica. If I have to take her to heaven with me, I will."

Wonderful, I think. *Take me!*

October 20, 2014

We mention to Dad that we are going to Arizona for ten days.

"Well, that puts cream in my eyes. At least they're not out loud."

One thing I've been noticing is that Dad has a million ways of saying "crying eyes." Sometimes he's crying out of his nose. Today, it's "cream" in his eyes. I could write a blog about it and call it "50 Ways to Say I'm Crying." In fact, I'm going to take special notice of this during our visits with him.

"Both of you," he continues. "You're the two most perfect persons . . . and the dog comes in next."

◆◆◆

Meanwhile, Lorraine is going on and on about something. White noise in the background.

Dad muses in reaction to Lorraine's prattle: "Man. It ain't the way it used to be." Then he reconsiders. "Well, it ain't bad. Maybe I overlipped it. I don't know."

Overlipped it. Cute way to say "exaggerated."

◆◆◆

"I like my family. There's no doubt about it." Dad nods to me. "I have good times with your boys. I have nothing bad to say about them." To Halsey, he adds, "I might let you drive home alone. I like her pretty bad." He nods in my direction again. "I'm not going to ditch her."

◆◆◆

Lorraine is still going on and on. Now she's repeating, "Abraham. Abraham. Abraham."

Abraham is Lorraine's primary daytime helper, just like Dad's primary daytime helper is Ben.

"There's no end to this," Dad says, in response to Lorraine.

And now all the residents are chanting, "Abraham. Abraham."

It's a political rally.

"Abraham. Abraham."

Abraham tries to calm the crowd.

October 28, 2014

"Don't worry, Monica. You're my chick. Monica, you're right up front. And Halsey, you're right behind her." Dad starts laughing. "Not a 'behinder'!"

He enjoys his play on words.

◆◆◆

"Is that your sister?" Shirley asks Dad as she points at me.

"She's my everything," Dad replies.

My heart melts.

November 1, 2014

It's hard to believe, but I realize Dad has been here at McKenna for almost a full year.

Dad says to Halsey, "You're my friend. You're my buddy. They don't come any better."

In between these endearing comments, I can't help but notice Dad has a bit of a limp today.

"How's your hip? Does it hurt a little bit?" I ask.

"It hurts a lot a bit."

I make a note to keep an eye on this.

"Look at that daughter of mine," he says now. "I wouldn't push that in a corner."

November 6, 2014

Dad and I are sitting at the table in the Commons as Halsey comes to join us from having signed the visitor log in Dad's room.

Dad sees him coming up the hall. "You know that guy?" he asks me. "You'd know him a mile away. I would too."

♦♦♦

"I like those nice white teeth."

This is becoming Dad's standard greeting to me. It seems he's forgotten the word *smile*. I think the last time I heard it was maybe three or four months ago, but he still knows *teeth*.

♦♦♦

On Thursdays, the Arbor has sing-alongs after a visit with the chaplain. Gwen, the former schoolteacher, tries to coordinate the singing.

Finally, after a few grimaces, she says to the fellow resident next to her, "Are you harmonizing or just off a note?"

November 22, 2014

Dad's talking about Mom and us kids. He follows up with, "And you, too, Halsey. You're one of the children. I respect my family. Monica, I have to give you credit. You're lovable. I don't ask for much as long as I have my people."

He points to Halsey.

"That's my son or son-in-law. And Monica? Bananas don't even compare."

Bananas?

◆ ◆ ◆

We're watching football, and a player gets tackled.

"I'd just as soon see a person live forever," Dad comments. "Whatever they look like. Life is funny. It's nice, but all of a sudden, you're lying there, and you're gone."

Isn't that the truth? I find myself nodding at so much that Dad says.

◆ ◆ ◆

"It's my own head," Dad says. "Have another nut look me over. If I can find you two, you can come with."

Another nut? Does he think he's a nut?

And *us* too?

Is Dad cracking a joke?

November 27, 2014

"I think about it but don't put the wires together."

◆ ◆ ◆

"And Greg? He's OK, but he might be locked up."

He might be revisiting something back in time. Or more than likely, Greg hasn't stopped by to visit lately. Maybe Dad's just trying to come up with a reason why. "Locked up" seems a bit of a stretch, but so is a lot of what he says.

◆ ◆ ◆

"That one joker was picking on me. I was the lonely one in there."

❖❖❖

We take Dad to the Thanksgiving buffet. Another holiday dinner in the downstairs restaurant.

"Dad, save some room for dessert," I say.

"Keep telling me that periodically—but not every time my mouth opens." He licks his fork over and over again, until it's spotless. "OK. This will be ready for service now." He takes another bite.

"Good to the last bite, Dad?"

"I was just going to say that."

"Do you want your cranberry juice?" I ask, thinking it would be good for any urinary infections.

"You can have it," he replies after the words have hardly passed my lips. Then he looks up at Halsey. "You'll never be forgotten."

❖❖❖

We make our way back up to the Commons. Dad's shaking off the red glitter that has fastened itself to his shirt.

Bob notices the glitter. "Ish."

Dad gets a little defensive and points to some loud people next to him. "There's a lot of 'ish' over there."

November 30, 2014

"My history is ninety percent good—unless I've got that reversed."

December 4, 2014

Dad gestures to me.

"She's a good girl. I know I'm good, and if *I'm* good, then I know *she* is too."

❖❖❖

"There's nothing better than a big family partnership, and there's nothing wrong with that—unless you're nuts."

I think he uses the word *partnership* to mean "joint venture." As in, there's nothing better than a big family joint venture. We're in this together. Through thick and thin.

And there's nothing wrong with that—unless you're nuts.

Amen.

◆ ◆ ◆

The radio has been playing loudly. A staff member comes over to turn down the volume.

"They turned the radio down, so they're holding their nose shut," Dad explains.

◆ ◆ ◆

Laura, the recreation coordinator, can be heard talking in the background, telling someone a story. "I was sweating my butt off," she says.

In her no-holds-barred manner, Shirley says, "And you still have plenty."

◆ ◆ ◆

We're chatting about not much, and something I say hits a chord with Dad.

"I think you're right," Dad says. "And I don't think I can make myself right."

◆ ◆ ◆

"I don't know anything, and it makes it easy."

◆ ◆ ◆

"There's nothing I wouldn't do for my children—and my dogs too. I'd run a mile for them."

That's saying a lot, considering Dad is hardly able to get up and around even with his walker. Not only that, but I doubt Dad ever ran a mile in his life. Running wasn't his thing.

December 7, 2014

"I like my life, really. And I love my children. I like my two partners here." He nods to us. Then he hiccups. "Excuse me." He blows it over his shoulder. "I like my children and your children. I like your teeth."

There's *teeth* again. Also *partners*. Again, I think he sees us in this together.

◆ ◆ ◆

"I hope I live long enough to have you all see me. There's not that much to see," he adds.

◆ ◆ ◆

Dad keeps talking, and I keep trying to follow along.

"I just want to be with you as much as I can. That's my goal. And I don't want to show off. I keep telling both of you—I love you extremely. And Mom leaving—almost out of nowhere. Like my family. I love them. It ain't just *liking*. I like those nice teeth too."

◆ ◆ ◆

I ask Dad whether he's getting hungry. Halsey chimes in to say that *he* is.

I turn to Dad. "Does it look like Halsey's starving?"

"He looks a little overbuilt."

◆ ◆ ◆

"Monica's a good girl," Dad says." Always was. I don't think she got a lickin' in her life, unless she was a baby."

No, I think. *I didn't ever get a lickin'. But I came close to getting one . . .*

Chapter Twenty-Two

All Around the Mulberry Bush

I follow rules. Always have. It's what I do. I'm the oldest child. There did, however, come a day that I broke the rule. It was 1965. There was an unspoken rule in our house: "Honor thy father and mother." The Fourth Commandment. Or in our case, "Do not sass your mother."

But I did.

I didn't mean to sass her. I don't even remember what I said. All I remember is that she accused me of something I hadn't done. When that happens, I start to simmer. And to make matters worse, she had apparently shared her theory with Dad. Not fair! Two against one. So the words spilled out, and I couldn't grab the tail end of them and stuff them back in.

Neither of my parents said a word. Mom continued washing the dishes, with her back to me, but her hackles raised. Then at once, Dad pushed back his kitchen chair.

This was not good. I dropped the dish towel and hauled myself out of there, down the basement stairs—with Dad in hot pursuit.

With my heart in my throat, I started circling the Ping-Pong table, running as though my life depended on it. And I was sure it did. I couldn't let him catch me. I just couldn't. I'd never been spanked, but my brothers had been often enough for me to know it wouldn't be in my best interest.

The floor was slippery. Mom must have just recently waxed the linoleum. My stockinged feet had no grip as I rounded the corners. I tried to upright myself by holding on to the corners of the table.

Round and round I went with Dad chasing me and getting madder by the moment. I could feel his breath on me as he got closer. In my panic, I dropped to my knees and slid, passing under the table to the other side to double the distance between us.

The move caught Dad off guard. "You little shit!"

I thought I heard a chortle in his throat.

I jumped to my feet—pop! goes the weasel—and peered through my scared eyes across the top of the table. Sure enough, Dad had a sideways grin, which he dropped off the minute our eyes met.

I do not remember a spanking that day.

There were repercussions enough in the pursuit.

Chapter Twenty-Three

Bubbles in My Eyes

I've begun my annual Christmas letter, which I send to faraway friends. I start with a quote I picked up somewhere:

Christmas is a necessity. There has to be at least one day of the year to remind us that we're here for something else besides ourselves.

Then I continue on . . .

> *I am reminded of that with each visit to Dad at the memory care unit. In fact, I have peace within those walls with the other residents who live with my dad. They are a family of individuals who have nonvoluntarily shed the outer world from their lives. And there's a certain balm because of the surrender of all that outside chaos. I have found the memory care unit to be the "something else besides ourselves."*

December 9, 2014

McKenna Crossing offers a fine-dining experience three or four times a year in the dining room for those in assisted living and the memory care unit. These dinners are held in a separate area located between the Arbor and Arbor Ponds.

Family is invited. Tables are set with linens, and plated dinners are served by the staff. Live background music provides ambiance. It's our special "date night" with Dad.

Dad asks me to try his sparkling red grape juice.

I take a small sip.

"You don't have to suck it all," he reprimands me.

◆◆◆

For the special event, I'm wearing my hair tied in a ponytail.

"You have a little twister back here," Dad says as he flips my ponytail.

♦ ♦ ♦

"I like my family together," Dad says, looking around our table. "I like your cooking better, though."

♦ ♦ ♦

To Halsey: "I'll be kissing you from day one until the end."

He points to me next.

"And that girl—I'll keep you forever. You'll really miss me when I tip off."

Yes. I'll miss you forever, Dad.

December 18, 2014

Dad lights up when he catches his first glimpse of us. "If I could, I would carry you from here and hell and gone. And I would still love you."

We chat after we settle in at his table in the Commons. But then Dad starts struggling with words.

"I can't talk anymore," he says. "And I don't have horns or anything."

♦ ♦ ♦

After a few moments of quiet, he suddenly says, "And your teeth! They're awfully beautiful."

Again, there's his special laugh.

"Dad, I love it when you laugh," I say.

"They all love me for that," he replies.

"Yes, they *do* love that about you."

"I know they do."

♦ ♦ ♦

Dad starts talking to another resident. "You're a good man. I've known that for years now."

Dad met him last week.

Patting the other resident on the back, Dad says, "That's my boy. Even if you are old."

They're the same age.

◆ ◆ ◆

I kiss Dad goodbye on the top of his head.

"Hmm. I might take you for a banana split or something."

On our way out, Mary recommends checking into a Lidoderm patch for the pain she's noticed Dad has been having with his hip.

December 21, 2014

Mariah, Trent's wife, has been a choir director for the church's six- and seven-year-olds this season. She brings her young choir to sing at the Arbor. In between songs, fourteen-year-old Akaya, my oldest grandchild, narrates with passages of Christ's birth from the Bible.

Dad and I sit in the circle of residents who are the audience for this concert. As sweet voices lift upward to sing "Away in a Manger," I drape my arm around Dad, with my hand resting on his shoulder.

Suddenly, my hand starts to buzz. There's a vibration—like a silenced cell phone in a pocket. I feel it before I hear it.

Dad is singing! I can't believe it!

Dad has actually forgotten that he doesn't sing. Not at birthdays. Not in church. Never ever in the years he's been my dad has he sung.

He continues to join this little choir as they move into another carol.

"Silent night, holy night." He reverently sings the chorus as if he's been singing all his life. "All is calm, all is bright."

I motion with my head to Trent across the room. I nod his attention to Dad and mouth, "He's *singing!*"

Trent looks at his grandpa and smiles warmly.

Maybe it is calm and bright. Really, I believe it is.

◆ ◆ ◆

"You're so nice," Dad says to Halsey. "I'm going to touch you. You're my son-in-law."

"Dad," I say, "if I could be as happy as you as I get older, I'll be in good shape."

"Oh, I think you already are. And if not, I'll take care of it. Ooh, I like my children. Especially these two." He pats Halsey. "My son-in-law."

◆ ◆ ◆

"Dad, how come you're missing a sock on your foot?" I ask, looking down at his one bare foot.

"I don't know. No chicks in my car."

I laugh. To be honest, I'm not sure what he's really saying. Does he mean "chicks," as in cute girls? With a bit of disrobing going on? Or does he mean chickens?

Either way, it makes me laugh.

◆ ◆ ◆

He pulls his sweatshirt sleeve up to his elbow to show some bruises.

"It's getting choked up here," he says.

He's probably referring to his sleeve being so tight around the elbow.

But where did he get the bruises? Did he fall again?

I'm initially alarmed, yet I know how easily we bruise as we age.

December 25, 2014

It's Christmas day—also Dad's birthday. He's sitting at his table in the Commons.

"Happy birthday, Dad!" I say as we approach him. "Do you know how old you are today?"

"Not really."

"You're eighty!"

"I am?" he asks. "How did I get there?"

◆ ◆ ◆

"I get bubbles in my eyes when I get to see you," he says.

(More poetry to describe tears.)

"My family's the main thing. I like everything else, too, but family is number one."

◆ ◆ ◆

He's chewing on a piece of caramel. It sticks to the roof of his mouth, making it hard for him to talk.

"Sticks," he says. "But feels good, though."

♦ ♦ ♦

"I think I'm learning more," he says as he slowly reads his birthday card. "That's what you do to me."

I'm so pleased he's still capable of reading, even if with a bit of a struggle.

And evidently, the card touches him. That's perhaps what he means by "learning more." He's reading how important he is to us.

♦ ♦ ♦

"My whole life I had everything good. I always did love and care for my family."

Family. Again.

Always.

♦ ♦ ♦

"You two sure are the lovemakers," Dad tells us. "I even got a little tear in the eye on that. I think I'm getting pushed aside by myself."

How I love this—we're the "lovemakers." What a beautiful comment!

And what about "I think I'm getting pushed aside by myself"? How do you push yourself aside? It's kind of like being a guest in your own life and realizing life's not what you thought it was.

He says things that just get me thinking deeper.

♦ ♦ ♦

"What I like most about the two of you is that I don't feel like I'm being used," Dad tells us.

This statement is about us as much as it's about other people he's encountered in his life.

Many years after Mom's passing, Dad found companionship with another woman. He reassured me no one would ever take the place of Mom. I didn't need the reassurance; I was just happy he had someone with whom to share his time.

However, he told me he sometimes felt used by her, as if he was just someone to pay for her dinners out. Dad was frugal. I mean, when he and Mom dated so many years ago, he'd take her to the Try-Y drive-in for an ice-cream cone. After he took her home, he'd go back to the drive-in for a burger by himself! Of course, he was only nineteen, with not many bills in his wallet.

This woman (who was very nice, by the way) had also asked Dad to do various handyman jobs at her house. She suspected she had bats in her house, so she asked him to sit in her downstairs to keep watch for them one night. So, off she went to bed, while Dad sat up all night with only a newspaper to keep him company—waiting for the bats to appear. Which they never did.

Overall, I guess he just felt he was being used.

Dad was also concerned about how the church would hit him up for donations. They even sent a deacon out to apply pressure. Dad can hold his own ground. He felt his donations more than covered his own obligation. "I took the number of families in the congregation and divided them out," he once told me. "I figure I'm paying for myself and covering four other families besides myself."

There were others too. In any situation, Dad just didn't want to feel he was being taken advantage of.

Halsey and I don't ask anything from him. I've never asked for a handout. Ever. And Dad knows that. We're here not to *take* but to *give* of our time and ourselves, plain and simple. No strings attached.

He trusts us.

◆ ◆ ◆

We move over to join the residents forming a circle with their chairs around the piano. It's another caroling sing-along. Once again, Dad joins in the singing. I'm still not used to hearing him sing.

I just have to say, "Dad, I love you."

"Every time you see it or think it, it's more than just blowing bubbles," he replies.

Chapter Twenty-Four

Juicy Eyes

When we were kids, Greg and I looked forward to New Year's Day, when Grandma Marge would visit. We always enjoyed her visits, but New Year's Day was special. Grandma Marge was Mom's mom. She waitressed at Charlie's Cafe Exceptionale in Minneapolis, which was a high-class restaurant in its day, until it closed in 1982. Whenever we were in Minneapolis, Dad would make a point to drive by Charlie's. It felt a bit scandalous with its naked dancing nymph statue in the fountain.

Grandma works there?

On New Year's Day, she would come bearing party favors, whistles, and hats from the various parties she had served the night before. She also came with stories of how so-and-so was there. "You wouldn't believe the tip he gave me!" she'd say. Cedric Adams, a noted local newspaper columnist, was there often. So were other celebrities, including Vikings football players. The names didn't mean much to us at the time—but boy, did we have fun celebrating when Grandma came, bearing the noisemakers!

These days, the New Year comes and goes. At one point, I tried to watch the ball drop in Times Square on television. But why? It feels so artificial. A bunch of people whooping and hollering and kissing strangers?

I'd rather use this moment of transition to reflect on where I've been, how I've grown, what I've learned, and what I need to change.

(Having a noisemaker, too, would be kind of fun, though.)

January 6, 2015

"If I die and am still alive—hang in there," Dad tells me. "Maybe I want you with me."

Hmm. That's interesting. If he dies and is still alive . . . ? Is Dad going all philosophical on me?

January 9, 2015

Sue is a regular visitor to the Arbor. She's probably in her late fifties and lives with her mom (whom I've never met) in the assisted-living unit at Arbor Ponds. Sue comes over frequently with her dog, Daisy. The residents love it.

She joins our table today at the Commons.

"He talks about the Ford plant all the time," she comments about Dad.

"I quit today," Dad adds.

◆ ◆ ◆

Shirley is inspecting the black top she has on.

"Why did I wear this?" she asks out loud. "It shows every speck of white."

She snaps and tugs at her shirt in an attempt to pop off the sprinkle of dandruff across her shoulders.

"It's very beautiful, though," Dad says, ever complimentary.

January 18, 2015

Dad has many one-liners. Nothing tied to anything.

"I still respect my religion," he says out of the blue.

◆ ◆ ◆

"Went on the farmlands today," Dad tells us. "Made it bigger so farmers could have more to work on. Lawrence wants to get involved—today. It didn't last. One turn. I shouldn't pick on him," he adds. "He does try."

"Another thing," he begins. Then he pauses. "Ah. Lost my memory. It was clear as day until I just said it."

◆ ◆ ◆

Dad's been fiddling with Halsey's pocket flashlight. He gives it back to Halsey.

"I think I'll let you park it," he says.

January 20, 2015

Fine-dining again. The room is set up with many tables, again with white linens for a feeling of elegance. People stream in, all looking at the placards in the center of the tables to find their family member's name. Every once in a while, you hear, "Hey, we're over here," as someone tries to get another's attention.

"I would crawl to find my people," Dad says. He looks at me. "That's my girl. I couldn't find any better. That Halsey—he's a beautiful thing." He nods at us. "My kids—they don't come any better. Upside down or backwards. I love you better, and I want to keep it better."

◆ ◆ ◆

Dad takes a swallow of the sparkling red grape juice.

"It's so good," he says. "It's going right down my throat before I let it."

Maybe he feels the bubbles before the juice itself goes down?

January 21, 2015

Shirley's talking to Dad at lunch.

Shirley: "Do you want a bun?"

Dad: "No, I'm full."

Shirley: "I knew you would say that!"

Dad: "Then why did you try?"

◆ ◆ ◆

We're getting ready to leave. We push back our chairs, reach behind for our coats, and put them on.

Dad offers a string of goodbyes. "You got nice teeth too. I could follow you right out of here. Take care of yourself." He then says something inaudible as we step away.

"What did you say, Dad?" I ask as I turn around.

"That was too far away." He waves it away with his hand. "I can't remember."

January 25, 2015

Halsey shares that he needs a replacement pair of glasses and that insurance will cover $125 of it.

"Jerome, I get a hundred and twenty-five dollars for my glasses," he emphasizes to Dad.

"That sounds good."

"Well, Jerome, you got to take it when they give it to you."

"Well, it hasn't come home yet," Dad replies.

He then turns to me.

"How do you keep your teeth so nice? You look so good. You must be pushing it."

He turns back to Halsey. "And *you* have nice cheeks." He reaches out to pinch Halsey's cheeks for good measure.

◆ ◆ ◆

"I spent three times at the car wash. I scooted in and scooted out. I put my figures in. I'm not sitting on a stick."

Well. There's a lot being said here, but I'm not sure what. Let's break it down:

- ◆ "Car wash" we know. He worked at the Canterbury Car Wash.
- ◆ "Three times," though? Hmm. Maybe that's just his way of saying he spent many years at the car wash?
- ◆ "Scooted in and scooted out" might be code for putting in his time there and then choosing to retire when he was ready to move on?
- ◆ "I put my figures in"—he logged his hours.
- ◆ "I'm not sitting on a stick." That's a tough riddle. Maybe he's saying he's not just sitting around these days, even though he no longer works at the car wash?

If we put the translation together, we get, "I spent many years working at the car wash, logging my hours, and when I was done, I was done. But I'm still not sitting around."

OK. So maybe I broke this code.

But to be honest with you, I like it better the way he said it.

January 29, 2015

Today my hair is tied back with a black ponytail binder. Dad reaches over and flips my ponytail.

"You have a nice handle here," he says.

◆ ◆ ◆

I trim Dad's fingernails whenever they need it. The staff has a hard time keeping him in one spot to do it. He sits still for me, but that doesn't mean he likes it.

"I might have to get you a bicycle or something for your hard work," he says as I'm trimming. Looking at Halsey, he adds, "And she's got a blackbird on top of her head."

Again with the ponytail.

"That's my girl," he says. "Nothing goes to waste there."

◆◆◆

I'm complaining to Halsey about how he doesn't listen to my answer whenever he asks a question. (What is it with husbands?)

Dad listens, taking it all in. "I didn't look," he says, "but maybe I have it stuck in my pocket."

I think it's his way of helping Halsey get out of trouble.

February 1, 2015

Janet, one of my favorite residents, regularly sits at Dad's table. She leans toward me and says, "Your dad's cute."

"You notice," Dad tells me, "I try to sit next to her."

◆◆◆

Halsey and I muse about whether older generations understand what "hang out" means, so I test it.

"Dad, do you want to hang out?"

"I think I'll stay here," he answers.

February 8, 2015

"Poor Mom," Dad says. "She can save her moneys. My dad—he goes as deep as he could. Much more than I, even. He was a pretty angry man."

I think Dad's talking about *my* mom, not his. Grandma didn't have anything to do with money, because Grandpa was in charge of it.

Dad never told Mom what she could or couldn't do with the money she earned—she could save it or spend it, as far as he was concerned.

Dad's follow-up comment about "he goes as deep as he could" might mean Grandpa paid for everything in his marriage. Grandpa was a farmer. The farm is what paid the expenses.

I think he's making a comparison between the dynamics in the two marriages. Whereas Grandpa was the sole earner in his marriage, both Dad and Mom contributed financially to theirs.

But Grandpa was a "pretty angry man"? This is something I've never heard before.

"Why do you think that was?" I ask.

"He definitely was an angry man," Dad repeats. Then there's a long pause as he woolgathers. Finally, he says, "Everything I think about—I think I gain it, then it falls to the floor. And that's what I have. Zippo."

The words have left him.

◆ ◆ ◆

Later, though, Dad says, "My dad had a good heart. I don't know how to say it because I forgot how to read it."

All I, myself, know is that Grandpa was stern. When he told us not to play in the boxcar with the loose corn, that's exactly what he meant.

I heard stories that Uncle Lawrence didn't always like Grandpa's rules. But breaking them didn't serve Lawrence well. My dad was ten years younger and learned vicariously. He knew exactly how *not* to push his dad.

◆ ◆ ◆

"Monica, you're such a good girl. My eyes are starting to get juicy."

Juicy. Hmm. That's yet another way to say "crying." I add it to the list.

February 13, 2015

I usually don't go on and on about birthdays. And I rarely announce mine. In fact, I'm always a bit fearful that my husband or my boys will forget mine. I prepare to be disappointed.

Suddenly, I wonder where that comes from. I think maybe because of my ex-husband. He liked to *pretend* that he had forgotten my birthday. He wouldn't mention it all day—and then at sundown, he'd pull out a card and gift and say, "Oh, hey. Happy birthday." Meanwhile, my whole day was a disappointment.

But today, I feel like bringing up my birthday. It's a milestone year, after all. Something for both of us to share together.

"Dad, I just had a birthday," I tell him. "Do you know how old I am? You're not going to believe it—sixty!"

"Sounds a lot, but it ain't that bad. Did I say that right?" he checks. "And you got nice teeth too. You can't miss that."

◆◆◆

"See much of Monica?" Dad asks me.

He immediately realizes his mistake.

"No," he answers for me.

And he laughs.

◆◆◆

"Greg shows up all the time, I have to say. Usually in the day."

I'm glad to hear Greg comes and that Dad realizes it.

Then he says something I don't catch.

"What, Dad?" I ask.

There's a pause. "I forgot what I said. I think you would have liked what I said. At least you got the taste of it."

I don't think I got a taste of anything.

February 19, 2015

There's a lot of commotion in the Commons. Chitchat among the residents.

"Sounds like all little kids," Dad says.

In the middle of it all, Lorraine is keeping up her steady chatter, all of it meaningless. Sputtering like a broken sprinkler.

"Sh!" says Gwen, not overly fond of Lorraine.

"You shut up," Lorraine answers.

Gwen, in turn, responds, "I'll shut up if you do."

A few moments pass, then Lorraine continues her chattering.

Gwen finally asks her, "Do you know how to whisper?"

Long since retired from teaching, it still comes out in her.

February 21, 2015

As we sit at our table and look around, it's not hard to notice that everyone has gray, silver, or white hair. Of course, they do. These are all senior citizens. And while Presbyterian Homes has a hair salon, I don't think many, if any, of these residents color their hair. So, it's a monochromatic view.

Dad nods in the direction over my shoulder. "Yep, that's the Silver Group."

Sounds like a bowling team, if you ask me.

◆ ◆ ◆

"I want to keep moving. If I stop, it's the end."

This just makes me want to linger. Savor the words. What comes to mind on this quip though is Mom. She achieved so much in her life—almost as though she knew her time was running out and that she had to pack in as much as she could. Before she couldn't.

Keep moving.

◆ ◆ ◆

Janet has been sitting with us. Lorraine bothers her with her constant "Here. Here. Now. Now."

"She should be long gone," Janet says to me on the q.t.

Dad laughs.

Halsey wants more of Dad's take on the issue. "Jerome?" he prompts.

"I'll stay out of it," Dad answers.

Wise man.

Chapter Twenty-Five

Where's Dad? And a Bottle of Beer

March 2, 2015

When we come today, Dad isn't in the Commons. We check out all the hallways, then I finally find him in his room.

He's sitting on a bench—all knotted up. He has his arm up and through the neck opening of his T-shirt. His left shoe and sock are off. His pant leg is up over his knee. He's wrapped up in his undershirt and an infinity Ace bandage. His lower teeth are on the floor next to him, and his upper teeth stand at attention on top of the dresser behind him.

My heart plummets to see him so helpless—and of his own doing. He's so disoriented that he can't find his way out of the mess.

I get him untangled.

"God, you've got nice teeth," he says.

On our way out, I report Dad's entanglement to the appropriate personnel. Dad is on a new patch for the pain he experiences when he tries to get up from bed. It's called Salonpas, and it's over the counter. The staffer says it might be the cause for his confusion.

March 3, 2015

Halsey and I are debating the "better bagel."

After listening in for a while, Dad says, "I made up my mind I wasn't going to stick my nose in it. I didn't want to get everyone all juiced up. Not that I don't like you."

"I know that, Jerome," Halsey says.

"I know that too," Dad replies.

March 6, 2015

Dad sees me taking notes as I play the stenographer, jotting down the nuggets he shares.

"Look at that pretty writing," he says.

"Oh, I don't know about that, Dad."

"I do. God, Monica—I think you should turn your house around and aim it at mine, and then we could all have fun."

◆◆◆

Meanwhile, at another table, Shirley and Gwen are going at it, tête-à-tête. Shirley's met her match.

Having been beaten down by Gwen, Shirley finally asks, "Do I have *any* good points?"

"Two," Gwen retorts.

◆◆◆

"I don't want to throw you out the window," Dad suddenly tells me.

"Well, Dad, *I* don't want you to throw me out the window either."

"I'd throw myself out," he says.

◆◆◆

Halsey, Dad, and I are discussing the merits of coffee.

Dad sums it up with, "It's really good. But you won't get drunk."

"Nope, Dad," I agree. "Not on coffee. Now if it was beer . . ."

"Call me up," Janet quips.

This response is perfect. Sharon and Diane, Janet's daughters, told me they once put a bottle of beer in the small refrigerator in Janet's room—just because they know how much their mom enjoyed beer. Janet let it sit in there for months, as it gave her a simple pleasure just to see it.

Then one day, Hanna, the resident services director, requested a meeting with the two daughters in her office. On her desk sat the bottle of beer—half-emptied.

Immediately, Diane and Sharon exchanged a look. It was not one of remorse.

Hanna informed the daughters that Janet had popped the cap off the beer, taken a few swigs, then sashayed through the Commons, beer in hand, nipping at it now and again.

Sharon howled.

Hanna frowned.

Sharon countered with, "Don't you see? My mom had the wherewithal to know it was a bottle of beer! And she knew what to do with it. I take comfort in that!"

Hanna is a professional and did not share in their glee.

March 10, 2015

"You can't find more benefit-type people than you two," Dad says to the both of us. Then he turns to me. "You are a cutie. Don't go sitting in another place, now."

◆ ◆ ◆

We're scheduled for a meeting with Optage. We meet in Dad's room. Room 131. Pat's our Optage nurse today.

Blood pressure: 106/62. Low.

Pulse: 72.

Oxygen saturation in the lungs: 97.

Weight: 125.1 pounds. Stable.

There's phlegm in his throat.

"Let's listen to see if anything is going on," Pat says as she puts the stethoscope to his chest.

"I'd just as soon not know," Dad comments.

"Breathe in. Breathe out," Pat coaches him.

"Sounds like a windmill," he says.

"Lungs are fine," she concludes. She moves on to check his ears and throat, which also look good.

"You have nice, soft hands—and eyes too," Dad says to Pat. "That's enough that way. I'm not going to go play on the floor."

Whoa, Dad! What does *that* mean?

Pat notices that Dad clearly tenses up when she moves his leg. She explains to us that the tension is a protective mechanism.

She also notes that three months ago, Dad used to get up a little more smoothly. He had to push less.

"And I've got Halsey over there," Dad says. "He'll protect me."

Dad's last blood work was on October 14. Pat will order new blood work to check the thyroid. Could maybe even get it drawn today.

Dad's still getting the nebulizer every night.

Lastly, Pat makes a note that a Salonpas patch is placed on his hip at night and taken off in the morning.

"Thank you, Jerome, for letting me visit you today," she says.

"You can come every day if you cook," Dad replies.

After Pat leaves, Dad turns to me: "You're the nicest girl. You remind me of your mother a lot. That's a big part of my heart." Then to Halsey: "You're a nice guy. Good guy." Back to me: "And even your nice little white teeth. That's my girl."

I start chuckling.

Rubbing my arm, Dad says, "She's vibrating now. Nice smile. You're not going to find that in any city block. I even told my father that when I was a teenager—and it worked!"

What "worked"? I wonder. Did Dad use some sort of one-liner to pull a fast one over his father when he was younger?

I'm reminded of a time I tried to pull something over my parents. I can picture a lone hobo hat sitting on a counter almost fifty years ago . . .

Chapter Twenty-Six

The Woods, the Hobo Hat, and the Chalk

It was a ho-hum summer day in 1967. Terry Hogan came up with a great idea. "Why don't we work our way to the other side of the Woods?" he said. "Way down there. We've never done that before."

The Woods was three banks of trees at the end of our street, Market Street. The trees marked off different acreages of farmland.

We kids instinctively divided ourselves up into two groups for building forts in the Woods. Two groups for the two neighborhoods, I guess. At the start of the summer, you had to be the first group to get down to the Woods so you could pilfer the other group's materials—lumber, carpet remnants, old sheets—from the year before.

Then we'd scout out a new hidden location for our fort. We'd clear an opening tucked into a clump of bushes around the base of a tree. We'd use branches to hoist ourselves up, scraping our arms and legs on the rough bark in the process.

An assembly line ensued. Someone down below would pass up a two-by-four, maybe fifteen inches long. Then a hammer and some nails. We'd climb farther up with the same momentum—passing the board and tools upward, upward until we found the perfect perch. Once nailed securely in a nice fork, the board became a lookout tower. We all took turns up there, gazing out and over our territory.

"They're coming!" someone would announce when the other group was spotted.

We'd all scramble down the tree, whispering to those below us to hurry up. More scrapes as we slid down the bark. Then we'd scurry to take cover in the bushes, making sure to sweep our footprints in the dirt with a tree branch, erasing all signs of life—just like the Indians used to do in *Bonanza*.

We weren't the only ones who used the Woods for a hiding spot. The women's reformatory makes its home in Shakopee. We'd often get news flashes that an inmate had escaped and was headed for the Woods.

A bit of alarm would creep inside of me whenever a warning came out. Who escaped? Could it be Pearl? With a knife? She wouldn't even need a knife. She had a brute strength that could rival anyone. I knew because we played softball against the inmates from the reformatory. Pearl was a huge black woman who pitched. The other inmates called her "Big Pearl."

And now Terry was suggesting we go to the other side the Woods . . .? A nagging thought went through my mind: I probably wasn't allowed to go that far. I quickly waved the worry away.

Why not? I thought. It would be fun to traipse through the Woods, cross over the cornfield, go into the next crop of woods, and do some discovering of our own. We could see what existed outside our usual stomping grounds.

Off we went. It was great. Unexplored terrain. We loved it. We followed the remains of an old trail through the Woods. We imagined it had been left there by the Indians. Maybe we were the first white people to find the path.

I wonder if any of the ancient Indians know we are trespassing on their grounds, I thought.

As we followed along the overgrown path, we would hold back low-hanging branches for each other. Otherwise, they would slap the other person hard in the face. Once Terry forgot, and a branch slapped *me* hard. It smarted, but I held back the tears. A twelve-year-old girl doesn't cry in front of a twelve-year-old boy.

We could tell we were nearing the end of one section of woods. There were fewer trees, and they were kind of straggly. As we ducked our heads under the last of the branches, the world opened up to an old abandoned junkyard just across a field.

We shared a look. I saw heaven written all over Terry's face. My own eyes widened as well. We had hit pay dirt.

We kicked our feet up and took off through the field, eager to explore the junkyard. It was a treasure hunt.

We admired the junked cars. Years of cobwebs and dust and dirt covered the interiors. These cars had to have been there forever! We marveled at how someone could just leave them here.

On the grimy dashboard of a rusted-out Studebaker, Terry found a bedraggled brown hobo hat. After brushing off a good share of the field dust, he plopped it on his head.

I busted out laughing. It hung low over his forehead and rested on his ears, making them stick out even farther than they normally did.

We continued on, rutting through glove compartments. We found the occasional photograph, a spare key of some sort or other, pop bottle lids, a screwdriver, matchboxes. So much for the taking—it was unbelievable! Terry took off that dirty old hat so we could fill it with our prizes.

In one of the last glove compartments, we found a box of chalk. The box was red with white lettering: *C-H-A-L-K*. We couldn't believe our good fortune.

"This is like new!" Terry said, holding up the box. "Who would leave all this stuff here?"

We made our way home, careful not to lose any of our precious cargo as we maneuvered over the ruts of the cornfield, tripped on a tree root here and there, and passed through the Woods.

When we got back to the bank of trees at the end of our street, Terry handed me the hat filled with our treasures.

"Here," he said. "Take it home and put it somewhere safe. I have to go in for supper."

With a nod, he went his way and I went mine.

As I neared my house, I thought about where I could store the booty. It was too dirty to bring into my bedroom. I'd have to clean everything first. There wasn't enough time for that, though. I, too, had to get in for supper. For the time being, I decided to slip that hat into a hiding spot in the corner of the garage.

Mom had made beef roast with mashed potatoes and gravy. Dad was up to his usual pranks as we sat around the dinner table.

"What the heck is that under the table?" he said to Greg.

As always, Greg fell for it. He peered under the table. As soon as he did, Dad stretched across the table, tunneled into Greg's potatoes with the back of a spoon, and quickly buried a small dab of horseradish.

Greg looked up, confused, then carried on eating. The rest of us just waited for his reaction. It was always good for a laugh.

As we neared the end of the meal, Dad turned to Mom. "Glor, there's something I want you to take a look at in the garage after we eat."

There was a tone of secrecy to his words. It's that same tone all parents use when communicating in code in front of their kids. Parents think they're being sneaky, but kids always catch on. They know something's up.

In my case, I knew exactly what was up. The hobo hat. He found it. My heart flopped with guilt.

I tried not to look guilty. But why did I feel guilty? Did I really do something wrong by taking that hat and the little treasures? They were abandoned in a junkyard.

Feeling unsettled, I finished the last few bites on my plate. It happened to be the green peas, which I couldn't stand. (The middles are so dry. Peas look so pretty on the plate, but they're never good, no matter how much butter you put on them. I usually scattered the last of them to various spots on my plate, as if I had overlooked the stragglers. Sometimes I could get away with it. Other times, Mom would ask me to scrape my plate together for one more spoonful.)

This time, my scattered peas went unaddressed. So did Dad's invitation to check out the mystery in the garage. Mom seemed to have her mind on Library Night.

Every Wednesday, she and I went to the library together. I loved it! It would be just the two of us—without my brothers, who always smelled like sweat.

I prayed there'd be a new Betsy-Tacy book to check out. But first things first, I needed to make a quick stop in that garage—before Dad could lure Mom there and before she and I would head out for Library Night.

I quietly excused myself from the table and nonchalantly strolled my way out of the house, trying not to draw attention to myself. I felt eyes drilling holes in my back, but when I looked behind me, I did not see my parents watching me. I slipped into the garage, snaked up the hobo hat, slid out the back service door, and put the hat *behind* the garage.

There.

I still wasn't sure what I did wrong or why I was covering my tracks. But on some level, I must have known I had done *something* wrong. I guess I didn't want to disappoint Dad.

I ran down the alleyway and rounded the corner. The neighborhood kids were already playing Scrub. Tom Hogan, Terry's older brother, was playing too. I knew I had a little time before we would head out for the library, so I joined in.

It was a blast whenever the older kids played; it didn't happen very often. The older kids hit the balls farther, sending everybody scrambling after them. And when fielding, the older kids actually caught some of the balls we were lucky enough to hit.

Thirty minutes into the game, I heard Mom calling my name from the front step. "Monica, time to come home!" Within minutes, all neighborhood moms were yelling for their kids from their front steps.

I skipped up the street to our house, opened the back door to the kitchen—then stopped short with a silent gasp.

There, shouting at me and smacking me in the face, was a bedraggled brown hobo hat strategically placed on the kitchen counter. Nothing else was on the counter. (Just like the lone bottle of beer that was sitting on Hanna's desk.)

How it made its way there turned out to be an interesting story—one I learned many years later.

As it turned out, Dad never saw the hobo hat in the corner of the garage, where I had originally placed it. That's not why he wanted Mom to go out to the garage. Instead, he wanted to show her a new scratch on the car. He assumed one of us kids had scraped a bike against it. But then after I moved the hat behind the garage, Dad stumbled upon it when he took some trash out to the alley.

When we try to cover our tracks, sometimes we reveal the truth.

Mom stood with her arms crossed and her mouth a thin line. I knew it wasn't good, but I wasn't quite sure what wasn't good about it.

"What is this?" she asked.

I hung my head. "Oh. Just some stuff Terry and I happened to find," I muttered.

"*Just some stuff*," she repeated, emphasizing my own words back to me. "And just where did you *happen to find* it?"

"In some old cars at the end of the Woods," I mumbled, picking at some dried gravy that had dribbled and dried on my T-shirt.

"And you thought you could just take these things?" She paused for several long seconds before adding, "That's stealing."

The Seventh Commandment: Thou shalt not steal.

I tried to brush that thought aside. I started justifying myself.

Stealing? How could it be stealing when it was obvious those cars didn't belong to anyone? No one even lived there.

The Seventh Commandment: Thou shalt not steal.

"Young lady, everything belongs to someone. These things do not belong to *you*, do they?" Mom could hardly muster the words. Her distaste was so evident. "Therefore, they belong to someone else, and you need to take them back. Now."

I shuddered. It was nearing dusk. I knew I couldn't go through the Woods alone. Anyone could be lurking, just waiting for a young girl carrying a bedraggled brown hobo hat. Someone like Big Pearl.

"Can Terry come with me?" I asked meekly.

Mom conceded with a nod. "I think that would be a good idea."

So, I stiff-armed my way down to Terry's house, carrying the hobo hat out in front of me, making sure no part of it touched my skin. It was evil.

It was hard to believe how giddy we had felt only a few short hours ago. We had taken turns cradling the hobo hat as if it were a prize from the county fair. Now it was the spawn of Satan himself.

When I reached the end of the street, Terry was waiting for me.

"Here. You carry it," I told him, all too willing to relinquish my hold on it.

I now realized that my self-disgust had been escalating ever since Dad's mention of wanting to show Mom something in the garage. I had broken the Seventh Commandment.

I couldn't figure out how I could have done something so horrible without even knowing it was horrible. What if I was doing other horrible things—or even *worse* things—that I didn't have a clue about?

Would God ever forgive me? If I didn't know I was doing something wrong, I couldn't ask to be forgiven, could I? What was I supposed to do with those unknown sins?

That night, Uncle Lawrence and his wife, Connie, came over to play Five Hundred with Mom and Dad. From my bedroom, I could hear the four of them laughing and placing their bids.

How could they laugh while I was lying in bed with a heaving heart? Worse—were they laughing at *me*? Did Mom and Dad tell them what I had done? Was that why they were laughing? I blushed at the thought. I wanted to die.

And then, I poured my heart out in song:

Hear, O Lord, the sound of my call. Hear, O Lord, and have mercy.
My soul is longing for the glory of you. O hear, O Lord, and answer me.
Every night before I sleep, I pray my soul to keep.
Or else I pray that loneliness is gone when I awake.
O Hear, O Lord, the sound of my call. Hear, O Lord, and have mercy.
My soul is longing for the glory of you. O hear, O Lord, and answer me.

Over and over I sang.

Much later, I would learn that as we grow in Christ, the Holy Spirit reveals the sinfulness of attitudes and actions we may not have initially recognized as wrong. But that day was much further down the road.

Tonight, I needed Jesus to know how sorry I was. I needed to know He would forgive me.

The tears dried on my cheeks as I sang myself to sleep.

Chapter Twenty-Seven

Ann's Monster

March 13, 2015

Walking unsteadily with her little back hump, Ann is being chased by a past memory. She keeps looking over her shoulder as she scuttles her way through the tables in the Commons. Her eyes dart to the left. To the right.

She reaches me, trembling. She spits out just loud enough for me to hear: "He's going to get me. Help me. I don't want him to see me. Please don't let him see me."

Rather than try to convince her it's all in her mind, I decide to concur with her and comfort her.

"Ann, you come right here and sit next to me," I say. "I'm not going to let anyone hurt you. We'll block his view with my purse."

I help her sit in a chair right next to me, and I position my purse on the table to shield her from her attacker's view.

"He comes home every night and beats me," she confides.

"Who does, Ann?"

"My dad. He's drunk. Don't let him see me."

My own dad is sitting in a chair directly across the table from Ann. I can see from his facial expressions that he's trying to follow the story. Witnessing her fear, Dad sees her as a child—even though she's a good ten years older than him. He, too, wants to calm her and give her peace.

"It's OK, little girl. Grandpa here will take care of you." And he gives her his little wink.

So many thoughts go through my head. Wasn't it bad enough that Ann had to hide from her abusive, alcoholic father when she was a little girl? It's not fair that she has to live that nightmare all over again now—how many years later? Maybe seventy? Eighty? What sense does that make?

I want to protect her. My dad wants to protect her. We're all in this together. We put on our armor to protect Ann from her monster.

Seeing Ann's fear turn her into a little girl, I suddenly find myself in a similar transformation. I, too, am a little girl afraid of a monster, though my experience pales in comparison to Ann's. Thankfully, my monster isn't my father.

Mine is under my bed . . .

Chapter Twenty-Eight

The Monster under My Bed

It's scary to go to bed at night. My room is at the end of the long, dark hallway.

With heart increasing in its beat, I walk down the hallway in trepidation. Once my bare feet reach my bedroom, my hand gropes in the dark for the light switch. I flick it on quickly.

I glance to make sure my closet doors are closed. If they are open, I do not look inside the closet. I just close the doors swiftly.

Something might be hiding in there. I'm terrified of eyes looking dead straight into mine before straggly old arms reach out from under a moth-ridden coat and grab me.

Something could be under my bed, too, waiting to grab my ankles. It makes bedtime a process.

I sneak up to my bed, keeping a safe distance from the frame. I reach as far as I can to snatch the bunny-shaped pajama bag from the middle of the bed.

Quickly, I move to the middle of the room, temporarily safe from monster arms. I unzip the bag, snag my pajamas, and remain there in the middle of the room as I change into them. Once I've donned my pajamas, I fold my clothes and set them on the rocking chair near the door.

I used to properly kneel at the side of my bed to say my bedtime prayers. That was before I figured out that the monster was under there, just waiting for me. Since then, I've been saying my prayers in bed.

Getting *into* bed is quite the physical feat. It requires some preparation. Maintaining as much distance as I can from the bed frame, I stretch my arms and pull the covers down from under the pillow. I make sure to angle a corner back.

Taking a deep breath, I then reach to turn off the light, race toward the bed, launch myself into the air three feet away from the bed (so no one can grab my ankles), and slip my legs into the pulled-back sheets without disturbing the rest of the covers. It's all one fluid motion.

I whip the angled flap over me and bring everything up to my chin, making sure the edge of the sheet is folded over the blankets. I want only the sheets to graze my chin.

As a pleasant distraction, I notice the sheets smell fresh. It must be clean sheets day—the best night of the week. Mom must have hung these sheets on the line to dry.

Turning over on my side, I chicken-wing my arm and place it between my head and the pillow. But that leaves my hand hanging loosely out behind my neck. One fast yank, and I could be dragged under the bed. I quickly cup my hand and fold in my wrist, safeguarding my hand under my neck.

I pray softly: "Now I lay me down to sleep. I pray the Lord my soul to keep. If I should die before I wake, I pray the Lord my soul to take." I then remember the part Mom always tells me to add: "God bless Mommy, Daddy, Monica, Greg, and Stevie. Help Monica, Greg, and Stevie be real good kids. Good night, Jesus. In the name of the Father, and of the Son, and of the Holy Ghost. Amen." I don't want nightmares coiled underneath my pillow.

If I should die before I wake . . . It drifts through my mind like vapor.

I tuck my hand in farther.

Chapter Twenty-Nine

Dandelions

We are all dandelions. Persistent. Resilient. *Our various shades of yellow-to-orange flower heads are open in the daytime but closed at night.*

Yellow fairly shouts with youth! It symbolizes clarity and communication, and with it, alertness of thought. A quick wit.

Our younger years.

As we grow older, our flower heads mature into downy spherical seed heads. Blowballs. Children delight to blow them away, counting how many little puffs it takes before a wish can be made. Little parachutes.

Some blowballs are more attached and have full crowns of fluff. None, though, are the bright yellow blossoms they once were. Instead, they are all white puffballs. White—a symbolic color of new chapters of an aging life. In a field of dandelion blowballs, you can see hundreds of weeds or thousands of wishes. In the memory care unit, I see wishes.

Each day, I watch the white fluff that is Dad wisp away, leaving less and less of the little parachutes intact . . .

These thoughts come to me almost like a dream. They cause me to stop, to pause and ruminate on Dad and our visits.

There are definite themes to Dad's comments. Family. Smiles and teeth. Family. Happy crying eyes. Family. Baxter.

All these themes give us positive affirmation. How encouraging to know that he loves us and that our visits bring him joy!

But then . . . there's the theme that Dad *knows* that he doesn't know.

This one gets me every time. It's heart-wrenching that he knows he's being held hostage by his own mind.

With each day, it's more evident that his white blowball is disappearing. It's happening to all the residents we've come to love in the memory care unit. Janet. Bob. Charlie. Ann. Winnie. All the others.

I keep reminding myself to meet Dad where he's at. To tell him not to worry about how his words get stuck. To reassure him that I totally understand what he's saying. To let my eyes convince him of that truth.

Because once you immerse yourself into discussions with your loved one, you become one with them. It no longer matters what they're saying or what you're hearing. Fantasy becomes reality. What matters is that you have a heart connection. And you both feel it.

I've found this to be the truth with Dad and all the dandelions that have become part of our necklace. And I need to remind myself of this truth before *pouf*—the last wisps take leave, and they're gone.

March 15, 2015

I'm taking notes in my book as we chat with Dad.

"That's my girl," he says. "She's making notes of it. She has clean teeth. I don't see you enough," he says to both of us now. "That Monica and that Halsey—we all get along. We could build two bathrooms and join them together with a bedroom, and you could both move in."

Janet's sitting at the table with us, following this conversation. "*That* gives you something to wonder about," she remarks.

I choke back a laugh. Yes, it *does* give you something to wonder about.

◆ ◆ ◆

Later, Dad finds himself struggling with his words and thoughts. Again.

"I lost what I was going to say," he states. "And there was a lot up there."

March 17, 2015

Halsey and I collect Dad for another fine-dining outing. Melissa, the campus administrator and a very wonderful person, walks by in a formfitting red dress.

"She's nicely put together," Dad says.

Ten minutes later, Melissa walks by again and stops to greet us.

"She has nice legs," Dad says as she walks ahead to greet another table of guests.

◆ ◆ ◆

We're finishing up with dessert.

"My teeth feel like they're filled up," Dad says. But then he continues to put another forkful in his mouth.

"I thought you were full, Jerome," Halsey comments. "Now all of a sudden you have room for more dessert."

"That's rather streaky," Dad replies.

◆ ◆ ◆

We take Dad back to the Arbor so the night staff can continue with their routine of getting the residents to bed. They come to collect the residents one by one from their tables in the Commons.

"That's my girl," Dad tells me. "I hope she knows it."

"She does," I answer.

"That's good. That's my girl."

"That's my dad."

"You betcha."

◆ ◆ ◆

As we sit and wait for Dad to be collected, he notices the bud vase with a single rose in the center of the table. He inspects the rose and refers to it as "this here chicken coop."

◆ ◆ ◆

Dad says to me, "You are a beauty."

"Dad, Dad, Dad," I say, beaming.

"I don't chew baloneys," he replies.

March 19, 2015

Toward the end of our visit today—and out of nowhere—Dad says, "Those that are still hungry will have to scalp their own potatoes."

Scalp? Or scallop?

Mom used to make really creamy (and delicious) scalloped potatoes. Does Dad realize that the reason she made them this way was to make the potatoes "multiply" so there'd be enough to feed more people when there was company?

Operating on a shoestring budget when they were young parents required some ingenuity. I remember a lot of creamed dishes—creamed peas, creamed corn, creamed tuna. Mom was clever.

And apparently, Dad was aware of it.

On the other hand, maybe he meant "scalp," as in "stealing" their own potatoes? Like farm boys did back in his day—run through the potato fields, bagging stolen potatoes to whisk home to their family. Too many mouths to feed, too meager the portions.

March 23, 2015

Dad has a series of little random thoughts. I quickly pluck them from the air and tuck them into my notes:

- "Someone was backing me besides me."
- "It's my people that keep me going and doing my things."
- "Oh, Monica. I'm so happy."
- To Halsey: "If it wouldn't be for the help of *you* . . ."
- "I don't think I hit him. He looks too big for me to hit. That's my boy." Rubs Halsey's head. "I wouldn't do anything bad to you."

◆ ◆ ◆

"There must not have been good cops around then," Dad is saying now. "I had them, and I was trying to get away. I was a teenager. I wanted to save this woman—or girl. From there, I went to the hospital."

Hmm. This is something I've never heard before! Dad was trying to get away from someone? All to save some woman? And he ended up in the hospital?

I guess I'll never find out the story behind this. If there even is one.

◆ ◆ ◆

"Must have been that time of year," he says. He then points to his face. "The tears are starting to wrinkle. Even now, I have to be very pinchy with my eyes, because they could explode into the glass."

The sensation of wanting to cry. A small wrinkling, a tickling, before the tears actually form.

And explode.

◆ ◆ ◆

Dad's having trouble with his memory. He's aware of it.

"I don't know," he says. "And it ain't because I'm stupid, either. It's just the way it is. I can't come up with it. I'm running low."

◆◆◆

I sneeze.

"It does hurt me and hurts God too," Dad says of the sneeze. "And I'm sure it hurts the dogs too. And the eyes feel like they'd jump out and go for a ride." He pauses. "I must sound like I'm some sort of a nut."

◆◆◆

Halsey's wearing a sweatshirt that says "Halsey's Athletic Apparel." Dad points to it.

"I'd have a very tough time kissing you, but I think I might have to. It's my lifestyle."

◆◆◆

Dad's been sniffling with a cold. "Starting to run out of my nose, and I can't help it," he says. He blows his nose.

Janet has been sitting with us and tolerating Dad's sniffles. "Thank you," she remarks after he finally blows it.

◆◆◆

"Life sure isn't all heaven," Dad says with a heaviness.

A thought streaks through my mind. *He used to say we were living in hell now, on earth.*

I understand why . . .

Chapter Thirty

Red Owl and the Unraveling Glove

1973

I was back in the breakroom. You can stand in one spot for only so long, and four hours standing behind the register as a cashier at Red Owl was enough for me. Time for a break.

Besides, I loved hanging out with my coworkers. We weren't exactly friends outside of work, but we had built a camaraderie there at the store. We could pal around in the breakroom. Out on the floor, however, we couldn't show any signs of enjoying ourselves. Or each other. Otherwise, we'd get *the look* or a head gesture from Mr. Gosling, the owner.

Mr. Gosling was very uptight. In fact, everything about him was tight—he had a tight haircut, tight clothes, tight lips.

Several times an hour, he'd flit his way across the store. He'd start in the produce aisle on the left, head to the meat aisle, then move along the back wall, then worm his way along the dairy aisle on the right. The whole time, he'd swing his head back and forth like a double-jointed turkey, furtively looking for someone who might not be on task. He paid closest attention to the bag boys, who really didn't care whether they held on to their jobs or not.

So there I was in the breakroom, laughing at Scott, a bag boy who, in particular, could crack me up with just a stupid look on his face. For example, at the end of a shift, he'd say, "OK, time to beat feet." Maybe it was just me, but I got a real kick out of him. Pretty much made the four-hour shift go quicker.

Then suddenly, Mark Peterson busted through the door.

"Monica," he panted, out of breath. "You gotta come. Your brother's in the hospital. I'll take you there."

I rolled my eyes, annoyed at the interruption. Mark liked attention—especially mine—by telling jokes that were, in hindsight, pretty rough. (But truth be told, I was flattered by his attention—unless he'd go overboard.)

"Yeah. OK, Mark," I said. "Are you kidding? Is this a joke? I suppose I'll get all the way there to the hospital and then—"

"No, really," Mark cut me off. "I'm serious."

One look at his ashen face, and I knew this was not a game.

When I got to the ER waiting room, Mom and Dad were clutching each other. Our family doesn't clutch. There was pain written all over their faces—just a raw pain.

Immediately, the afternoon sun went down. A dark void blanketed our little area in the ER and encased the three of us.

"Oh, Monica."

My name, said so flatly. Hollow.

I watched as whole beings dissolved in front of me. I looked first to Mom and then to Dad. Looking for questions I didn't want to ask and answers I didn't want to know.

"Mom? Dad?" I could hardly call them by name, I was so scared.

"It's Stevie." Choked out.

It's Stevie. It's Stevie. It's Stevie. It's Stevie. A broken record resonating in my head.

"He's not going to make it."

Not going to make it. Not going to make it. Not going to make it.

Just then, the ER doctor somberly came through the doors, went over to my parents, lowered his chin to his chest, and placed a soft touch on each of their shoulders—shoulders tense and afraid of what they might hear.

"I'm so sorry."

Did he actually say those words? Or did I just *know* by seeing the touch?

The wails cut loose from both of my parents as they collapsed into each other and folded themselves against the rest of the world. Otherworldly sounds racked up their throats and out of them. Sounds I didn't even know were within a person. Naked, anguished groans. Horrible animal sounds. It was soul destroying. Until that day, I had never heard my dad cry. And now hearts were gushing out of both my parents.

In my head were my own internal screams. *How is this possible?* I had no information, yet I had too much information. I couldn't process it.

The words just kept hammering and hammering. *It's Stevie. Not going to make it. I'm sorry. It's Stevie.*

Mom struggled to raise up her anguished face. "We need to get Greg," she said to me.

She needed me. Here was something tangible for me to grasp from this world that was spinning out of control. Mom and Dad would not break free from their spin for a long time. Years. But someone had to break out today.

I took the saving grace thrown to me and put my mind on finding my other brother. This was 1973. People did not have cell phones.

Greg was up at Big Sandy with some friends, biking and camping for a week. That much I knew. I called friends. And friends of friends. God was in the room with me, because somehow I was able to put those calls through while I was in that waiting room of despair.

I had graduated from high school just two weeks earlier. I have a photograph of the three of us kids standing on the front steps of our three-bedroom rambler. Stevie was reaching up, trying to adjust my cap and tassel, right when the picture was snapped.

Eleven-year-old Stevie, the one I brushed off with annoyance just a month or two earlier. He had made a belt for me, crocheting cream-colored yarn around plastic bath curtain rings. I was impressed and told him so. I didn't know how to crochet. And I told him that too.

Well, he was all over me then, full of pride. "I'll teach you how. When can I show you?"

He was relentless. And I was a too-cool, just-getting-ready-to-graduate eighteen-year-old girl.

"Sure, sure. Just not now, OK?"

How many times had I told him that? I never did make the time to learn from him. I still have the crocheted belt in a box labeled "My Memorabilia" with a red marker. It numbs me every time I go through the box.

Stevie didn't make it. And it changed all of us. That was the day the finely knit five-fingered glove of our family began unraveling, beginning with the severing of the baby finger.

Three weeks after we buried Stevie, I went to South America for a year as a foreign exchange student. My parents didn't want me to miss out on an experience of a lifetime. At the same time, I missed out on the grieving process with my family.

Three weeks after we buried Stevie, Greg went from being the middle child to an only child. He had always felt lost between his older sister and a spoiled younger brother. "Well, Monica's *perfect*," he would complain to Mom and Dad. "Well, Stevie's the *baby*." He had always felt invisible before; now he was in the limelight in front of everyone. Be careful what you wish for. He found pot to make himself invisible again.

Mom was the darning needle that tried to keep the rest of the unraveling glove together. It worked for a while. Mostly it didn't.

It became a lonely house.

And Dad? Dad's world became a hell.

There is no hell when we die—we are living it here on earth.

Chapter Thirty-One

Janet and Sliding and Humming Along

Janet is shaking she is laughing so hard. The mirth is rolling off her, and her eyes are leaking tears. She sits directly across from me at one of the four-square-foot dining room tables. Eyebrows raised, she invites me to join her. I'm already laughing with her, and I don't even know what we're laughing at.

I love Janet.

Our eyes meet, and we read each other, as we often do. With a nod of her head, she's trying to get me to look over my right shoulder.

In my peripheral, something streaks from the right and behind me. It's Virginia, tooling by in her wheelchair. With her tail on fire, she's in a hurry to get somewhere. Determination is written all over her, and her Grandma Moses bun goes right along with her.

I don't know why exactly, but it's hilarious. Maybe the set of Virginia's jaw and the clench of her teeth? Her clutch of the wheels as she turns them with her worn hands?

I look back at Janet, and she is rolling. I am too. A few precious moments shared without a word spoken.

Then Shirley pipes in from another table. "Hey, you two over there—what's so funny?"

"You don't need to know," says Janet.

And a whole new round of laughter erupts.

◆ ◆ ◆

Janet is not fond of Lorraine.

Lorraine comes over and pulls out a chair to sit down.

Janet lays down the rule. "You can sit down, but not for long," she instructs.

"Dad tries to get along with everyone . . ." I gently comment.

"That's the way it should be," Dad replies.

Halsey initiates a different conversation. "Jerome, remember Whoopee John?"

Dad lights up.

Whoopee John was a professional polka musician. He and his band reigned in Minnesota, enjoying popularity in the '40s and '50s. And of course, Dad played his accordion to a number of the pieces he heard Whoopee play on the radio.

"And how about Cedric Adams?" Halsey adds. "Do you remember him?"

This is the same Cedric Adams who frequented Charlie's, where Grandma Marge worked.

"Oh, yeah," Dad says. "My dad liked him too."

He tries to say more, but he starts stumbling over his words.

"I can't put it together," he finally says.

"How does that work?" I ask him.

"Not good," he answers.

March 26, 2015

We're at the Commons for one of our usual visits. We find that coming at about three o'clock gives us a solid hour to an hour and a half before staff starts steering the residents to their favorite dining table. Once the food starts appearing, it makes for an easy break for us to leave Dad.

At the start of our visit, Dad says, "I'm not the kissing type, but I still love you. If I put you in the ground, I'll go in right next to you."

A pretty easy one to decode: *If you die, I'll die right with you.*

♦♦♦

It seems we talk about age as we get older. At least that's what we're finding we do. Is it because aging is something to be proud of? Because we've weathered the storms—and pretty much unscathed?

It's actually kind of ridiculous, I think. Still, it's just small talk, which is what you resort to when trying to make conversation.

So I remind Dad of his age.

Dad's comeback: "I'm eighty? I don't think there's anyone out there who would want a part of it."

March 29, 2015

It's a Sunday. We come to visit Dad right after Mass. It's our routine.

Our conversation today is just bits and scraps. When Dad chimes in, most often with unrelated comments, we just go with the flow.

At one point, he interjects, "All I can do is talk smart or don't talk."

◆◆◆

"Monica, you're such a nice-looking girl."

"Oh, I don't know, Dad . . ." I reply.

"I do." His eyes start tearing up. "I got water bags under each eye."

◆◆◆

He's struggling with words again.

"Right now, I'm kind of warped," he finally says. "I don't know what I'm going to do, but I'll give it a lot of whirl."

A lot of whirl! I could just kiss him on the top of his sweet head.

Dad did everything with "a lot of whirl." Thirty years working at Ford Motor Company. Clock repair. And in his free time, Ping-Pong, slot car racing, shuffleboard, darts, remote control airplanes.

All with "a lot of whirl."

"I'm running out of power," he says, though. "It ain't good."

◆◆◆

"It's a pretty big box," he says, "and we can't get anywhere."

This is something else out of thin air. Is he reflecting? Is the "big box" the world?

And "we can't get anywhere"? We *can't*? He obviously doesn't mean the obvious—he isn't talking about getting places with cars, trains, boats, airplanes.

I try to read his facial expression. He's not giving me much to work with.

Does he feel as though *he's* not getting anywhere? Treading water? Not making any progress? Just sitting day after day after day? Am I trying to read too much into it?

Sometimes, you just have to let it go.

"I don't know where Lawrence is. He just plain escaped."

Halsey pats Dad on the back.

Dad reacts with, "I probably need a lot of that banging."

◆ ◆ ◆

"What am I going to get you for Christmas?" he asks me.

It's March, but I don't tell him.

"And the rest of the family?" he adds. "And Halsey too?" He pats his heart. "He's one of my products too."

One of his products.

April 2, 2015

We greet staff members as we pass by their station and make our way over to Dad. Halsey sits as I get Dad some coffee.

"I don't like to do anything wrong," Dad is telling him as I approach. "And I don't want to be dragged into something—like when I was younger."

Aha! Sounds like Dad might have hung around with some people who got him involved in something he otherwise wouldn't have gotten involved in. I wouldn't be surprised.

I am suddenly reminded how, back in his teenage years, Dad and some of his friends gathered around Tony Dearborn's parked Chevy while Tony was in church. The story is, they had some dead sparrows—maybe two or three. They opened the driver's door, pulled down Tony's front window visor, and wound a cord around the sparrows' legs so they were hanging from the visor like icicles. Then they stood behind some trees, waiting for Mass to end and for Tony to reach his car.

When Dad told this story, he had you laughing through each step.

◆ ◆ ◆

"Monica, you've got the nice looks. Maybe you have whiskers I don't know about," he adds. "But I think you're perfect."

Nope, Dad. No whiskers.

Yet.

April 5, 2015

After greetings and a rub across Dad's shoulder, he says, "I'd like to take you home for life. I love my peoples. You're perfect. And I'm not just bragging. I don't want to lose you."

◆◆◆

"God," Dad says, "I hope I don't ever get old so I can slide along."
  I think we slide because we get old.
  "I should change my ways," he continues. "I kind of just hum along."
  Sliding and humming along.

◆◆◆

"I don't think I've ever had it better than this," Dad says.
  Then someone sneezes.
  "Was that a dog barking?" he asks.

◆◆◆

As he reaches over to rub my back, he runs into my bra clasp.
  "Oh, Monica. Such a nice girl. And here's a nipple. Wrong side, though."
  Oh, boy . . .

◆◆◆

He looks at his hands.
  "Yeah, the young man is getting old."

◆◆◆

We're looking at a book with wonderful illustrations of national parks.
  "Dad, have you ever been to Yosemite?" I ask.
  "I'd have to know how to spell it first."

April 12, 2015

As we near Dad's table today, he greets us with, "I'm looking for you every time I walk around. It's sure fun to be up in the air with my family."

Being "up in the air" never sounded so good!

◆ ◆ ◆

"I'm getting old," he says. "Everything's coming out. Nothing's coming in."

Is he commenting on how his memory is slipping away?

He points to Halsey and me. "But I'm sure enjoying the people who are enjoying me." Now he tears up. "I get heavy eyes, but they don't fall yet. And your smile helps," he says to me.

Seeing me take notes, he motions to my notepad and winks.

"Make a little note."

◆ ◆ ◆

Dad tries to initiate a conversation with, "So, what else don't I know?"

Halsey laughs. "That's a good one, Jerome."

◆ ◆ ◆

"Everything escapes so fast. I have cries in my eyes."

The meaning is sad, but the words are awesome.

◆ ◆ ◆

I overhear a staff member mention having a hoedown.

"You gonna dance, Dad?" I ask.

"I'd feel guilty," he replies.

"Why is that?"

"Mom's not there," he says. "That's a mystery."

I find the smile I had started with now turns upside down. "Poor Dad."

"You don't have to 'poor' me. I'm just a widow. I never used that word before, but I think I'm right."

He is right. Neither *widow* nor *widower* has ever been part of his vocabulary. It's incredible, really, that this exact word found its way out, considering that most words escape him.

Then to Halsey, he says, "I just look at you and laugh and smile."

April 15, 2015

Again, Optage comes for a visit in Dad's room. Room 131.

Observations: Doesn't want to stand without support. There's an indication that there's pain when getting up.

Lungs: Good.

Oxygen: Good.

There have been two or three times within the last month when he didn't want to get up from bed.

All in all, though, doing amazingly well regarding pain and managing it.

He's getting 2000 units a day of vitamin D. Before, his levels were as low as the nurse has ever seen. He was at 7.4 mg/mL, and a level less than 12 mg/mL indicates vitamin D deficiency. He's now at 20. That's an improvement. The goal is 30.

On Tuesday and Thursday, she's going to have him get 2000 additional units to see if we can get his level stabilized. He'll need another blood test in a month to see where he's at. At that time, the Optage nurse will have the additional units removed from his chart.

◆◆◆

The Optage visit ends, and we move back to the Commons to visit. We pull up our chairs to sit at his table.

"He's my better friend," Dad says about Halsey.

Not *best*. But *better*.

As he continues, he gets tangled in his words. "My words aren't worth a talk," he finally proclaims.

◆◆◆

"Everything you do, Monica, I feel I should be doing it," he says. "I love my girl."

I'm not sure what he sees me doing that he thinks he should be doing. His thoughts are somewhere, but he hasn't opened a window for me to see them.

"I don't like the strange people staring me up and down."

Though I don't know which "strange people" Dad is referring to, I do know that he never did like to be put on display. I have to chuckle when I think about a Sunday Mass way back when we were a young family.

It was time for Communion. Dad got out of the pew, stood back, and let his family out one by one in front of him. As he walked down the aisle behind us, he could feel something creep down the inside of his left pant leg. He inched his way in the Communion queue, wondering what the heck was crawling down his leg.

When it was nearly his turn to receive the host, he felt something finally escape his pant leg. He looked down—it was a sock. Dad was mortified.

We thought it was great.

April 19, 2015

Bob walks by in his yellow Iowa Hawkeyes sweatshirt.

"I like him so much," Dad says, "I love him throughout."

And then the most thought-provoking words come forth from him. I get the sense a few words are being left out, as if he's beginning in the middle of his sentence.

" . . . when I'm living, until once I'm sealed into what I am."

Not sure what he means, but I love the sound of it!

♦♦♦

"You have nice wings." He's referring to my hair as he pats his own hair. Then he trips over his next thought. "Now I'm stuck in the mud again."

"That's OK, Dad," I say.

"To you it is. Not to me."

♦♦♦

They're getting ready for dinner, which is our cue to get ready to go.

"You're going to leave already?" Dad says. "You're killing me."

April 23, 2015

We nod to staff members as we make our way over to Dad. He starts the conversation by turning to Halsey.

"Don't kill any of them," Dad tells him. "And if you do, take them down to the river."

Wow. There's that mention again of taking people down to the river.

What's running through his mind?

◆◆◆

About Halsey, Dad says, "I'm going to hold him for the rest of my life, because he's the best." Then Dad pauses, pats my arm, and says, "*Second* best." He follows it with a wink.

In the background, I hear Shirley say to Laura, the recreation coordinator, "Boy, you have a big nose."

Laura and Shirley are yapping in the background so much that Dad loses his concentration.

"Oh, shut up for a minute," he reacts.

April 26, 2015

Dad sees Halsey and me coming in to visit.

"Those are some nice teeth you have," he greets me.

Then his eyes fill up. "Hot waters on my eyes." He points to his eyes. "With that move, I lost my head. I can't do anything, because I'm afraid I'll go shooting up into the sky."

The blowball of a dandelion. Wisping away.

Bit by bit.

Chapter Thirty-Two

Making Moments

While Alzheimer's destroys some brain cells, it uncovers others. Some have discovered artistic abilities. Dad uncovered a poetic nature. His words are priceless—they're original quips and thoughts pouring out of his mouth. Fragments. Poetry. They become better and better as time passes. The more we visit, the more musings we get. I continue capturing them in writing to preserve them.

We've learned how to become even more a part of this Other World. With our visits, we do not create memories for Dad. We create *moments*. Moments that won't stick five minutes after we leave the room. But they're still moments.

We're still giving him something.

April 30, 2015

Sadly, we find Dad sitting alone at his table today.

I'm always thrilled when I see Janet sitting with him at his table. Or Bob. I'm even comforted when Shirley, at the table directly across from Dad, is piping something into the conversation.

Occasionally, though, we find him alone like this. A solitary figure with nothing in front of him to pass the time.

Today I observe him as he planes the surface of the table, smoothing out any wrinkles that are in his mind. His hands run the length of the table, cupping the edges, remembering what his mind cannot. Braille.

Meanwhile, some other residents cluster together, busy with the recreation coordinator. *Can't Dad be brought over to watch and admire?* In another area, some of the men discuss current events. *Can't Dad be sitting there with them, nodding with their conversation? At least pretending to be a part of it? He can still* hear.

However, Dad is separated and alone.

My empathy is with him. I feel certain he wants to join in, to be part of the group. Or to *feel* he's part.

But then again, maybe he just longs to be invited first.

Once more, I remember how his long-ago five-year-old daughter sat at the end of the driveway on Market Street, willing someone to come by and ask to be her friend.

◆ ◆ ◆

As we circle around to join Dad at his table, he greets me with good news.

"You have such a beautiful face—you don't have anything crooked."

I smile. *Well, that's nice to know.*

◆ ◆ ◆

Dad is going on about how he'd like to see more of us.

"I'm here every couple of days, Dad," I say in defense. Maybe I'm still feeling guilty about not sticking with my promise of never putting him in a home.

"I can't get enough," he counters.

◆ ◆ ◆

Dad tries to bite an Oreo, but then he pauses because of the struggle with his loose dentures.

"If I fall through and hit bottom, at least I have my people," he says.

"Dad," I say, "go ahead and eat your cookie." I know he wants to.

"I'm going to enjoy looking at it first." He studies it a moment. "It's tough. It doesn't go anyplace. It's like a rock."

At least it's not bending his teeth, like it was last summer.

◆ ◆ ◆

Dad looks at Bob in his yellow Iowa sweatshirt and calls him Trent.

"Dad, that's Bob. Trent's my son."

As soon as I correct him, I remember I had vowed not to do that.

"But he still makes a mark," Dad says. "Everything I have makes me feel love."

And there you have it.

Everything I have makes me feel love.

Chapter Thirty-Three

Tears That Bite

May 3, 2015

There was a time when we rescued a baby fawn. It was a few years ago—when Dad was still living in his house and we were building ours next door.

Trent told me that he had spotted two orphaned fawns on the other side of the chain-link fence at the edge of our property. They'd been there, alone, for five or six days. He thought maybe the mother had been struck on the freeway, which was a short distance below.

He invited me to join him in a rescue. I asked my neighborhood friend, Dar, to join us, because she's also an animal lover.

When we arrived at the property, Trent was on the other side of the fence, approaching the fawns. Dad was on our property to observe.

Dar climbed over the fence first. I followed. I stretched my leg up and over the fence, using a nearby tree for balance. But when I put my weight on a branch, it snapped. My inner arms dragged down the tree bark as I hugged it to break my fall. My right foot landed in a hole.

I knew it wasn't good. Not good at all. I eased myself up from the fall and tried to stand, but my ankle folded.

"I think I really messed up my ankle," I muttered under my breath to Trent. I didn't want to make a big deal about it, though, because I didn't want to scare the baby fawns away.

Dar and I managed to help Trent lift one of the babies, then we passed him over the fence for Dad to take him.

Dad wasn't quite sure what to do, so Dar climbed over to his side to help with the handoff. It was a bit of a struggle. The fawn was all legs—and, of course, he was resisting. Trent climbed over to assist. I decided to limp my way around the chain-link fence instead of taking my chances crawling over it again.

Somehow, we carried the fawn across the yard to the granary, where we could secure him. Then Trent, Dar, and I went back for the other fawn. Dad stayed behind with the rescued fawn.

I discovered that if I walked backward, it didn't aggravate the ankle as much. So, backward I went, dragging my injury through the high grasses. We searched for the second fawn for about half an hour, but it had disappeared. So the three of us went back to the granary.

Dad, Dar, and I made friends with the fawn while Trent went to the grocery store to get a baby bottle and some goat milk. When he came back, we took turns feeding the poor thing.

He couldn't get enough! He sucked and sucked with goat milk spewing up his face. Droplets on his eyelashes. He was just lapping it up. Whenever we passed the bottle, the fawn would follow the bottle with his eyes and mistake someone's chin for the nipple and try to suck it.

I don't even have words for the experience. We all felt the same—and Dad was right there with his grin. I snapped a picture of him kneeling down with his arm embracing the fawn's shoulders.

About four hours later, the ER confirmed that I had a high ankle sprain. "What took you so long to come in?" they asked.

Hoping to jar this happy deer memory for Dad, I've framed that photo and brought it with me today.

When we sit down for today's visit, I present it to Dad.

"I get tears in my eyes," he says as he gazes at the photo. "They almost bite."

Tears often do that, don't they?

◆ ◆ ◆

Chad recently bought a new truck. A Ford. We share this news with Dad.

"I like when they let me do something for them," he replies.

Does Dad remember that because he retired from Ford, his family members are able to take advantage of the Ford employee discount and get quite a good deal on new vehicles? Or is it a bit simpler, that he knows Chad likes Fords because of his grandpa?

Whatever Dad meant with the comment, it's clear he knows he had something to do with Chad's new truck.

◆ ◆ ◆

We overhear some arguing at a back table in the Commons.

"Well," Dad says, "they didn't bubble on that one."

◆ ◆ ◆

"Monica, you've got the nicest teeth," Dad says. "Nice and shiny." To Halsey, he says with a wink, "You're over the hill."

There's no time to even react to *that* one, because Dad quickly churns out more.

"You're my child again, and I'll take him. I love him. You're all good children—as long as you don't pee on me. I never had any trouble with food on the table. And my family—I feel so good that everything came out all right. Poor Monica. You're too good to be good."

I'm too good to be good. I love that!

"Greg's floating around someplace," Dad adds.

And I love that he thinks of Greg.

◆ ◆ ◆

Now two other people are talking loudly nearby.

"I wish they'd move down the road a ways," Dad says. And he laughs.

◆ ◆ ◆

To Halsey: "Don't worry about Daddy here. He'll make it work."

To me: "I can't help but love you."

About tearing up again: "It's in this eye—it's wiggling. And the other one's waiting for this one to get done, and then it'll start."

Wiggling, like a caterpillar.

◆ ◆ ◆

Halsey pats Dad's back. It must be a bit too forceful.

"He's knocking it loose," Dad says to me with a smile. "Why?"

◆ ◆ ◆

I make a comment about how a certain friend of mine is a *really good* friend.

"Thank you, and thank you again," Dad says to me. "She's a good person."

To be thankful for *someone else's* blessings—this is gratitude.

◆ ◆ ◆

"He's got a nice-looking wife too—not that *I* want her."

Who is he talking about? I wonder. We're left guessing who this man is, let alone who his wife is!

May 15, 2015

Today when we visit, Dad starts rubbing his heart.

"I'm going to keep you in that area that doesn't go anyplace," he says to me.

He's going to hold me in his heart—in that "area that doesn't go anyplace."

May 17, 2015

During our visit this afternoon, Dad shakes his head and declares, "I need a vacation. I can't even talk of it anymore, so it must be over."

◆ ◆ ◆

To yellow-Iowa-sweatshirt Bob: "You're a good boy. You're so good everybody else got up and moved out."

Makes me laugh out loud.

◆ ◆ ◆

Dad tries to whistle.

"It's getting so bad, I don't want to blow it out anymore."

◆ ◆ ◆

Halsey rubs Dad's back. "You don't have to do everything I say," Dad says.

"Oh, OK," Halsey replies, teasingly. "I won't." And, he stops rubbing.

Dad wants to pull back his words. "I'm trying to talk smart, but I'm getting down in the woods."

Halsey resumes with the back rub.

May 19, 2015

There's a fine-dining event tonight with live music in the background.

"I love my girl," Dad says at the end of the meal. "I have tears in my eyes right now. It can't get any better than this."

"Did you have enough to eat, Dad?"

"Yes, but I never have enough of my girl."

◆ ◆ ◆

Dad and I return to the Commons, and Halsey follows us a few moments later.

"Hi, there!" he says as he joins Dad and me.

"Oh hi, son," Dad says.

Halsey and I bask in the words.

May 24, 2015

Dad is leaning into the conversation the three of us are having at the table. You can see his eagerness to become one with us.

He says, "Oh, Monica—I want to take you home with me." To Halsey, he adds, "And I might take you along with me. I'd be lying on the floor if I didn't have one of you."

"No, that wouldn't happen," I answer.

"You're right—because one of you would take care of me," Dad replies.

There's no doubt in his mind. He knows it.

◆ ◆ ◆

Dad is thinking about Mom, his wife of forty years.

"Mom's dead, isn't she?" It's more statement than question. "That shouldn't be." His eyes tear up. "They're kind of greasy," he says, pointing to his eyes. "I'm trying my own system, and it didn't work. I can feel it in my eyeballs that something's wrong, but I'm not going to break myself up to figure it out."

◆ ◆ ◆

Dad knows he doesn't know.

"Day to night, the clock up here isn't working right." He points to his head. "The Good Lord should turn me loose and let me go. The Good Lord is taking pretty good care of me."

◆ ◆ ◆

"We couldn't find your dinner," Dad tells Halsey and me. "We all looked for it, and we couldn't find it. And then we found it by the curb. It was all still there. We checked."

That's right, Halsey. You better go get it before it's gone.

◆ ◆ ◆

Mary, one of the staff members, drops a cup in the workstation, causing a lot of noise.

Dad looks around, checking over his shoulder. "I don't see any weapons," he says in all seriousness.

May 30, 2015

When we visit, sometimes we fall into a nice quiet after our greetings. Sometimes we recognize that what's said doesn't matter, and what matters can't be said. Today, though, Dad tries to fill this quiet.

"I don't know anything to talk about," he says.

"Well, we can just sit next to each other and look at each other," I answer.

"That's true," he says. "But I don't want it that someone looks nice at me, and then I have to do something for them."

Ha!

◆ ◆ ◆

Dad, dumbfounded by it all, says, "It's quite a world. We're forced to do this and that—and we don't know how."

It is a puzzling world, Dad. I have to agree.

June 3, 2015

Sitting around our table, Halsey makes some useless comment.

I point at him. "He's losing it, Dad."

"*He* is?" Dad asks.

"Yep," I answer.

"I thought *I* was," Dad replies.

There are still moments of lucidity.

◆ ◆ ◆

Occasionally, little preschoolers come in to mingle with the memory care residents in the Commons. This is fascinating to watch. Such a wide age gap, yet two are as one. They delight in each other.

Today, one is wearing leggings. Dad takes notice.

"Look at that tight little bumper," he says.

June 10, 2015

I wave to Janet as we head over to sit with Dad. Not far into our conversation, Dad says, "My eyes are getting wet—and there's another falling. I want my girl to take care of me so that I can be with her when I'm gone."

This is just so sad. He must feel so alone.

What does he think about as he passes time, sitting at his table? *Are* there thoughts? Or do words just free-fall? Does one word get hung up, and then another piles on, and pretty soon there's a bunch of words just heaped on top of one another?

I think of a bowl of alphabet soup. But instead of letters, words.

Words on a spoon.

◆ ◆ ◆

"I'm all done with school," Dad says. "Legally."

Well, now . . .

We must be back in eighth grade, when Dad graduated from parochial school. Since he lived on a farm, he could now quit school and help the family with farming.

◆ ◆ ◆

As Dad finishes his applesauce, I comment, "Good to the last drop, huh?"

"And beyond," he replies.

◆ ◆ ◆

Another Optage visit. We take Dad back into the Sun Room for some privacy. The nurse shares some observations.

A lot of talk in the distant past; the more-present reality is going.

> The more he uses his wheelchair, the sooner he will forget how to walk.
> BP: 136/68. Good.
> Oxygen: 93. In the 90s is good.
> Pulse: 66.
> Pressing Dad's fingernails: Good circulation.
> Pressing his thighs: Muscle mass is clearly diminished.
> Eating is not an issue.
> Humming is his way of controlling anxiety.
> A very slow decline.
> Significant amount of time for a life span.
> Dad is to be seen in another two to three months, with labs (kidneys and nutritional status) in six months to a year.

June 14, 2015

When I go to sign the visitor log in Dad's room, I see that he still has the picture with the fawn. It makes me smile.

I join Dad and Halsey at the table.

"You're a nice girl, and I love you," Dad says. "I like your teeth too. And I'm not humbucking, either."

He pauses and considers this new word, *humbucking*.

"That's good!" he exclaims. "Woopy doo! I just came up with that and thought it would fit right in!"

◆ ◆ ◆

"Everyone knows I'm a one-person man."

Out of the blue, but I think it's obvious he's saying no one could ever take Mom's place.

◆ ◆ ◆

"Hard to do something when you don't have anything to do it with. I'm trying to make corners."

Maybe "making corners" means trying to do something differently. Not always in the same straight line.

June 21, 2015

"I do love my life," he says with a slight nod of emphasis.

June 28, 2015

During visits, Dad and I have most of the exchanges. Halsey refers to it as the Mutual Admiration Club. He jokes that he often feels like an extra person at the table. (But a very important extra person!)

"Monica," Dad purrs.

He then looks at Halsey.

"Do you like her too?"

He continues to look at Halsey.

"I wish you'd talk a little bit more."

◆ ◆ ◆

Dad tries to say something but loses the thread.

"I just forgot it . . . just let it roll."

◆ ◆ ◆

Lorraine shuffles over to us, cradling a baby doll in her arms, snuggling it close to her chest.

"Here, here. Now, now."

Dad peers over at the baby doll, admiring it. He looks up at Lorraine. "Is it a puppy?" he asks innocently.

She snaps at him in disgust, like he's an idiot. "No. It's a *cat!*"

Dad realizes he made a mistake. I can see his thoughts wrestling across his face.

"Dad, you were nice to her," I comment as Lorraine toddles away.

"I was?"

"Yeah. She was showing you her baby doll, and you were very nice."

"Don't feel bad if I screw things up," he replies. "I can do it easily. I'm just a little boy."

There is such an innocence in the disease.

◆ ◆ ◆

"And we went home together," Dad says. But then he quickly clarifies. "Not 'to get her' but 'together.'"

Too funny. Dad has been struggling with words and is on a steady decline—yet suddenly he could be a game show host.

July 5, 2015

Dad always likes to diddle with Halsey's keys. So last night, we filled up a key ring with spare keys, hang tags, and so on for Dad. This will give him his own set—make him feel he's in charge.

When we give it to him, he just beams.

"I can't put it on any scale at all," he says.

He's *so* happy that he starts to tear up again.

"My eyes will escape," he says, "and I'll look like hell."

◆ ◆ ◆

We start talking about Dad's old Hudson from way back when.

"Can't find it anymore here." He points to his head.

Is the memory of his Hudson now fading—and he realizes it?

◆ ◆ ◆

I try to keep up with the flow as the words tumble out.

"You two are just immaculate."

"Monica, I think you need to come to my house and stay with Daddy."

"My memory's not too good, but I still know my people.

"Oh, Monica, I don't know. I want you at my house at all times."

"My gut's jumping." He laughs.

His eyes start to tear up. "My eyes are running out of my eyes."

Wow.

July 9, 2015

We're off to a late start in getting to the Arbor today.

"I can't believe the Good Lord is pushing you two to come to my room," Dad greets us when we finally arrive.

Truth is, I don't need much of a push. These visits have become my life!

July 16, 2015

A week has passed since I last journaled during our visits. Dad is popped out more than usual today.

"I wish I could put together and cook so I could feed him on top of the car," he says as he rubs my back.

Really?

Now he plays with his keys. "Then we'll go down and hook him some trees—if everyone wants to use them. Then we'd get no smell."

He goes on to call a cookie a hot dog, a table a bird.

"We can make good perspedesprians," he says.

He's convinced of whatever he's saying, but I have no idea. This isn't a matter of decoding poetic language. Sadly, it's a deterioration of language.

◆ ◆ ◆

Thankfully, a few exchanges are easier to follow.

"I never had it so good," Dad says.

"Didn't you?" I ask.

"Not *that* good."

◆ ◆ ◆

The AC comes on overhead. Dad hears it.

"Wind must be perking up."

◆ ◆ ◆

"You can kick me if you want," Dad says.

"I wouldn't do that!" I answer.

"You can think about it. That's my girl. And I ain't drunk, either."

And of course, it's good to see that some themes never change.

"That's my girl, yes sir," he says. "You have nice clean teeth." He points to Halsey. "This is one of my good people too."

July 17, 2015
We have a care conference today. They are moving Dad to the next level of care. Level 3. More hands-on. More extensive toileting and morning care.

We saw it coming.

Chapter Thirty-Four

A Kingle Family

July 18, 2015

Dad is petting my arm.

"That's my girl. That's not going to run away."

Pet. Pet.

Dick, another resident, observes this. "You've been locked up too long," he says to Dad.

◆ ◆ ◆

"That's charming!" Dad exclaims. "That Monica—she can build anything. And then she can teach Halsey, and we can go camping."

Charming? I've never heard my blue-collar dad say anything was "charming."

◆ ◆ ◆

"In my face and my body, I *like* what I've got."

◆ ◆ ◆

Somewhere in our conversation, I say, "No one's laughing at me."

"How do you know?" Dad answers quite seriously. "People could be laughing right now."

Well, that's pretty astute!

He then calls my ponytail a "tube-ling" as he flicks it.

And that ends that little conversation.

◆ ◆ ◆

"I want my Monica and my Halsey too!" Dad says. "You are a very good girl, and I'm a good dad too."

"Yes, you are!" I wholeheartedly agree.

"I like nothing better than my own children. Could put me and all my partners together, and we'd all have a nice life. I have my ways too."

He pats Halsey.

"That's my dad," he says to Halsey.

Hmm . . .? Maybe it's a role reversal. Father Halsey taking care of son Jerome.

◆ ◆ ◆

Dad pets my arm again.

"You're nice and smooth and salt. I can't get myself going for fuel for our own party. I feel my eyes sweating. You take good care of me. You're a good little girl."

July 21, 2015

It's another fine-dining event, and we're seated with table linens, music, and ambiance.

"I hit my dad once, and I still feel bad about it. I hit him with a hamburger." He makes a hammering motion.

I rather doubt he ever hit his dad with anything. Much less with a hamburger.

Cute.

◆ ◆ ◆

Dad points to his butter knife.

"Can you prevent yourself from getting hurt with that?"

◆ ◆ ◆

The water glass is sweating in front of Dad.

"It's like alfalfa," he remarks.

◆ ◆ ◆

He's struggling with his words.

"The words aren't coming?" I ask gently.

"They're coming," he says, "but they're down here, and they're not coming up."

◆ ◆ ◆

Nearing the end of dinner, I ask, "Are you all done?"

"For today."

July 26, 2015

Again, we're in the Commons, sitting at "our" table.

"My house is not the same without my people in it," Dad says. He shakes his head.

I imagine he's seeing himself alone. Without Mom. Without Stevie. Greg and I are still here, but we live with our own families. Dad's house was once full of his people. Not anymore.

I try to divert the conversation into something more pleasant.

"Dad, remember when we used to go to the Yulefest at St. Mark's and have beer and popcorn and play bingo?"

"That's how I got an ingrown toenail," he responds.

◆ ◆ ◆

"Beat my children?" he says out of the blue. "I'd take my house down before I'd do that."

◆ ◆ ◆

He's trying to remember something.

"I don't think I can," he finally admits in defeat. "That's what I miss. I don't know how to approach that."

◆ ◆ ◆

"I want my family to stay the way it was. I don't want to bleed my eyes."

◆ ◆ ◆

We overhear Winnie—with her freshly curled hair and her papery hands—at a neighboring table.

"Are you going to kill me?" she asks.

"Yes," another resident at that table calmly replies.

"Why are you going to kill me? When are you going to kill me?" Winnie pleads.

"Tomorrow," the other resident answers.

July 30, 2015

As I enter the code and pass through the door to the Arbor, I notice there's a photo of Dad "bowling" pinned behind the display case. One of their activities in the Commons, I guess.

I wish I could've seen it in person. He looks so engaged.

◆ ◆ ◆

"I'm going to put you up to heaven and keep you up there for a while," Dad tells me. "And then I'll bring you back with me."

What could he mean? It feels like it's a good thing—but I can't even put regular words to it.

◆ ◆ ◆

"We will look out for him, because that's what I do."

I don't know who he's looking out for, but I *do* know that that's what he does.

August 2, 2015

I have the same thought every time we enter the Arbor: *There's Dad!*

It's like being at the state fair. You see all the other people, but your eyes scan over everyone else until they light on recognition.

(Of course, we don't have far to scan here at the Arbor—Dad sits in the same spot every day.)

◆ ◆ ◆

"I'd like to have the whole works as a kingle," he says. "All my family."

A "kingle" sounds nice . . . but what is it?

Oh, why not? A "kingle" family.

August 6, 2015

We've had a nice visit with Dad, and it's time to leave. They're setting up for dinner. When I push back my chair, Dad asks if I'll be staying to eat.

"No, I'm not staying to eat," I tell him. "I have to go home and cook."

Bob, still wearing his Iowa sweatshirt with the frayed collar and cuffs, says in response, "That makes a hard job to have a pleasant experience."

You got it, Bob.

August 10, 2015

When we enter the Commons, I notice it's emptier than usual. Well, today is Monday. We usually come on Tuesday. Maybe Monday is a slow day.

Dad seems a little more withdrawn today. He does say to me, though: "That's my girl. Forever. Don't forget it. You're just a young chick."

August 13, 2015

It's a hot one today. Once Halsey parks the car, I'll make a mad dash to get inside McKenna Crossing, where it'll be cool again. Halsey won't be dashing. He's not a dasher but rather a dawdler.

"I like my family," Dad says as soon as we join him. "That's you and myself."

"I love your new shirt," I compliment him.

"I love *you!*" he answers. "Your teeth—I like them too. I definitely want them with you. You're so cute I can't eat my cookie. I might wink my shoulders."

How can you not just smile when you hear this? I feel the grin on my face.

"I like my tears," he continues. "They don't feel good all the time, but I like them. Until they drip once in a while."

◆ ◆ ◆

Crabby Joyce comments on another resident's blouse: "It looks like a rag."

"It's not a rag," the other resident counters.

"*You're* a rag!" Joyce says. "Smarty."

August 17, 2015

I notice the television is on quite loud across the room. I look around to see if a staffer will attend to it, before I need to go to take care of it.

Oh, good. There's Laurie. She's on it.

Meanwhile, Dad has been talking to Halsey. I turn back in time to hear him finish by saying, "That's my boy. And I want to keep him that way."

♦ ♦ ♦

"I like myself when I do this"—Dad waves his hand up and down and across his front. He laughs. "I'm a wicked old man. Am I nobbling you? I like your nobbling. And you know I'm nuts!"

♦ ♦ ♦

"Look at those nice little arms," Dad says to Halsey about me. "I can't help but touch her. Do you ever pepper her?"

I'm not so sure about this. Might not want to go there.

♦ ♦ ♦

The Minnesota Twins baseball game is on in the background. (At least it's not blaring like earlier.) Dad sings "God Bless America" with the TV. Every word.

He's singing again! He knows the words! I'm thrown for a loop. I guess that some things, such as songs, are so deeply etched in our memory that they spill out when called upon.

♦ ♦ ♦

Janet is peering down at a fox in a book. There's a puzzled pucker between her eyebrows. She squints as she makes her way closer to the book to inspect it.

"He's got a bad hangy thing on his butt."

"Janet," I say. "That's his tail."

She roars.

August 18, 2015

As we join Dad at his table, I see he's crying. Not just tearing up with his "eyes running out of his eyes." He's actually crying. This is rare.

I ask him questions, trying to understand.

Dad shakes his head at himself. "I don't know how to answer anything anymore. I just don't know what's going on. I don't know what to say or what to do. It just ain't right."

No, it absolutely is not.

I feel like joining him. God hears the tears you will not cry.

He sniffs up his runny nose. "Snot's still there, though." He blows his nose. "Nothing works. Sounds like a horn. I don't think Greg would help me like this."

I'm rubbing his back, trying to soothe him.

Finally, I want to change the subject, so I announce my age: "I'm sixty!"

I'm not sure why I feel the need to always proclaim it. Here we go, talking about age again. I don't get it.

"If I have to, I'll give you a ride in my arms," Dad says. "You're in good shape. I couldn't see you. I was floating around on top."

◆◆◆

Another Optage Visit.

I'm told that Dad's been combative before getting in the shower. He will be given Ativan beforehand to calm him.

Also, he is to be given Seroquel for sadness.

His heart and lungs sound good.

◆◆◆

Later in the evening, I get a call at home from Vicki, the nurse. Dad crawled out of his wheelchair and positioned himself on the floor. He was "fixing" the underside of the table. They had to use a lifting strap to get him back to his chair.

"Did your dad spend much time fixing things?" Vicki asks me.

All the time!

He did a lifetime of bodywork on cars.

He fixed old clocks.

How many times did he fix Mom's twenty-year-old dryer when all she *really* wanted was a new one?

He also knew how to fix the small household problems I had as a single mom. A few immediately come to mind.

- ◆ Problem: A light bulb broke in the socket, and now the metal base is stuck.
    - o Solution: Needle-nose pliers. Still stuck in there? Rusted? A little spritz of WD-40.

- ◆ Problem: When screwing into a piece of wood, the hole is bigger than the screw.
    - o Solution: Break up a toothpick, stick the pieces in the hole, and now screw in your screw. The screw will grab the toothpicks for a nice, snug fit.

- ◆ Problem: Too much static on the radio.
    - o Solution: Make an antenna out of aluminum foil.

Over the years, there was nothing he couldn't fix. Yet now here he is, unable to fix his own mind.

Chapter Thirty-Five

Hog Riding

August 27, 2015

We're back in the Commons, visiting at our old hangout. Dad looks over at Halsey.

"You *still* look good," he declares.

Then Dad starts rubbing my back.

"I better not do that anymore or I'll give you a master fever on your neck."

August 30, 2015

We're browsing through one of the coffee table books in the library section of the Commons. We run into a picture of the *Titanic* and try using it to start a new discussion.

"I don't know how to get back there on that side," Dad says. "My mind won't leave."

Think about that. He's basically saying he can't move his thoughts to another topic. It's as if his mind is roadblocked.

◆◆◆

"How late are you staying?" Dad asks.

"Oh, another half hour," I answer.

"The most you can. I can't have it too much."

◆◆◆

"I can't mention anything. My mind is all bubbled up."

◆◆◆

"I'm going to keep her—if I have to go in the hog barn," Dad says to Halsey about me.

I don't know the last time I was in a hog barn. Oh, wait. Fifty-some years ago, we went to visit some cousins in Cambridge, Minnesota. My mom's cousin, Pat, and her husband, Cy, had six or seven kids—everyone's named started with a J. They had a farm.

I loved it when we went to visit! They had barns with hay bales we could build tunnels through. And the biggest thrill was when I rode a fat hog.

You can't just walk up to a hog and hop on. The hogs don't enjoy it. And apparently, they're mean, which I didn't know at the time. Otherwise, I probably wouldn't have been so adventurous.

The trick is to straddle yourself with one foot on each railing that flanks the path in the barn. You have to hold your balance—and then when a hog runs under you, you drop down on its back.

Hold on!

When we came back in the house after my brave ride, the women were cackling at the table in front of Pat's wood-burning stove. The J kids came running into the kitchen, interrupting to announce, "Monica rode a hog!"

The ladies let out a collective "What the—?"

I shyly peeked out at the back of the group. I was rumpled with dirt smeared everywhere. I was still blinking out the dust.

Everyone in the room slapped their legs and busted out laughing.

I guess hog riding isn't something you should attempt. I think I was put up to it.

◆◆◆

"My mom never swore," Dad remarks.

"Did she ever get mad?" I ask.

"If she did, it was a whisper."

September 3, 2015

"Jerome, how are you doing?" Halsey asks as we approach Dad's table.

"Oh, hi, sweetheart," Dad answers. He then turns to me. "Look at those good-looking teeth." He motions my attention toward Halsey. "This guy is a good guy."

"I'm glad you feel that way," Halsey says with a smile.

"I *honestly* feel that way," Dad emphasizes.

He starts petting Halsey.

"I like this man. I call him Dad—he's worth much more than that."

There it is again. He called Halsey his dad not too long ago. He must be referring to how he feels about Halsey. The love. Someone who is looking after him.

Still looking at Halsey, Dad says to me, "Look at this, sweetie—he even likes *me*."

Maybe Halsey has made it into the Mutual Admiration Club after all.

Dad speaks to Halsey again. "I'll watch over you." He points to me. "And Gloria—she'll give you food."

First time he's called me Mom's name.

"She'll probably even let you have this scoop," Dad says as he fingers my earring.

◆ ◆ ◆

Halsey: "Jerome, there was a squirrel climbing on our window screen today."

Me: "Do squirrels do that, Dad?"

Dad: "Evidently, they do."

September 6, 2015

I bring Dad a cup of coffee from the staff station in the Commons.

"How's that coffee—pretty good?" I ask. "Does it hit the spot?"

"If it doesn't," he says, "it's pretty close."

September 11, 2015

"Monica, you're my little girl and I love you."

◆ ◆ ◆

"I don't know if I'll get out of this," he says after blowing his nose *a lot*.

He blows his nose again and looks at his tissue.

"That baby's almost full."

◆ ◆ ◆

All of a sudden, he says, "Peanuts."

Even he doesn't know from where he pulled this out. He laughs at himself. "What the hell next?" he says.

◆◆◆

"I'm going to stay there," Dad says. "And if I can't, I'm going to crawl under a wheel."

◆◆◆

A tear falls from his eye. He calls the tear a "drip of wine."

◆◆◆

Dad looks across at another resident. "That's the one who doesn't like me. Thanks, buddy."

September 14, 2015

Shirley is sitting at Dad's table this Monday afternoon.

"Should we get married?" she asks Dad.

"I don't have time yet," he answers.

"What do I know that I don't know?" she asks. "I always knew you were a woman flacker."

September 25, 2015

Dad appears to be reflecting today as we visit.

"I enjoyed you," he says to Halsey. "I like my life. Couldn't be better."

Dad rubs my back. "I just keep letting you know where I stand." He rubs my arm next. "And you have the nicest legs."

Nope. Those are my arms, Dad.

◆◆◆

"Oh, Monica," Dad says, "I hope you like me half as much as I like you."

September 29, 2015

As we make our way into McKenna, we comment on the news we just heard on the radio: Caitlyn Jenner officially changed her name from Bruce and her gender to a woman. We shake our heads and agree this isn't worth mentioning to Dad. He would never get it.

We enter the code and weave our way to Dad's table. I smile big in his direction.

"You've got such nice clean teeth and such nice clean whooptushes," he says.

Whooptushes?!

"That would cause me a big lip," he adds.

By the sound of it, maybe it should! Whooptushes. Ha.

◆◆◆

Dad starts coughing.

"Sounds like tin in there," he says.

October 6, 2015

As we pass through the secured doors, we check out the bulletin board—just to see if there are any more photos of Dad. Not today.

We join Dad at his usual table.

"I'm getting juicy flakes." He points to his tear-filled eyes. "I know Monica will take very good care of me, and I'll take care of her. I like her teeth."

October 11, 2015

When I study Dad across the table, he doesn't look too well.

"Dad, do you feel OK?" I ask.

"Looking at you, yes. Definitely."

◆◆◆

Dad makes an observation: "People go through so much before they die. I don't know how they do it."

I don't know either.

◆◆◆

Dad points to his head.

"Seems like I'm getting cedar-break—or something."

Does he mean *senile*? *Cedar-break*. *Senile*. Kind of sound the same.

I think I'm reaching.

But that was always his fear. "I don't want to get senile," he'd say . . .

October 19, 2015

Dad popped a lens out of his eyeglasses, so I took them in for repair.

When I bring the repaired glasses back to him, he says, "Oh, Monica. I can't help but love you. I don't know what I'm going to do with you. I just love you."

October 22, 2015

Sometimes we find it hard to come up with things to chatter about. This time, Dad comes up with something.

"What's this?" he asks as he pulls the loose skin of his neck.

"That's your neck," I answer.

"It's getting bigger all the time."

And he pulls some more.

October 24, 2015

As we get up and prepare to leave at the end of our visit, Halsey rubs Dad's neck.

"Are you choking me?" Dad asks.

"No, I'm rubbing you."

"Is that a good choke or a bad choke?" Dad continues.

"It's a good choke," Halsey says, giving in.

"Oh, OK. Thank you."

October 28, 2015

We find that residents in the memory care unit hang on to compliments. (Really, doesn't everyone?) Knowing this, we pass them out frequently.

"You look good, Dad," I compliment.

"Aw," he reacts. "That'll take me a long ways."

November 8, 2015

We can hear the football game before we even round the bend into the Commons. The Vikings are playing the Rams.

Dad sees us as we approach. "My people! I *do* like my two people."

"You were watching the Vikings, weren't you?" Halsey asks Dad.

"I'll have to say I don't know."

◆ ◆ ◆

I smile at Dad.

"Look at them pretty teeth she has!"

I smile again at him.

"And her teeth seem so nice and soft. I like my daughter a little bit more than other ones." To Halsey, he adds, "You have a good wife. You couldn't find a better one."

"I know it," Halsey replies.

"She's good to *me* that I know," Dad says.

◆ ◆ ◆

The TV is set too loud. Again. We've been competing with the Vikings game during the visit. Dad finally gets fed up and tells the TV to shut up.

◆ ◆ ◆

"Look at these hump bumps," he says, inspecting his knuckles.

◆ ◆ ◆

He calls Halsey a girl, then laughs at himself.

"Don't worry," he tells Halsey. "I'll be on your racetrack."

November 15, 2015

As we pull up our chairs to the table, we see Dad is fiddling with something in his hand.

"Jerome," Halsey says, "what do you got in your hand?"

"Something I put in it," Dad says.

We gently unclench his fingers and find a balled-up tissue.

◆ ◆ ◆

"You know that Greg is a pusher," Dad says to Halsey.

There must have been an altercation. Or is Dad chewing on something from the past? They often butt heads, and Greg tries to push his point home—sometimes a little too forcefully.

November 18, 2015

I think when Dad sits alone at his table, it gives him time to reminisce. I'm not sure how that actually goes for him, though. Maybe words escape him, but I think he's warmed with feelings.

As if to prove my point, Dad greets us today with, "I like my girl, and I love my Halsey."

"I love you, too, Jerome," Halsey replies.

"Oh, you can if you want."

"I *do* want to."

"And it gets bigger and bigger and bigger as times goes on," Dad says. As an aside, he looks over to me. "I like you. You know I do."

Once again, proof that Halsey *is* in the Mutual Admiration Club after all.

November 20, 2015

We meet in Dad's room with Kari, a nurse practitioner from Optage.

Weight: 124.8 pounds. Down quite a few from June, when he was at 136. Kari suggests that I bring in extra Boost or Ensure so Dad has enough to receive it twice a day.

COPD.

No evidence of acute pneumonia.

Nebulizer: Twice a day right now.

Kari will write an order for an evaluation for physical therapy with his wheelchair. Using the wheelchair has been a struggle for Dad. His feet used to get tied up in the foot pedals, so the staff finally removed the pedals. Now his arms are starting to get chafed because of the cracked vinyl padding on the rests. Kari will also talk to the wheelchair provider about sheepskin padding to cover the armrests.

She mentions the Wilder Foundation in Saint Paul, which offers healthy aging and caregiving services.

December 8, 2015

Dad points to his head.

"It's up here but can't get it out. It doesn't work out of my pocket."
He now points to his mouth.
What a great idea—to call your mouth a pocket.

◆ ◆ ◆

"Should we do a little thinking?" Dad asks.
I love this! Yes! Let's do that!

◆ ◆ ◆

Jean, another resident, always has polished nails. I notice that while the nails on her right hand are beautifully manicured, the nails on her left hand are all chewed up. I comment on this to her.

She lifts her left hand. "This is my regular world to live in."

Makes sense. And we always find comfort in our "regular" world.

Laurie, a staff member, replies with, "And your other hand is your fantasy world?"

"You too?" Dad interjects.

◆ ◆ ◆

We talk again about Dad's red Mustang that he had back in the '60s.

"Mom smashed in the front end." He's very clear. "A *couple* front ends."

◆ ◆ ◆

We're most successful with conversation when we use prompts from long ago.

"Didn't you use to watch *Bonanza?*" I ask Dad.

"It would be fun to slop around with them," Dad answers with a fun grin.

Chapter Thirty-Six

Love—and Bullying by Geese

It's a brisk late-fall day. On my morning walk, I smile as I think about the Mutual Admiration Club. What it is is love.

I wear this love as a perfume, letting its essence linger after the visit so it may waft to my other family and friends I hold so close to me. Love is meant to be emitted. Love is meant to be spread. The more love is given, the more there is to give.

I see love at the Arbor. Dad and the other residents perhaps don't know it by name, but they all hunger for love and recognize it when it approaches them. Their eyes light up when love greets them. Their eyes follow this visitor, this love, around the room.

Their eyes are flat, though, when someone greets them not out of love but out of obligation. They know love is more than a hurried visit, a pat on the back, and a "See you next week."

Love is a magnet. Its force pulls you and draws you in. You cannot resist, nor do you want to.

Love melts fear.

Love comforts the lonely.

Love cannot be matched as it grounds the Alzheimer's patient.

Love builds bridges over rivers of lost words and memories.

I come upon a gaggle of geese up near the top of a huge open area. There must be fifteen to twenty of them. I notice how they're all part of the group and very content with one another.

Three more geese appear from above—latecomers to the party, or so it seems to me. They arc their way down to the other side of the open area, respectfully keeping a bit of distance from the initial group. They start eating from the ground.

Then all at once, the entire large group decides to greet the latecomers. The whole gaggle starts waddling over.

I smile to myself. What a welcome—it's as if the latecomers are celebrities. Perhaps this is their Mutual Admiration Club.

But then, in one fluid movement, every goose in the bigger group lifts its neck and freezes. Since I have never observed the habits of geese, I have no idea what this means. After pausing in that position for about fifteen seconds, the entire gaggle storms the latecomers.

It isn't so friendly now. With necks lowered to the ground, the geese steam-shovel and scoop their way over to the three strays. Every movement is in tandem—perfectly orchestrated. This is not admiration—mutual or otherwise. It feels hostile.

The three strays do their best to act oblivious to what's going down. They continue pecking at the ground, pretending not to notice the rapid, aggressive approach of the other geese.

Will they ever become part of the larger group? Or will they be forced to leave?

The scene plays out before me until the geese move farther down the open field, away from me. I can no longer see how the three are faring.

I continue on my way now, sidestepping a flattened frog pressed like a paper doll on the asphalt trail. I note that the sumac is showing signs of red. The high tips of trees are beginning to don their fall finery. Colors of orange and yellow are starting to blaze. Clusters of pine cones have sprouted on top of evergreens. I spot a partially deflated beach ball.

I see all this as I see flashbacks.

I know how those three geese feel . . .

◆ ◆ ◆

We didn't call it bullying back in the '60s. Or at least not that I'm aware.

There was a core group of three or four girls at St. Mark's School. The boys called them the Dog Pack. Whenever the group would pass by, the boys would bark. Amazingly to me, the group took it as a compliment.

Occasionally, the pack would let two or three other girls into their circle. But then, for no reason at all, they would turn on one or another of the girls, and she would be ousted. I was one who would occasionally be allowed into the group but then soon after kicked out.

When they kicked you out, they would make snide remarks as you walked by. Or they'd snicker and roll their eyes when you were called on in class to give an answer. Or glare in your direction with smirks behind cupped hands.

I remember one particular time when the bell rang and we began exiting the classroom. The leader of the pack shouldered me into the coat hooks in the back of the room. The hook rammed into my temple and stunned me. What truly stunned me even more than the push was the shock that someone could actually do this to another.

At recess, teams needed to be chosen for softball. As the picks neared the end, the pack would groan about how only the "losers" were left.

Two of the girls consistently left until the end were farm girls. You could smell they came from the farm—and the pack would make a big point of holding their noses in disgust whenever they walked by.

One of the farm girls was my third cousin. We were in seventh grade, yet she would stomp her feet and cry like a young child when she saw she was last to be chosen. Crying was a mistake on her part. It was a call for the pack to ridicule her all the more and push her into a snowbank.

Eventually, I found two other girls to befriend. I realized I didn't need that treatment anymore, nor did I deserve it. No one does. I didn't want to be associated with anyone who treated others that way.

My two new friends had pierced ears, so I asked Mom if I could get mine pierced too. I was so excited when she said I could. When I got to school, proud to be sporting a pair of pierced earrings, the pack called me a slut. Because I had *pierced ears?*

At a class reunion almost forty-five years later, one of our male classmates made a comment to me how brutal that group of girls was back then. It was an unsolicited remark, out of the blue.

This classmate affirmed for me that that treatment really did happen. On some level, you try to convince yourself that you just imagined it. You move on. But deep down, you don't forget.

◆◆◆

Trent also had a bullying experience. It still pains me to think of it.

He, too, was in seventh grade. We were new to the school district. At lunch, he sat down at a table to join some classmates. But then the leader of the group asked, "Who at this table doesn't like Trent?" They all raised their hands. Trent got up, took his lunch tray, and moved to a different table in the cafeteria.

I cried when he told me about it. How do you parent when your child has been bullied?

Many years later, I heard Trent mention the ringleader's name. Trent was hanging out with him.

"Wasn't he the kid that—" I started.

"Yes," he interrupted. "Mom, I've forgiven him, but I still haven't forgotten."

I'm proud of Trent. Anyone can hold a grudge, but it takes character to forgive. In forgiving, you release yourself from that burden.

It's important to realize, though, that forgiveness doesn't mean what happened was OK. It just means you have made peace with the pain and are ready to let it go.

Even though I can't see them, I can hear the honking of the geese as they go off and circle in the opposite direction. I hope the three latecomers have made their peace too. I hope they find their way to a Mutual Admiration Club.

I hope they find love.

Chapter Thirty-Seven

The *H* Word and Eating Hangers

O ur visits with Dad continue as fall gives way to winter and 2015 gives way to 2016. In mid-January, I get a call from a Cindy, who introduces herself as the hospice nurse. She gently tells me it has been recommended that Dad be put into hospice care.

My heart jolts. Hospice. The *H* word. Kind of like the *C* word.

But Cindy is so kind; she makes hospice sound like an elevated status for Dad. He will now receive some one-on-one attention. I've been advocating for that for a year—though I never for a minute imagined that such attention would have to happen within the framework of *hospice*.

Three hours a week, he will receive either a chaplain visit, a social service visit, a nurse and/or doctor visit, massage therapy, music therapy, or a pet visit. (It makes me want to sign up for hospice myself!)

I still feel the initial shock, but my mind is slowly also making way for joy. Hospice care sounds so perfect for Dad.

Yet on a deeper level, I know that it means he's dying.

◆◆◆

I don't know how to wrap my head around this new status with hospice. What I do know is that I want Dad to receive Communion regularly. Bottom line: I want to fill him with Jesus.

I speak with the chaplain who will be visiting Dad every two weeks. She is not Catholic, but I ask if she could give Dad Communion.

I understand that different denominations have different beliefs about the Eucharist. I could be wrong, but I really don't think Dad made a distinction between a Catholic and non-Catholic Communion, though. He never got into it that deep.

And here's how I see it: if we were to give Dad non-Catholic Communion, the power of his own belief that it *was* the actual Body of Christ would override anything non-Catholic about it. Differently put: if I were dying on the side of the road and found a crust of bread, I believe I could declare "This is the Body of Christ" and take it as Communion, and God would see the intent. Maybe I'm way off base.

However, I need to double-check with a Catholic priest to find out the church's position. I've lost my truths before and had to round them up.

And while I'm asking about this, I can also make an appointment to have Dad receive the Anointing of the Sick. If hospice is the beginning of the end, I want Dad to be prepared.

So on February 6, 2016, I send an email to the local priest, explaining Dad's situation. The priest kindly replies back to explain that this can't happen. It would be inappropriate for a non-Catholic to bring Dad "communion bread" from another religious group or Christian denomination.

"Catholics are not to presume anything to be the sacramental Body and Blood of our Lord unless we know it has truly been consecrated at a Catholic Mass," he writes. "Your father has had the right to the True Body and Blood of Jesus ever since the day of his First Holy Communion. And it would have to be from a priest, a deacon, or a lay Catholic who has been trained as an extraordinary minister of Holy Communion."

I grapple with this answer. I agree Dad has the *right* to a consecrated host. Does that mean nothing else will do?

I want to share more about Dad with the priest, give him a better sense of who Dad is. Isn't Dad's need—his human need for the Divine—more important than human regulations and rules?

Or is this a Divine rule? Now I feel as though I'm wrestling with God. Doesn't Jesus know what's in our hearts? I know that the Creator is always greater than the creation.

A flicker of a Bible study flashes through my thoughts. What of David in 1 Samuel 21:1–6? Ahimelek goes against the law to give consecrated bread to David. And later, in Matthew 12:2–4, Jesus honors the spirit of Ahimelek's decision.

But I accept this priest's explanation.

◆ ◆ ◆

It's 3:20 a.m. I try to get out of bed.

It's something you do automatically. You throw off the covers and swing out your legs as you raise your upper body. Then you swivel to the side of the bed and plant your feet on the floor.

But not this time.

The blankets don't do their part as I try to throw them off. Instead, they cling to me and wrap around my legs. So when my legs are supposed to swing out, they don't. That makes for a big problem. Unaware that my legs are trapped in the blanket, the rest of my body swivels out—and then promptly propels to the floor with an odd sort of twisting.

Halsey wakes up when I hit the ground. He asks if I'm all right.

Well, I am. But I know I'll pay for it in the upcoming few days. I can already feel where some muscles have been pulled in directions they haven't been pulled for many years.

When I climb back into bed, I try to fall asleep. But it's been way too long since I've had what I would call a "great night's sleep." It's always just snatches of a couple of hours, interspersed with long hours when the clock moves forward but sleep eludes me. Sometimes I'm so tired that I just want to cry.

Eventually, I do fall asleep.

In my dream, I'm married to Patrick Swayze. He's stuffing his mouth and swallowing clear hard-plastic hangers with metal hooks, like the ones you get at Target sometimes.

Obviously, it isn't easy to swallow them whole. Some of them break in half before he swallows. But even so, he keeps at it. I yank one out of his mouth, but he's already swallowing another.

Then he starts to gag. The hanger won't go down—but it won't come up either. He grasps his neck, trying to work the hanger down by sliding his hands along his throat. He's retching. Holding his throat. Trying to swallow it down.

"You can't eat that!" I shout.

My shout wakes me up. It's 5:10. I can tell by Halsey's breathing that I've wakened him as well.

After about fifteen minutes of me trying to sort out the dream on my own, I tell him about my dream. He's usually pretty good at interpreting them, and I want to hear his thoughts.

"Well," he says, "you're looking for answers to questions about your life that you don't have the solutions for."

I absorb that and try to understand what he's getting at. After some thought, I know he's right. Unbidden tears trickle down the sides of my face as I lie wordlessly on the pillow. I didn't realize I felt so fragile.

"I think that might be it," I finally say.

Every part of my life has taken unexpected jags, especially in the last few years. I don't even recognize myself anymore. It's not as though I'm disappointed with my life. I just feel as though I'm walking in someone else's shoes.

◆ ◆ ◆

I understand how family dynamics need to change when life throws you a curveball.

The first curveball actually came in 1995, when Mom was diagnosed with brain cancer. She had limited time. So I made a choice. I divided my time between her and my teenage boys.

Maybe I should have been around more for the boys. Maybe I would have had a better read on choices they were making.

But then Mom unexpectedly passed away. My time was now divided again. This time between my sons and my dad, who needed to be taught how to take care of himself.

Then Trent and Chad started having families of their own.

And that's about the time I met Halsey. My attention was now redirected to him—though I still tried to incorporate my sons, their growing families, and Dad.

Then the dementia hit Dad, and my focus was directed back to him.

None of these changes of direction were in my plans. So, Halsey's explanation makes some sense. I'm eating hangers. Heck, I've been eating hangers for twenty years, when I think about it.

If you want to see God laugh, just tell Him your plans.

Then again, a piece of me also wonders if the hangers are the unconsecrated "communion bread" I wish I could fill my Dad with.

Chapter Thirty-Eight

Communion and Eyeglass Repair

Hospice has brought a much-needed rhythm to all of our lives. We need this soft landing, a cushion to catch us, after the last few months of Dad's decline.

We have fallen, just like Dad's delightful poetry, which has now fallen into almost unrecognizable Alzheimer's language. We have fallen, just like Dad's teary eyes, which now "escape" and "wiggle" like "drips of wine" more and more often. We have fallen, just like his shoulders, which now slump as he sits alone at his table.

We need something to catch us and comfort us, just like Dad, who is now being cradled in the arms of hospice.

January 24, 2016

Again, the three of us are sharing a cup of coffee and some conversation in the Commons.

"Dad, your brother Lawrence is ninety-one now," I tell him.

Dad is overcome with surprise. "Wow. I hope he's not going to drop in my bed or anything."

He must be concerned about Lawrence dying.

◆ ◆ ◆

Halsey steers the conversation to Dad's Hudson. "Jerome, you used to have a Hudson."

Dad lights up. "I used it to show off."

This makes us light up too. Last time we mentioned the Hudson, he didn't seem able to uncover those memories.

"You used to have a Hudson Hornet," Halsey says again.

Dad nods. "Definitely."

February 2, 2016

Dad has an announcement to make at the table: "I'm just an honest little boy."

"You're a good man, Jerome," Halsey adds.

"Yeah. I'm surprised at myself."

February 7, 2016

There is one thing we agree on each time we visit. And today, Dad nails it.

"We like each other," he says. "I like my children."

◆ ◆ ◆

Dad points to his head.

Halsey asks, "Is there a lot going on up there, Jerome?"

"I'm not there that long," Dad says.

So interesting. It's as if he knows that thoughts take time to develop and communicate, but something pushes him out before his mind can complete that work.

◆ ◆ ◆

"And Monica, your teeth! They're just perfect," Dad says. "Oh, Monica—I don't know what I'd do without you."

"Well, you don't have to worry about it," I say. "I'll always be here with you."

◆ ◆ ◆

"Dad, are you happy?" I ask.

Dad is petting me. "More than happy. That's my girl." Pet. Pet. "I don't want to mess you up. I'd like a little pootin'. Not much. Just a little."

I'm trying to figure out what "pootin'" means.

◆ ◆ ◆

"I enjoyed my work 'cuz I had my daughter and that helps one hundred percent," Dad says. "Should I change it or not?" he continues. "Or should I just let it whistle on its way?"

Change what? I do like the sound of letting something just *whistle on its way,* though.

"It just moves things the way they should be—down to my feet. Shoes off," he finishes.

February 9, 2016

I talk to Chaplain Jen and Kevin, the recreation director, about getting Dad on the list to receive Catholic Communion. Kevin also tells me that two volunteers, including a Catholic nun, lead the rosary each Wednesday in the quiet Sun Room. Dad has been attending these rosary prayers weekly, though he mostly just participates by listening.

Kevin is certain that these familiar rituals—praying the rosary and receiving Communion—connect deeply within my dad's spirit. At his suggestion, I ask that Dad receive Catholic Communion with the deacon on the first and third Thursdays of each month. I just want to fill him with Jesus.

(Not hangers.)

February 11, 2016

I'm not sure what Dad's been doing with his glasses, but today they are beyond repair. He's bent his frames this way and back again, like a piece of origami artwork. I wonder if he thinks he's "fixing" them.

There was a time when he would have been horrified to realize what he was doing.

I head to Shakopee Vision with the mangled glasses. They have to put his lenses in a spare frame they find in the back room. It's become a joke.

"That Jerome!" they say.

I return to McKenna with the repaired glasses and hand them to Dad. He looks at them with suspicion.

After ten minutes, he says, "You look really good. I don't know what you shovel in there."

I change the subject. "So, do you like my fancy socks?" I wiggle my feet to show him my new socks. *Girl with a Pearl Earring* is featured up the side of each sock.

"For you, they're nice," Dad says. "Not for me, though."

February 13, 2016

I ask that my Bible study leader put in a prayer request for my dad since he is now in hospice care. I ask that he may continue to live each day in a positive frame of mind. That he may continue to see joy in the small things. And, above all, that he may know Christ is his Savior—even if Alzheimer's is limiting his knowledge of what truly *is*.

February 28, 2016

A staff member walks by our table.

"Must be looking for somebody who doesn't got anything," Dad says.

◆ ◆ ◆

"That's my daughter, and I like her. And that's Halsey, and do I like him—woo hoo!" He does a little air whistle through his teeth.

"I love you, Dad," I reply.

"I love you too. And more."

March 1, 2016

Another Optage visit in his room.

Kari, the Optage nurse practitioner, suggests that I ask Cindy, the hospice nurse, about massage therapy.

Dad's taking two tablets of aspirin, 81 mg each, for his heart. Kari feels we could drop down to one or eliminate it entirely. Aspirin makes platelets slipperier—which could cause problems if he fell. At this point, that's more of a concern than heart problems are.

The increased Zoloft has been good.

"He seems to be thriving in hospice," Kari says. "He's so much better."

March 4, 2016

We're in the Commons with the rest of the residents at surrounding tables.

"Both of you are the cutest, best-looking people," Dad says to Halsey and me. "You're a pretty chick," he adds to me. And to Halsey, "You're a good family."

◆ ◆ ◆

"I had my fun, but I'm not going to make it," Dad says.

This comment puts a lump in my throat, but I answer with a smile, "None of us are going to make it."

"Nice white teeth. I like it."

March 10, 2016

It gets harder and harder to see how Dad has declined. I went to Target last night to find something he can fiddle with. It had to be something he can manipulate himself and that won't hurt him or cause him to choke.

I went into the baby department. Isn't that interesting?

So today when we come to visit, I bring the little music-making toy with me. I put it in his hand.

Dad replies, "I'd like to put *you* in my hand and talk and talk and talk until there's nothing left."

April 14, 2016

We still visit regularly, but sometimes there's just not enough for me to write down. For the last two weeks, we've mainly just been in each other's presence.

Today, however, he says, "That's my girl. No one's going to be packing in my suit. I like my family. That's a humdinger."

He pets my arm.

"That's my Monica. That's mine. You got nice teeth. What a nice family I got."

♦ ♦ ♦

Dad gestures to me. "Poor girl. I like her. You get so turned around. And I got another boy over here," now gesturing to Halsey. "I like him. That's a really nice boy. I'm not going to give up on him. I like my people."

"That's my dad, and I'm going to keep you," I respond.

"I don't mind."

♦ ♦ ♦

Dad's beginning to look heavy lidded.

"Dad, are you going to sleep?"

"If I can, I will. If I can't, I can't."

April 17, 2016

"I like your eyes. I like your teeth. And I like your tea-totes," he adds as he dangles my earrings.

April 19, 2016

Today, I'm greeted with, "I know you're my soul—and more, even. That Monica."

◆◆◆

Janet, my laughing partner, is sitting at our table. Halfway into our visit, she sputters. "I'm trying to do it."

"What are you trying to do, Janet?" I ask.

She giggles. "That's what I'm trying to figure out!"

May 5, 2016

"Ray! Ray!" Shirley shrieks out from across the way. "Will you marry me?"

Ray is silent.

Shirley isn't giving up. "I'm talking to you. Will you marry me?"

Ray is silent.

"I don't think I can take this," Janet mumbles at our table.

May 11, 2016

The hospice team calls me after each visit to give me an update on how their visits go with Dad. I've received calls from the music therapist and from Chaplain Jen.

Today, Cindy calls and shares her observations about Dad being a linear thinker. She sees how he puts things in order as they happen to him, then talks about it.

"It's a very sequential manner—like a straight line," she says. "It's the easiest way to get from one point to another. But when he sees only part of something, his learning becomes disabled," she explains.

She shares other little observations as well. "He's always building and rearranging place mats." And "He moves the wheelchair by turning the little wheels in front."

She informs me that Dad seems to be thriving. I'm happy that he's happy.

But my poor, sweet dad has lost so much weight. Back in November, he weighed 124 pounds, and he now weighs 107.

He receives Communion.

May 12, 2016

"The girls all went on the cookie wagon," Dad remarks.

Halsey's ears perk up at the mention of cookies. "Oreo cookies?" he asks.

"I don't think so," Dad says.

◆ ◆ ◆

"That Monica. I love her. She's a good daughter." He looks at Halsey. "You got to try that periodically. It works good."

I pat Dad's back. (This is the Mutual Admiration Club, after all.)

"He's a good dad," I say.

Dad agrees by remembering his own dad. "I think he is. I will never give up my dad. I like him."

May 15, 2016

As we sit down today, I notice that Dad's nails need to be trimmed.

"I like my little family," he begins. "These two right here. That's more than enough."

I think this might be a good time to slide it in. "Dad, should I cut your fingernails?"

"I don't think so."

He's still not a fan.

◆ ◆ ◆

"I like my little daughter. They're hard to come by. I like the good ol' days. Oh, Monica, what a wonderful person."

May 16, 2016

That's the end of Dad's glasses. Again. Back to Shakopee Vision I go.

May 26, 2016

As Dad pets my arm, I look over at Halsey. "I think Dad loves me."

"I do!" Dad says.

"I love you, too, Dad."

"Woo hoo!"

May 31, 2016

While petting my arm today, Dad says to Halsey, "What kind of help do *you* need?"

Apparently, Dad thinks I'm here only to help him, so now he's wondering who's going to help *Halsey*.

◆◆◆

"I like your teeth and everything. Look at those pretty buds. Can't go through every dot and tiddle."

◆◆◆

"I like children. I got a whole nest full."

(Well, he really doesn't have a whole *nest* full. But it's great that he likes us!)

June 9, 2016

It's Thursday. I'll be running a bunch of errands today, but I want to stop in quickly before and after to check on Dad.

"Hey, Dad. Father's Day is coming. Are you my father?" I tease.

"I hope so," he says.

"Dad, you're going to see me two times today. Can you put up with that?"

"I'm going to have to," he replies.

The reason for the second visit? Yep. His glasses. I need to take them in again. He must have it in for them.

June 12, 2016

Halsey starts in singing the Brylcreem jingle: "A little dab'll do ya! Brylcreem!" He pats Dad on the back, keeping rhythm.

Dad nods. "Sounds familiar. Sounds snacky and sounds good." To Halsey, he adds, "Good stuff—and that's *you*."

◆◆◆

"You might get sick of me," Dad says.

"Oh, that will never happen. Will you get sick of me?" I ask.

"Oh, I hope never."

◆ ◆ ◆

Halsey decides to needle Dad a bit. Remember, Dad has a thirty-year tenure as a Ford employee.

Halsey: "Jerome, do you know who makes Corvettes?"

Dad: "I can't come up with it."

Halsey: "Chevrolet."

Dad: "Oh, you little shit."

Chapter Thirty-Nine

Father's Day and Pig Pogs

June 19, 2016

This year, I have to read his Father's Day card to Dad. He's no longer able to read.

"Dad," I read, "I think you already know how special you are to me, but just in case you forget that once in a while, I hope you'll remember this card. It's here to remind you that I love you far beyond any simple words I can say.

"I want you to know so many things that my hugs and smiles have tried—over the years—to tell you. Things about gratitude, closeness, admiration, and hope. Whenever it seems like the world is short on heroes, I think of how much I look up to you. I've got my very own here, and I always have . . ."

I pause. I look into Dad's eyes. "Dad, do you know who I'm talking about? Do you know who this important person is?"

I can read it in his face and eyes. He knows. He's fairly glowing.

"Jesus?" he answers with innocence.

Oh, Dad. I love you!

"Look at that Monica of ours," Dad says to Halsey.

"You're the best," I tell Dad.

"Yeah," he agrees.

◆◆◆

As I give Dad a Father's Day back massage, he happily groans aloud.

"*Ohh!* That's valuable."

◆◆◆

"The lice are running to beat hell. If it's bad, tell me about it," he says to me.

The lice are running to beat hell . . . ? You got me.

Words aren't what we know them to be anymore. We're pretty solid on "teeth" and "I like my family" and "that's my girl." We have all the niceties down pat.

But if a rose can be a "chicken coop" and earrings can be "tea-totes," then who knows what "lice" are?

◆ ◆ ◆

"Well, I like myself," he says.

We laugh.

"That's my little girl. I like her and her husband."

June 25, 2016

Janet is sitting at our table. For whatever reason, she has her index finger poking straight into her ear. Not moving it. Just poked there. For about three minutes.

"Janet," I finally comment, "you have your finger in your ear. Does your ear hurt?"

Janet pulls her finger out, looks at it, and busts out laughing, apparently not knowing it has been in there.

◆ ◆ ◆

"I'm going to take good care of you," Dad says to me. For reassurance, he says to Halsey, "Don't you think?"

◆ ◆ ◆

We're toying around with connector squares, plastic building blocks, which start to fall.

"Hang tight," Dad says.

Halsey then builds a tower with the connector squares.

Dad compliments him. "You do nice work."

"I have to straighten it up a bit," Halsey says.

"Probably."

It's so nice to see this companionship between my dad and my husband.

◆ ◆ ◆

Halsey gives Dad a massage.

"That does feel good in the salt water," Dad says. "Go down south."

"About here?" Halsey asks, moving his hands down.

◆ ◆ ◆

"The dirt was sitting on the floor, and then it moved. I ended it."

Maybe he thinks he's still working at the car wash? Cleaning up after his shift?

◆ ◆ ◆

"That's my girl. She's the best—I know."

June 27, 2016

Halsey shakes Dad's hand in greeting as we join him at his table.

Dad winces slightly. "That's a good hand."

◆ ◆ ◆

"Look at that beautiful girl," Dad says about me. "You've got a nice face too," he adds to Halsey. But then he's back to me. "That's my girl. I just love the hell out of her."

"You're a good person," I respond.

"Not as good as my children."

"You taught us."

"With my back rat," he says.

I nod, somehow understanding. "You did so much with your life, Dad."

"I did it for you, darling."

Darling? Does he think I'm Mom?

◆ ◆ ◆

"You look so good I want to take you on a cookie change. I like people if I feel like I can get something to help out."

◆ ◆ ◆

"I like girls. You can play with them."

Hmm . . . Tease them? Wink at them?

June 30, 2016

Eyeglasses are a problem again. I pack them up in my purse to take them to be repaired. I might have to order a heavy-duty pair. Work glasses.

◆◆◆

"Jerome shouldn't be doing that stuff," he says about himself, "but I've got to get rid of it myself."

◆◆◆

"I picked up one of your old habits, Jerome," Halsey says.

"Just one, huh?" Dad replies.

"I sit outside the front door and watch the traffic go by now," Halsey says.

We used to get a kick out of Dad sitting just inside his opened garage door, puffing on a cigarette, watching the traffic go by. Now we're doing the exact same thing. Side by side in Adirondack chairs on the front porch every afternoon, until I have to go in and start cooking dinner.

I still have thoughts of how nice it would be to have a third chair with us.

◆◆◆

"They've got rheumatisms."

What? And who?

◆◆◆

"I don't need the big-top ones," Dad says. "I can't do it myself. Even if I want to do it, I can't do it."

◆◆◆

Halsey decides to be stubborn about something this afternoon, so I say to Dad, "Sometimes Halsey can be a little ornery."

"Don't listen to her, Jerome," Halsey counters.

Dad matter-of-factly weighs in: "Well, I don't know what you were doing."

◆ ◆ ◆

"I'd like to look at you for at least a month," Dad says to me.

That could become a little uncomfortable.

◆ ◆ ◆

Dad starts laughing at something. "That's enough to bring you in half. I was chewing on them."

I don't need to understand. His laughter is enough for me.

◆ ◆ ◆

Winnie is sitting near us. "I'm scared. I'm scared," she says in a tight voice.

Dad tries to comfort her. "Maybe I can let out a nice tone for you."

◆ ◆ ◆

Dad is fumbling with silverware. Dinner won't be served for another thirty to forty minutes.

"Here, Monica." Dad hands me a spoon, even though I won't be joining him for dinner.

"Thanks, Dad."

"You're more than welcome."

◆ ◆ ◆

We've had a dry spell for the last couple of weeks.

"I wish it would rain," Halsey remarks.

"Bingo," Dad replies.

◆ ◆ ◆

Winnie is now grunting. "I'm scared. I want to go to sleep."

◆ ◆ ◆

At the table, Halsey and I have a quiet side conversation. Suddenly, Dad interjects with his own reply. We're surprised he can hear us.

"Jerome, there's nothing wrong at all with your hearing," Halsey says.

"Not now," Dad answers.

◆ ◆ ◆

"Takes all my power to move and get up the chimney," Dad says.

◆ ◆ ◆

"I'm going to carry you around," Dad says to me. "I like my girl. You do look cute, from the top of your head to the 'ottoms of your home."

Makes sense to me!

July 4, 2016

Today when we come to visit, Halsey greets Dad by shaking hands.

"That's nice," Dad says. "I like that."

◆ ◆ ◆

We reminisce about dating. About girlfriends and boyfriends.

"I did some of that too," Dad quips.

◆ ◆ ◆

I just love how hard Dad tries to be a part of the conversation. And good for him!

Even though his replies rarely line up with what we're saying, we nod. We smile. We agree. We want him to feel like a part of our group, and we encourage it. You can tell by the spark in his eyes that we're giving him a lease on life—even for a moment.

This time, Halsey makes a comment about a football game.

Dad replies, "It was something I thought of, and yet I didn't."

◆ ◆ ◆

I'm smoothing Dad's hair.

"Quit petting my friend," Shirley pipes in from her table. "You're spoiling him."

◆ ◆ ◆

Staff member Ben brings ninety-three-year-old Shirley a sweater because she's cold.

"That feels nice," she says. "I think I'll marry you."

"He's already married," another staff member says.

"Well, can't we get rid of her?" Shirley asks.

July 5, 2016

Cindy, the hospice nurse, passes by as we're visiting with our coffee and Oreo cookies.

"Your dad is at one hundred and thirty-four pounds," she tells me. "Real stable."

Oh, good. He's gained. Up from 107 in May. Big jump. Must be all the Ensures.

And Oreos.

July 7, 2016

We're talking today about Fourth of July celebrations.

We tell Dad how we used to spread a blanket on a hillside near the Children's Museum to watch the fireworks over the river in Saint Paul. An intimate number of people gathered there. It was a secret—until it wasn't. Then there were too many people, too many mosquitoes. We quit going.

I pause a bit to see if a flash of firework memories might pass behind Dad's eyes.

Instead, he says, "I'll wait for you—and wait and wait until I am."

Sounds so profound.

◆ ◆ ◆

A little while later, Dad contributes to our conversation with, "I myself don't know. If my dad was up in a tree, I'd skate over."

Then he reaches out and pets my arm with his apple-strudeled fingers.

◆ ◆ ◆

Halfway into our visit, I begin to sense some agitation with Dad.

"Are you getting irritated?" I ask him gently.

"No," he says. "That doesn't suit me."

◆ ◆ ◆

"You can't win everything," I overhear Leonard, another resident, say to Shirley.

"Why not?" Shirley answers. "Someone's gotta win."

"I did make it," Dad is saying. "Then I didn't make it. Then I went to bed."

Janet looks over to me and says, "I love you!"

"I love you, too, Janet."

Conversations have become pretty disjointed, but aren't they lovely?

July 10, 2016

Another visit, another vision of Dad lighting up.

"I like good people!" he greets us.

"That's why we like *you*, Jerome," Halsey replies.

"Well, I spit more," Dad replies.

OK, then.

◆ ◆ ◆

"I'm going to touch you, because I like you," Dad says to Halsey. "You're a good boy. And more, you're a good man."

I notice that over time, Dad has begun saying, "I'm going to touch you." But then he doesn't necessarily touch us.

Isn't that strange? Maybe he thinks expressing the idea is the same as doing the action.

Or maybe it has nothing to do with touching.

I think of how Halsey helps me interpret my dreams. When I start laying it out for him in the middle of the night (because I might forget it if I wait for morning—he *loves* this about me—ha!), Halsey strips away all the actual detail from my ramblings. He cuts to the chase, gets down to the rock-bottom basics. That one dream, for example, wasn't about eating hangers. It was about facing the difficulties of life—or maybe about Communion. I chuckle at the thought.

So maybe "touching" is just a symbol for "affection" to Dad. To just say it, *"I'm going to touch you."*

◆ ◆ ◆

There are more snippets from Dad. Some good stand-alone ones:

- ◆ "I'm just thinking, 'Hang on awhile—we still have got time.'"
- ◆ "I do like my family. I'm not glopping even in my own home."
- ◆ "God, you're so cute. I'm going to keep you and give Halsey the other half."
- ◆ "That beautiful pipe." (Batting at my ponytail.)
- ◆ "Dogs and cats, and we can all have our nursery."

◆ ◆ ◆

Dad's doing some reminiscing. "My own dad had so many benefits for so long. That's when we got Leo's car, and there it hangs."

I guess he's saying that Grandpa had a lot of strengths. Why he's tying that into Leo's car, I'm not sure. Leo was Dad's first cousin. They were as close as brothers.

Maybe it's just a run-on thought.

◆ ◆ ◆

I ask Dad if he wants to follow me out to the patio to get some fresh air.

"You're the nicest in the crowd," he answers. "That Monica. I've never seen such a beautiful dot."

◆ ◆ ◆

Dad first smacks his lips and then makes a clicking sound in the back of his throat. "Them cigarettes! They taste good. I don't think I got them twice, because I don't got them."

◆ ◆ ◆

"Monica . . ." he begins.

"Dad . . ." I answer.

"I hope so."

◆ ◆ ◆

We're still outside on the patio.

"Do you hear the birds, Jerome?" Halsey asks.

"No. Oh, Monica—I think you're the nicest bird I've ever seen."

With Halsey saying "bird," this is the first thing that can come out of Dad's mouth.

◆ ◆ ◆

While we're out here on the patio, Leonard is kicking the door from inside. Dad hears the sound.

"What's that?" he asks.

"That's Leonard kicking the door," I answer.

"Is that kind of different?" Dad asks.

"That's different," Halsey answers.

◆ ◆ ◆

"That's my girl. If you want chicken. If you want pigs' feet. That's my little girl."

◆ ◆ ◆

"Well, pig pogs could get in there, too, yet," Dad comments.

Pig pogs.

Pig pogs?

Sounds like something that belongs with Tweedledum and Tweedledee in *Through the Looking-Glass*.

♦♦♦

Leonard is kicking the door again.

"Sooner or later, it will be in the neighborhood someplace," Dad says.

What will be? The door? Leonard's not kicking it *that* hard.

Well, he kind of is.

♦♦♦

Natalia, a staff member, comes outside to bring Dad water.

"Do you work for Ford?" he asks her.

"No, I work for *you*."

"Oh, that's pretty nifty."

July 17, 2016

Florence, another staff member, asks Dad, "What makes you so happy?"

"You can do whatever you want, and that's good," Dad replies.

"You *are* happy today," I agree.

"*Every* day!" Dad says. "You're not going to get your be-boops."

♦♦♦

Halsey changes the subject.

"Jerome, I went fishing."

"Now that you bring it up, it ran some buttering in my ears," Dad answers.

♦♦♦

I have too much stuff. It's time to minimize. I've known it for some time. Even without Halsey's daily reminders.

"I have too much stuff, Dad," I announce.

"Oh boy, yeah," Dad answers. "I'm saying a lot. We don't mind."

Halsey grimaces. Maybe Halsey thinks that Dad doesn't see it as such a problem. "We just go along with it," he tells Dad.

Dad smiles. "That's right. That's my girl."

"What are we going to do about it?" Halsey asks Dad.

"I don't know how we're going to handle it." Dad turns to me now. "Monica, you're whining. I have some super oil."

Ha! I'm "whining"? Good plan of attack—get the super oil!

Halsey pats Dad.

Dad beams. "There he goes. He's a good man."

◆ ◆ ◆

I look over at the table next to us. Janet is holding Leonard's hand.

"You're getting me all shook up here," Leonard says.

◆ ◆ ◆

I kiss Dad's forehead goodbye.

"Come back anytime," he says.

July 21, 2016

When we visit today, we notice Dad has bruises up and down his arms. He points to them.

"These are all bullheads."

I have no idea what happened. It bothers me.

◆ ◆ ◆

"Gotta find a horseshoe so that you can park it."

◆ ◆ ◆

"He's there, waiting to become," Dad says about Halsey.

Aren't we all?

July 26, 2016

It's Tuesday. Halsey and I hop in the car to make our jaunt to McKenna Crossing. Once inside, we plop down next to Dad in the Commons.

I hunt for a puzzle that might give him something to fiddle. Then I remember the baby toy I bought him a while back. I get up to search for it in his room, but I come up empty-handed. Things disappear and end up in other people's rooms all the time. It'll show up down the road.

When I get back to the table, Dad is saying to Halsey, "Life ain't all that, either."

Well, sometimes I have to agree.

◆ ◆ ◆

"Cars are gone. They're not in the garage."

Hmm. We're back to talking about missing cars. It's been a while.

◆ ◆ ◆

Leonard pushes by in his wheelchair, wearing his straw hat. Dad catches sight of him.

"The head is a little messed up."

◆ ◆ ◆

"How are you feeling, Jerome?" Halsey asks.

"*Irish nun?*" Dad questions.

◆ ◆ ◆

"I have a good-looking house."

◆ ◆ ◆

Dad reaches over to pat my arm. "You little girl." He turns to Halsey. "I can't help but love her. That's my girlie, but I need more proof."

Halsey raises an eyebrow. "I *hope* you have more proof!"

◆ ◆ ◆

Dad says to Halsey, "You take care, and I'll do my best too. I think I'm over the hill, anyhow, now. I need people now. I like my family." After a bit, he adds, "I don't feel good. Nothing works right."

He lifts up his sweatshirt to check it out.

To me: "That's my girl."

To Halsey: "That's my man."

Janet, Stand Up

July 31, 2016

We're talking about putting up hay, and Dad says, "You got to take care of the back forty."

When he says this, it means nothing to me. Later, I look it up on the internet. Dad was spot on!

The "back forty" means the back forty acres. Most original homesteads were 160 acres, with two front forties and two back forties. Often, the back forties were left undeveloped, while the front forties were used for crops or livestock. A back forty very well could be mowed for hay!

I've never heard him talk about the "back forty." Not surprising, since he stopped working on his dad's farm when he was nineteen, got married, and went to work for Ford. Now he brings it up like he just did it yesterday.

◆ ◆ ◆

Staff member: *(kindly)* "Janet, stand up."
Again: "Janet, stand up."
Again: "Janet, stand up."
And yet again: *(same patient tone)* "Janet, stand up."
Shirley: *(piping in)* "You stubborn old bitch, stand up."
Staff member: *(still nicely)* "Stand up."
Shirley: *(rattled)* "She won't do it. She's stubborn as a jackass."

◆ ◆ ◆

"I like you, Monica. Don't change," Dad says at our table.

◆ ◆ ◆

August 15, 2016

Again, we're playing with connector squares. I build a box.

"Dad," I say, "it's a little doghouse."

"Not hardly," he replies.

◆◆◆

As we leave, I give Janet a hug goodbye.

"I love you," Janet croons.

"I love you, too, Janet." I kiss her cheek.

I walk over and stand behind Dad and kiss his forehead. "I love you, Dad."

Yes. I will wear this love as a perfume. Carry it with me.

August 19, 2016

Nothing really notable at our visit today. Before we get ready to leave, though, Halsey asks, "Want a back rub, Jerome?"

"I should think so," Dad replies.

I see he's getting used to the routine. It makes me smile.

August 22, 2016

When we visit with Dad today, I notice that his sentences are really loosely woven.

- ◆ "I like my girl. I told her until she dips, and I can see open."
- ◆ "I like my kids. I'll pull you into my little soak."
- ◆ "Normally, I'd slim myself."

◆◆◆

"Well, I haven't seen nothing of Lawrence," Dad says. "I don't know where he is."

As loose as his thoughts have been lately, this thought is nicely strung together and makes perfectly good sense. Dad still thinks of his brother.

◆◆◆

Dad pets Janet. She glares at him.

"Janet," I say, "he likes you."

Pouf ◆ 242

"That's his problem," she retorts.

Is she into Leonard now?

♦ ♦ ♦

"Cake a coo-ka," Dad says. "I'm not bumping on you."

♦ ♦ ♦

Shirley is sitting at our table.

"Are you my friend?" she says to Dad.

"They all are."

She gets up. "I suppose I should go find some mischief."

Exactly, Shirley. It's what you do best.

♦ ♦ ♦

I kiss Dad's forehead. "Bye, Dad."

"I'll be looking at you," he says.

September 1, 2016
According to Cindy, the hospice nurse, Dad seems sad these days.

September 2, 2016
We walk into the Commons and find Dad sleeping with his head on the table.

It's 4:30 in the afternoon.

September 3, 2016
Cindy says there was blood at the end of Dad's penis.

September 4, 2016
Dad is now being treated for a full-fledged urinary tract infection (UTI). That was the reason for the sadness. The infection has been growing for days.

He just can't understand when something's wrong. He doesn't know how to identify problems—and wouldn't know how to tell you if he did.

You have to pick up on his moods.

September 11, 2016

A week has gone by since Dad started his medication. As we head into the Commons, we expect to find him doing better now. We've followed up with phone calls to monitor him on the days we aren't there to visit, and staff has always reassured us.

When we spot him, we're relieved to see for ourselves that he's better. He's *back*.

"You look good, Monica." To Halsey, he adds, "And you're not so bad, either."

Yep, he's back.

We pull up chairs to visit.

◆ ◆ ◆

We decide to go out on the patio again and sit in the garden. It's a beautiful day. We position Dad's wheelchair so he has a view of the landscaping and greenery.

Dad points to a larger rock. "You might as well throw some of this rock stuff in my car."

◆ ◆ ◆

Dad makes a gurgling sound.

"What in the world was that?" Halsey asks.

"*Me*," Dad says in a small voice.

◆ ◆ ◆

We're back inside now. I point out the window to the patio plants, again commenting to Dad how beautiful they are.

"It isn't eating from your table," he remarks.

Does this mean anything? Is he saying he'd rather be sitting at our table at home with us? I should ask him—yet I don't want to feed what could be an unhappy thought.

September 15, 2016

Our visits have taken on an air of a "magical mystery tour." We've grown with it.

"If I can't handle my own payment," Dads begins, "I want it part of the pack. I like my family. Oh, Monica and Halsey, too. I like you all. That's my girl. But I wouldn't give you a tap oven."

◆ ◆ ◆

"I personally do think that I'm going to make your napkin."

◆ ◆ ◆

"It's what your mind it gives you a pop. And before I even get through it make some nice chicken. I really feel about my own stuff."

◆ ◆ ◆

"I help myself with these swing tuppies—or whatever you call them."

◆ ◆ ◆

"Look at this farm." He points to the floor.

◆ ◆ ◆

"Monica, you're such a sweet peeper. I want to keep you forever."
  "You can, and I'll keep you forever," I answer.
  "You can. I'll be laying in the corner back there," he says.

◆ ◆ ◆

"Look at this poor devil. I wouldn't duck a ray," Dad says about himself.
  "I know you wouldn't," Halsey reassures him.
  "She's a nice young lady," he says about a staffer. "And me too."

◆ ◆ ◆

Dad says something that I don't hear.
  "What did he say?" I ask Halsey.

"I forgot," Dad answers.

◆ ◆ ◆

"That daughter is absolutely perfect. Monica thinks I'm nuts. Monica, what can I do for you?" he asks.

"Just keep being happy, Dad."

"It ain't mine. I didn't buy it. Dust mates."

◆ ◆ ◆

"That Monica—do I like her, don't I ever!" Dad then adds about Halsey, "That's a nice, nice man. I want my children to be outside. If she wants to be outside, if it warms her up. Poor Monica and poor Jerome. I can't do nothing."

"Oh, Dad," I reply, "yes, you can! You can do whatever you want."

◆ ◆ ◆

"My ups and downs are pretty good, and I like that."

September 19, 2016

I hope today's visit is better than the visit a few days ago. His words were so muddled. I'm hoping that's not the case today.

When we greet him, he answers, "I was there. Then I wasn't there."

◆ ◆ ◆

After a big phlegmy cough, Dad looks up at the ceiling. "Oh, boy. Wicked stuff up there."

◆ ◆ ◆

"Oh, Monica, you are my chair. I like my people."

"We're a good group," Halsey agrees.

"I'm sure you are. I know you are." Dad nods.

◆◆◆

"Your teeth! You can throw them on this side and that side. Gum showder."

"I'm glad you're happy, Dad," I reply.

Gum showder . . . ?

◆◆◆

Dad coughs into his hand, looks at it, and says, "Where would you like to put it, madam?"

◆◆◆

"That poor Monica. She couldn't be broke loose."

◆◆◆

"I like it, and I don't like it."

◆◆◆

A small wooden building block is sitting on the table. It wasn't put away with the rest of its set. Dad pokes it.

"That poor little hobbit," he says.

◆◆◆

All this in the first half hour of our visit.

◆◆◆

Out of all that muddle, Dad says, "The nuns were really strict."

I don't know why he says this. Is he referring to his own experiences with nuns? Mine?

In my case, yes, some nuns were strict with their rules—and rulers. But what did I have for a basis of comparison? I'd only ever attended Catholic grade school.

I do know, though, that some people had difficult experiences with nuns. Not too long ago, my friend told me a story about how the nuns used to single out students. They'd come up to students, chalk in hand, towering over them.

"You *do* know the answer to this question, don't you, Mary Jane?" the nun would ask—all the while, taking her stick of chalk and grinding it into the top of Mary Jane's head, emphasizing each word with a twist of the chalk.

Could that really have happened? I found myself wondering as I listened.

My friend told me of another punishment where the nuns would single out a problem child and make them kneel on the metal strips of the furnace grate. Each metal strip carved into the child's knobby knees with the passing moments.

Personally, I didn't have those experiences. I loved my time at the parochial school. But it does cause me to wonder what kind of experiences Dad might have been able to share with us at one time.

But not now. Not anymore.

◆◆◆

"Well, *that* I know," Dad suddenly says with some confidence. "I can help you with that. I would move that and that and that and that. And it would work."

I don't doubt it would.

Chapter Forty-One

It's a Mishmash

September 24, 2016

I remember when Dad first made his home at McKenna Crossing—going on three years ago, back in November 2013. Back then, we were saddened by the fact that Dad couldn't really speak in paragraphs. Then it reduced to a sentence or two. Now, it's hard to call these sentences at all.

We still grab what we can while bending our minds around his words.

Dad nods at us as we join him at his table. "Look at that pretty good."

Before I sit down, I stick out my foot with its newly polished toenails. "Do you like my toenail polish, Dad?"

"I think they all are."

◆ ◆ ◆

We experience more disconnect.

"Jerome has good hearing," Halsey says.

Grinning, I joke to Dad, "Halsey has *selective* hearing."

"I can't change my mind," Dad says.

◆ ◆ ◆

But then, after a bit, sentences start to fall in place again . . .

"Your nails aren't cut too nicely," I tell Halsey, looking down at his hands.

Dad sticks up for him. "They look nice to me."

Maybe he's hoping Halsey will stick up for him when I get ready to pounce, nail clipper in hand, to cut at Dad's nails.

◆ ◆ ◆

The new rule at Gopher football games is that you can't carry a purse unless it's clear. So today I have my clear purse with me. Dad sees it.

"This is beautiful," he comments.

"I thought you would like it," I say.

"I wouldn't walk around the house with it," he adds.

"I know."

"You know? Then I know too."

◆◆◆

"Love your neighbor," Abraham, one of the staff members, says to Shirley.

"Who's my neighbor?" she asks.

Abraham points to Janet. "She's your neighbor."

Janet scowls.

Shirley and Janet tend not to see eye to eye.

"She doesn't look like she likes me," Shirley says.

◆◆◆

Dad gives me a cute wink. "You got nice teeth. I like them."

"I love your little winks, Dad. Those are special. They're your special trademark."

◆◆◆

Halsey gives Dad a goodbye back rub.

"It feels so good it itches," Dad says.

Dad turns to me. "You are so cute. Isn't she?" he adds to Halsey.

October 1, 2016

We're comparing arm lengths at Dad's table.

Like Dad's, my arms are long. I could push off the floor like a chimpanzee, no problem.

I pretend my long-sleeve blouses and shirts are three-quarter length, and I wear them with the sleeves pushed to the elbow. Otherwise, the sleeve length is three to four inches too short. It's ridiculous. But actually, I'm so used to it, it doesn't even bother me. I consider it "my style."

"I have my dad's arms," I say.

"I'm glad," he says. "If I did it for you, I forgot."

◆ ◆ ◆

Halsey gives his keys to Dad to mess with.

"I hate to take it away from you," Dad says, unsure whether he should take them, since they're not his.

"Oh, no," Halsey reassures him.

"Oh, yes. That wouldn't be good on my part."

Halsey lends Dad his own keys because the special set we put together for Dad has been misplaced. Probably in another resident's room.

I get to thinking about a time not too long ago when Janet and her two daughters were at another table visiting. Janet was all decked out in cheap rhinestones. Big, gaudy earrings. A rhinestone-studded brooch. Huge bangles. A ring on every finger.

Her daughter Diane looked over her shoulder at me and shrugged in confusion. "These don't belong to her!" she mouthed.

◆ ◆ ◆

"I'm going to run away from home," Shirley announces from across the room.

No one argues with her. She's silent for a spell.

A few moments later, she adds, "I had to have a beauty nap, but it don't help."

◆ ◆ ◆

I'm giving Dad a back scratch.

"That feels good," he says. "That feels really good."

I make my way up to his shoulder blade.

"Is it raised enough?" he asks. "It feels so good on top of it."

◆ ◆ ◆

We push our chairs back to get up and say our goodbyes.

"Have a good day, Dad," I say.

"I'll try. If I try too hard, then I'm done."

October 6, 2016
Yep. Another trip for eyeglass repair.

◆◆◆

Dad's rambling about something, then someone comes by wearing a bright-yellow top.

"Oh. There's that hupty-dupty one."

◆◆◆

Dad starts coughing. "It's loosening up. I don't see anything jump around, though."

◆◆◆

"Look how nice her teeth are," he says to Halsey. "We've got to keep her rolling." He pats my head.

Sixteen or seventeen times.

◆◆◆

Dad struggles with a word.

"I need some help here," he finally says. "Wipples and everything. And they're lying on the floor."

◆◆◆

"It's an adventure. Jeepers, peepers," he adds.

◆◆◆

The phone rings in the background.

Dad calls out, "Hello!"

Dad coughs.

"Next year," he says.

"I don't want Monica to get hurt," he says. He turns to Halsey. "You're a good boy."

"I love you!" I tell him.

"I think that even ties it up." He pets my hair. "Perfect. You can't help but look at her," he says to Halsey.

October 9, 2016

We've just come from Sunday Mass. Dad's sitting at his table, alone. We join him.

"That's my girl. She's got a nice face too." Then he suddenly adds, "Greg? What does *Greg* mean?"

Oh no. Is he now forgetting the names of his children? Or the association of who someone is to him? Will this be the new normal?

♦ ♦ ♦

"Look at him." Dad's referring to Halsey. "You don't want to hurt him. You don't want to give him a hong."

Dad laughs.

"I hope I get more than a hong," he adds.

♦ ♦ ♦

"She's got nice eyes," Dad says of me.

Halsey smiles at me. "And nice teeth too," he offers.

Halsey, you funny man.

♦ ♦ ♦

Dad is humming.

Cindy told us that humming sometimes indicates anxiety.

"Are you singing?" I ask him.

"I just wanted to see how far I could get with it," he explains.

◆ ◆ ◆

"I don't know what I can do for you," Dad suddenly throws into the conversation.

"You don't have to do anything. Just love me," I say.

"I do that all the time—when I can, where I can."

◆ ◆ ◆

"What do you think, Jerome?" Halsey asks.

"I don't know. What *should* I think?"

◆ ◆ ◆

"You have nice legs too," Dad says to me. He adds to Halsey, "I like her."

"I'm beginning to see that," Halsey says.

And here comes Halsey's turn. "That's my boy," Dad says. "I like him. He's got a nice face. That Halsey—he's a good guy."

"I'm sure glad you know it," Halsey says.

"Something's not right here," Dad replies with a puzzled frown.

I laugh.

October 13, 2016

Janet is picking food crumbs from her pants.

"I gotta get a Hoover."

Good one, Janet.

◆ ◆ ◆

Janet doesn't like one of the residents.

"Kick her in the butt," she snarls.

◆ ◆ ◆

Dad starts to pet me. Janet sees this.

"What are you doing?" she asks Dad.

"He likes me," I explain.

"Watch out now," Janet says.

Dad still pets me. "My little juba."

Juba?

October 17, 2016

We're enjoying another visit, and Dad throws out, "Oh, Monica. You are my little horse."

◆ ◆ ◆

As we leave, Halsey says, "I love you, Jerome."

"I know you do."

"See you soon!" I say.

"I hope so."

"You're a good man," I tell him.

"I try."

October 20, 2016

Sitting at our table, we attempt a conversation about past presidents. We mention Clinton. Then Bush. Then Obama. I tell him about Hillary Clinton now running for president.

"Dad, we don't want her to win," I add.

"Oh, God, no!" he agrees.

◆ ◆ ◆

"All hot to trot with no place to race," Halsey says.

"I'll run like hell," Dad smartly answers.

◆ ◆ ◆

"Everyone needs to laugh," I comment.

"I find it that way," Dad agrees.

He pets my arm.

"It's just like silk."

◆ ◆ ◆

At the table, Halsey and I debate about what color Christmas lights to get.

Dad, ever the peacemaker, says, "I like it whatever it is."

November 2, 2016

For today's visit, my friend Janice joins me. Only a few friends have offered to visit Dad with me. Janice is one of them. I will forever be thankful to her.

I'm more conscientious about Dad when someone is with me. I see him through her lens. Suddenly, I can see more vividly the parts that are missing.

I have to shake myself. *No. I'm going to hang on to the parts that are still there.*

And then, Dad comes up with a good poetry line: "I can always forgive it and start over."

Something we all need to do.

Forgive it and start over.

◆ ◆ ◆

"Holy smokers!" he announces over nothing.

November 6, 2016

We're sharing a cup of coffee and cookies with Dad. He's still having Oreos (which "bend" his teeth). I decide to go with the Fig Newtons. No teeth bending for me.

"I don't know what you're going to do to keep me whole," he tells me. "You look very, very, very, very good."

◆ ◆ ◆

"I ain't gone yet," he mutters to himself.

I wonder why he would even say that. Is he realizing he's slipping away from us? Yet at the same time, he's arguing that he's not "gone yet"? Is he doing battle from within?

"I got to put her in your hand," he instructs Halsey about me, "because she's a nice person, and I don't want her slapped around."

Dad is still being a dad. I love that!

◆ ◆ ◆

"I don't think they'll budge out."

◆ ◆ ◆

"I like certain things. I like my family. Don't worry," he adds. "It'll pop out. It'll be OK."

◆ ◆ ◆

Barbara wheels around quickly in her wheelchair, spinning out. If she were on a gravel road, she would have tipped over, gravel kicking out.

"She must be in a hurry," Shirley says from across the room. "She's really pumping the wheels."

◆ ◆ ◆

"You're a good man, Jerome," says Halsey.

"I tried."

And succeeded.

◆ ◆ ◆

"Have you seen Janet lately?" I ask Halsey on our way out.

Looking out for the other residents is just what we do. What we all do.

Families can't visit their loved ones every day, so we work together. For instance, if Sharon and Diane visit their mom, Janet, on a day we're not there, they keep their eyes on Dad. They fill us in about any observations or concerns.

We're very protective of all our dear loved ones there at the Arbor.

Halsey and I keep tabs on Janet in the same way. But I haven't seen her for three solid weeks now.

Periodically, residents come down with ailments that take them off-campus for hospital visits. Sometimes they're out for a week or two. Maybe that's the case here.

"Something's not right," I tell Halsey.

Chapter Forty-Two

Barbara, Followed by the Battle of the Walkers

November 14, 2016

After entering the code to gain access to the Arbor, we search for Dad. I see Barbara has cornered him at his spot at his table.

Dad has his head slightly bent downward. She leans toward him, wheelchairs touching and her hand occasionally reaching out to touch his arm to punctuate each sentence of her steady staccato.

We approach. Halsey takes a chair as I gently touch Dad on his shoulder to get his attention.

Slowly his head lifts as he turns to me. The veil over his eyes clears. Recognition greets me.

I'm so thankful I still have that.

"Hey, Dad," I say. "How are you?"

"That's my girl."

I take a seat next to him.

Barbara moves her wheelchair in closer to stake a claim at Dad's table.

Probably in her late seventies, Barbara maneuvers her wheelchair with a purpose. She cuts through the narrowest openings, barely missing staff members with plates of food as they attempt to serve the other residents.

With her white hair sleekly pulled back from her face and braided down her back, you can see the beauty she once wore. Her blue eyes look directly into yours. Without words, she can command you to get the hell out of her way.

She carries a lot of spunk. You can't take the New Jersey out of the woman. And she's happy about that.

Her left leg has been amputated at the knee. Most likely quite a while ago, as it is no deterrent in her movement or attitude. She is in command.

Barbara resumes her rhetoric to Dad. I'm fascinated with her *r*-dropping accent.

As I listen, I can tell she has it fixed in her mind that Dad is her husband. With presumed familiarity, she mentions that "Tom and Karen are coming for dinner" and "I hope they don't bring the kids."

I'm quite certain Dad isn't following a lick of what she's saying. He's gone back to his bent-head posture. He only slightly nods.

I attempt to find Dad, bring him back to me. I start by gently rubbing his arm and massaging my way up to his neck and shoulder.

"He doesn't like girls hitting on him," Barbara snaps at me.

More likely, you *don't like it.*

"We're older now and past that," she continues.

I let out a little gasp and chuckle. "Oh! I'm not hitting on him. I'm his daughter."

"You're not his daughter," Barbara declares. "I know his daughter, and you're not her."

I'm obviously not Karen—or whoever she said was coming for dinner. The exchange has become competitive, with Dad the much-sought-after brass ring on the carousel.

As I'm involved with Barbara, Halsey sets his keys on the table as a distraction for Dad. Like a magnet, Dad reaches for them. He explores each key, trinket, and reward card. They always hold a fascination for him.

After a bit, Dad sets the keys back down on the table. Barbara snatches them to her chest; they become hers.

Before we can react, Leah, a staff member, comes over and tries to remove Barbara from our table.

"She has a crush on your dad," Leah says over her shoulder to me. "C'mon, Barbara. Let's go to your room."

Barbara isn't moving. "I don't want to go to my room. Go to hell. I don't need this shit."

Panic sets in for Halsey as he sees his keys still firmly in her grasp.

"Don't worry. We'll get them back." I try to reassure him by patting his hand.

He's having none of it. He's twitting. "She'll lose them, and then we won't be able to go home!"

Really?

"Just let it be for a while," I say. "I promise you—she'll set them down."

Twenty minutes pass, and she still has them clutched tightly. Halsey's becoming more and more agitated.

Leah comes back, smiles, and suggests again that she and Barbara go for a stroll to her room.

"I'll distract her," she quietly tosses our way as she wheels off with Barbara—and Halsey's keys.

I quickly look at Halsey to see his reaction. He's now bristling. Such a worrywart.

"Just let things sort out," I say under my breath.

Barely ten minutes pass before Barbara wheels herself back to our table in a huff. Leah apologetically shrugs. The keys are now back in our sight, though not back in Halsey's hands.

I see Abraham out of my peripheral. Abraham works frequently with Barbara. They've developed a relationship. She knows and trusts him.

"Abraham," I say, beckoning with my head for him to come over. I explain the dilemma.

He squats down in front of Barbara's wheelchair to reason with her. "Barbara, these are Halsey's keys. He needs them to drive home."

"No," she pleads, now close to tears. "These are mine. Why are you doing this to me? You used to be such a nice man."

Abraham's head and shoulders slump. He ponders for fifteen long seconds. I can almost see his wheels turning with "what to do, what to do, what to do." He unhooks his keys from his belt and offers a swap.

Barbara agrees after some hesitation. She's happy.

Halsey sighs with relief; he's happy too.

◆◆◆

I stand up to kiss the top of my dad's head as we prepare to leave. "I love you."

He looks up. "Me too."

We head to the door but stop when we hear another ruckus in progress.

The Arbor has another Lorraine who has joined their family as a resident. She used to be a gynecologist. She deplores men, or so it seems. I like to refer to her as Lorraine2.

Lorraine2 and Bob are trying to maneuver their walkers through two sets of tables at the same time. It's only a one-way street, and Bob was the first to enter the lane of traffic. But Lorraine2 is forcing it into a two-way—with a bad result. Their walkers are tangled, and it's a deadlock.

Lorraine2 gets aggressive. Her apparent hate for men seems targeted on poor Bob. She thrusts her walker at his. Their wheels lock, and she loses her balance.

As if in slow motion, we witness her falling toward the floor. Just in the nick of time, another visitor extends his arm backward to hammock her and cushion the fall.

She's not hurt, but smoke is billowing from the top of her head. She's spitting and snarling at Bob.

He cowers. "What did I do? What did I do?"

It's the result Lorraine2 wants. She gloats.

The geese are back. The Dog Pack. The boys at the lunchroom table.

◆ ◆ ◆

As Halsey and I weave our way back to the door, I pause to pat Shirley's arm, ask how she's doing. I greet Mary and compliment her on how nice she looks. I catch Linda's eye and tell her to have a nice rest of her day.

In the background, I can hear Abraham imploring Barbara to please let him have his keys.

Chapter Forty-Three

2508

November 17, 2016

We're sitting in the Commons at our regular table. Just like a second Lorraine joined our family at the Arbor, so has a second Shirley. This Shirley I will refer to as Shirley2.

She's not as fun and spunky as the original Shirley. That Shirley has her own aura about her. Shirley2 tends to invade space and boundaries.

Today, she's put us in her sights. She makes her way over to us and begins asking us over and over if we know where she lives.

"Do you know where I live? 2508?" It might be her former house number.

Two minutes later: "Do you know where I live? 2508?"

As patient as I try to be, the repetitiveness starts to annoy me. Finally, I suggest she might enjoy watching TV. I point to the television set in the opposite corner.

She scampers off.

Five minutes later, we hear a loud voice from afar: "Do you know where I live? 2508? Do you? 2508?"

We crane our necks in that direction to see who's in her sights now. There she is, with her nose practically flattened to the TV screen, talking to the news commentator.

"Do you know where I live? 2508? Do you know where I live? 2508?"

He's not answering, either.

◆◆◆

Dad to me: "Hi, tootsie. I like you."

Dad to Halsey: "I like you too."

Halsey to Dad: "And I like you too."

Dad to Halsey: "I'm sure you do."

Ad nauseam to anyone within earshot.

◆ ◆ ◆

Halsey gives Dad a back rub.

"Oh, that feels so good," he says. "I mean it. It's nice and tasty."

◆ ◆ ◆

In an empty part of the conversation, I choose to say, "You're a good dad."

He nods in agreement. "A *bedpan*."

And then *presto*! All of a sudden, out of the blue, Dad counts to thirty. No problem! One number right after the other. A surge on his circuit board!

Just as quickly, though, a disconnect.

◆ ◆ ◆

A staff worker passes by our table wearing a dark work shirt.

"He looks like a priest," Dad says.

"What?" Halsey asks, confused.

"Yes, he does, Halsey—it's his dark shirt," I chime in to explain.

"See?" Dad retorts to Halsey.

◆ ◆ ◆

Halsey begins to give Dad his now-routine before-we-leave back rub.

"Oh, that feels good," Dad says.

"I know what I'm doing, don't I, Jerome?"

"I think you do. Don't run away on me."

"I might run away, but I always come back," Halsey says. He gives Dad a final pat. "You're a good man."

"I feel I'm pretty good."

◆ ◆ ◆

On our way out, I pass a staff member and ask about Janet.

"Oh, she passed away last month."

It takes my breath away.

No! Not my Janet.

Janet anchored Dad's table and anchored *us*, quite frankly. My heart sinks. It's beginning.

Chapter Forty-Four

A Grand Gesture

November 21, 2016

We're sitting at our table in the Commons. It's dinnertime.

Gladys is sitting with us. She's a very slow eater. She loads a fork and shakily attempts to balance the food as it begins its way to her mouth. Tries six times before the food actually gets there.

A staff member wheels Gladys from our table to another one. Gladys keeps her fork poised in the air, slowly moving toward her mouth, never realizing she's being moved and repositioned to another table.

She brings the fork back down at the new table, prepared for the next forkful.

December 11, 2016

Ray sits at the table adjacent to us. He wears a tattered football sweatshirt. (I guess Bob's not the only one. Come to think of it, Halsey has *his* favorite football sweatshirt too.)

"So, do you like football, Ray?" I ask.

"There's more serious things than that," he replies.

"I agree."

I look over at my sports-enthralled husband—in his tattered sweatshirt—to see if I get any reaction.

He ignores me.

December 12, 2016

Dad often inches his wheelchair down the hallways in his wheelchair. He still doesn't use his arms to wheel himself—he doesn't know how. Rather, he scoots with his feet, moving himself from one side of the hallway to the other.

He always pauses to inspect whatever catches his eye on the carpet. A thread. A piece of foil from a wrapped candy. A chunk from somebody's cinnamon roll at breakfast. It all deserves his attention.

He's "in charge of maintenance"—or at least that's what he perceives. Frequently throughout the day, he inches his wheelchair away from his table in the Commons to peruse the orderliness of his region. He's doing his "job." "Fixing" things. We praise him for the hard work and hours he puts into it.

Today we're coming for just a short visit. As we pass through the Arbor doors, Dad is straight ahead in the center of the hallway, hunched down and inspecting something he's plucked up.

He's alone in the hall—a lone bird on the wire.

As a daughter, I'm saddened. The staff members assure me he's very content; I take some comfort in that.

Dad's "job" also gives me some peace. He has a purpose. I know that Presbyterian Homes has goals of "pursuing purpose and living it out." They believe "it's the people that make the difference," and they strive to "make stepping stones out of stumbling blocks."

Halsey and I shorten the distance between Dad and us. I scooch up close so I'm at eye level with Dad. I give him a wide smile.

There's a slight pause. I can see his wheels turning in his head as he tries to connect who I am. Clarity begins pushing away the fog from his eyes. I hold my smile, realizing that my teeth are what ground him and remove the veil.

Unexpectedly, his long arms suddenly swing out. He wants to fold me into himself.

"Oh, Monica."

Oh, Dad!

This is not a motion I grew up with. Nor have ever seen. He has patted my knee. He has petted my arm. He has gripped my hand. But this grand gesture of taking me into himself is a rarity. A moment I want to last.

And it will.

Forever.

In my heart.

December 15, 2016

Linda, another resident, is sitting at a table next to me on my left. She gets up, walks behind me and around the table, and plants herself directly in front of Halsey, who is sitting at my right. She stoops down until she is face-to-face with him. Six inches away.

"Now I'm watching you," she says.

Oh, good. Halsey's gotta love that!

December 18, 2016

More drama in the Commons today.

"You're guilty," Shirley says to Lorraine, her archenemy.

"Of what?" Lorraine asks. "Being alive?"

"Well, yeah. But we can get rid of you."

Chapter Forty-Five

Dad's Haircut

December 20, 2016

Christmas is next week—and so is Dad's birthday.

During this holiday time, Chad and his wife, Faye, along with Freedom and Gloria, my grandchildren, have visited Dad to wish him a merry Christmas and a happy birthday. The kids made Christmas cards featuring the Elf on the Shelf for their great-grandpa. Trent, Mariah, Akaya, and Sterling have also stopped in for holiday visits at various times.

And because Christmas and his birthday are now right around the corner, today is a special day. We're taking Dad down to the Arbor's barbershop to get his hair trimmed.

As I study Dad's hair, I float back to a memory . . .

◆ ◆ ◆

I was nine years old and capable of traversing the long, straight country road for a full mile outside of town. Times were safer then.

I could see Grandpa's house in the distance—a lone farmhouse standing solidly against time. This two-story structure was built in 1860—Abe Lincoln was president.

Old houses often weren't built on footings. The root cellar walls were four feet thick, diminishing to about two feet thick as the cellar poked its head out of ground level. The support rock for the foundation was hauled from the riverbed in town, about a mile north. Mortar and dirt were thrown in for glue.

It was a fortress.

When we started the construction project on my grandparents' house back in 2010 or so, three engineers came to study the foundation to determine if a basement could be put in. The three of them stood staring down into the deep hole that had been excavated on one side.

(It reminded me of family gatherings years ago, when the men would pop the hood of a new car and gaze down at the engine. What they could see as they just stood there, staring, with bottles of beer in their hands, for thirty minutes or more, was hard for me to understand. I also didn't understand the value of kicking the tires.)

After staring into that great hole forever, one of the engineers came to a conclusion and said, "This is a happy house. I don't think you want to disturb the walls by trying to replace the root cellar with a basement. You could add a crawl space under the new construction, but leave these walls alone."

On my walks to visit Grandpa and Grandma, sometimes from a distance I could just barely make out the outline of Grandpa ambling back to the farmhouse after gathering eggs from the chicken coop. As was his habit, he'd stoop down and brace himself against the house with his free hand. Lifting one foot at a time, he'd run the bottom of his old brown leather boots down the length of a metal scraper he had rigged up in the ground to take off as much chicken poop as he could. Then he'd swing open the screen door, cross the threshold, and shuffle over to the old wooden bench to sit a spell.

Those worn-leather boots stayed on his feet all day, shuffling their way across Grandma's kitchen floor. I once overheard Mom wonder aloud to Dad how many times that linoleum floor had to be scrubbed. You certainly never considered taking your shoes off and walking on it in your stocking feet. ("Monica," Mom would say, "keep your shoes on when you go over there to visit. I don't wash clothes for my health.")

It was an old farmhouse floor, with old farmhouse chicken poop, and bits of old farmhouse straw scattered here and there. But you didn't care, because you loved your grandpa and grandma so much and they were always so happy to see you.

Within five minutes of my arrival, Grandma would toddle over to the second drawer next to the sink and pull out a box of snack cakes.

Oh, I hope she has Ho Hos, I'd think to myself every time. *Not those Little Debbie Chocolate Cupcakes with the thick chocolate frosting and the white swirly-swirl across the top.*

Little Debbie was pictured in the upper corner of the box, so proud of her Chocolate Cupcakes. But I hated them. Hated the frosting that was so thick and dry. Yet I would smile as I ate them, if that was all Grandma had. Because she would be just as proud of them as Little Debbie was.

Whether it was Ho Hos or Little Debbies, Grandma would hold out the box as she made small movements with her mouth, like old people do. In and out with their lips. Like they're going to say something but then don't.

Finally, she'd ask, "Do you want a cookie?"

She'd be so pleased just to make the offer. Those are the only words I remember ever hearing her say. She left the rest of the conversation to Grandpa.

As I would peel the cellophane from my "cookie," Grandpa would find his chair with the back of his denim coveralls and sit down without even looking. Those coveralls were stiff with old dirt—probably worn daily and washed monthly. I see that now but did not see it when I was nine.

His red tin can of Prince Albert tobacco would be down on the floor, off to his right, next to the pipe stand. While he tapped out his pipe and prepared it for a new round of tobacco, I would savor my Ho Ho.

As soon as Grandpa lit his pipe and took a few puffs to make sure it was well lit, I knew I could make my way to his side. He'd pat his right leg for me to hop up.

I loved it. Him puffing on his pipe; me feeling secure in his lap.

We would play our own little game. He'd place his left hand on the wooden arm of his rocking chair, and I'd try to slap it with my own little hand before he'd pull his away. He was too fast for me. I'd keep trying and trying. And giggling. And he'd sneak in a puff from his pipe in between our slapping rounds.

I'd look up into his craggy face. That white tuft of hair would be sticking straight up.

Just like Dad's is doing now.

◆ ◆ ◆

We make our way down the hall, through the Arbor's doors, and over to the elevators on the right. Halsey pushes the wheelchair and keeps prompting Dad with, "Follow Monica."

I lead the way, looking over my shoulder and smiling at Dad. Encouraging him to keep coming. I can see by his look of concentration that he's trying to do this right.

Is there a "right"? I'm sad that ordinary movements we don't think twice about require an ardent amount of focus for my dear dad.

We make our way into the salon. We call it a "barbershop" for my dad's sake. He wouldn't understand what a "salon" is.

Halsey wheels Dad to the station where he'll get his hair cut, then Halsey sits in the waiting area. I hunker down near Dad's chair so he can see me.

The tension leaves him when he has me in sight. The amount of trust he puts in me is humbling.

As Lindsay makes her first cuts, I praise Dad, chirping in his ear. "You're doing such a good job, Dad. Thanks for sitting still. You look so *handsome.*"

It's obvious he's pleased with himself.

Fifteen minutes pass. We're nearing the end.

"Oh, my gosh, Dad," I gush. "You look so handsome. Just look at that handsome guy in the mirror ahead of you."

He looks up, catches his reflection. Slowly, a surprised expression crosses his face. He looks back at me.

"Was he watching me the whole time?"

Yes, Dad. The whole time.

"I love you."

Chapter Forty-Six

Notes from Journals: Book Three

I remember remarking not long ago how Dad went from paragraphs to loose sentences. Suddenly, I realize he has gone from phrases, to handfuls of words, to lone words hummed here and there.

In my mind, I'm struck how language is a forest. This forest has thinned out. How could I have not noticed so many trees—so many words—disappearing? When we're so used to seeing a thick forest, maybe we don't realize it's made up of individual trees.

We can't see the trees for the forest, to turn around the old saying.

So now I receive any and all words Dad gives me—delighting in them and knowing they are for me. Often punctuated with a wink.

In rare cases, a string resembling a sentence emerges. I instantly transcribe it in my journal. Before, I captured Dad's best quips, poetry, and expressions. I filled two journals. Now, as I begin my third journal, I capture any fragment I can.

The less Dad offers me, the more I receive.

This paradox confounds me, yet it is the truth. The less Dad speaks, the more love I absorb from him. The more I am blanketed in a lingering embrace. The more I am blessed beyond measure.

I can see the last remaining trees so much more clearly. I appreciate them all the more, now that the forest has been thinned.

January 8, 2017

I'm giving Dad a back rub.

Barbara, the reckless wheelchair driver, chastises me.

"He doesn't like girls hitting on him."

This again.

January 12, 2017

Dad's not wearing his glasses today. I leave the table in search of them. This time, they're under his bed.

I go back to the Commons and put them on him.

First thing he says . . .

"You've got the nicest teeth."

◆ ◆ ◆

"I like our pieces."

I think he wants to say "family."

◆ ◆ ◆

"Boy, what a girl."

◆ ◆ ◆

Halsey pats Dad's arm.

"Wow, you wake up quick," Dad tells him.

◆ ◆ ◆

Looking out the window, I say, "It's a good old Minnesota winter."

Dad starts laughing.

◆ ◆ ◆

A new behavior has developed. And quite frankly, it's alarming.

Dad keeps trying to eat his fingers. Not just lick them, but *eat* them.

He also tries to crank his fingers off. He takes a finger and cranks it around in a circle and pulls. That's new too. And disturbing.

Today, I try to focus his attention away from his fingers by giving him a cookie.

He takes a piece of the cookie, makes an A-OK sign with his fingers while still pinching the cookie between his thumb and forefinger, then holds the cookie to his eye like a monocle. He telescopes the cookie out twelve inches from his face and reins it back in again to his eye, as if for further inspection.

◆ ◆ ◆

I kiss Dad goodbye on the top of his head, right next to the tan liver spot I'd never noticed before.

"That's my girl," he says.

January 15, 2017

We're in the Commons, and a Eucharistic minister is administering Communion to anyone who is Catholic and would like to receive it.

Dad receives Communion when the Eucharistic minister comes to our table. He receives both the bread and the wine.

"That has a bite," he says of the wine.

"I'm glad you received the Body and Blood of Christ, Dad," I say.

"I am too."

◆ ◆ ◆

I get up to leave. "Bye, Dad. I love you!"

"That goes two ways."

January 22, 2017

Odd how Dad's table has become, over time, the Adirondack chairs I envisioned the three of us sitting on out on our porch. We comment on whatever strikes our fancy.

"It's funny how people can blow things up, and it's still there," Dad says.

"That's my dad!" I say.

"That's my girl, Monica. She's a good girl."

◆ ◆ ◆

Halsey clears his throat. It's a big clear.

Dad looks at him.

"Wow," Halsey says, somewhat chagrined as he embarrassingly shakes his head, eyes downcast.

He's used to me commenting on his throat-clearing, and now he gets a look from Dad. I kind of feel sorry for him.

Then Dad clears his own throat. It's even bigger yet.

"*That* is a wow!" Dad says.

January 26, 2017

The sharp wind of January blows us from our car to McKenna's front door. We stomp the snow off our boots, drag our feet on the runner, and greet the lobby receptionist. I unwind the knitted scarf from around my neck as we make our way to see Dad.

After a bit of conversation, Dad reaches down to scratch his knees.

"Now my nubs . . ." he says.

◆ ◆ ◆

Suddenly, he announces, "I have to go pee-pee." A pause. "I have to go poopie."

We find a staff person to help.

January 29, 2017

Toward the end of our visit, Dad exclaims to me, "God, you look like yourself."

Well, that's reassuring.

"That Monica," he adds, "I'm going to keep her."

◆ ◆ ◆

Halsey gives Dad his goodbye massage.

"That feels good back there," Dad says.

"Does that feel good, Jerome?"

"It needs a little more. I'll be darned."

January 31, 2017

Another trip back to town for eyeglass repair.

February 5, 2017

"There's my little darling." With a wink.

◆ ◆ ◆

A staff member drops a dish.

"Jesus Christ," Dad exclaims.

"Kind of loud," I say. "Scared you, didn't it, Dad?"

"You bet."

◆ ◆ ◆

Halsey is playing around with a Tupperware toy—the red-and-blue hexagonal shape sorter for toddlers. He neatly puts the star piece in the star hole.

"No stoppage," Dad remarks.

◆ ◆ ◆

"Is it time for a back rub, Jerome?" Halsey asks.

"I could handle that, I think."

February 10, 2017

The Commons seems a bit sparse today. Not many people at tables. Dad is a fixture, though. Almost always at his table.

"That's my buddy," he says to Halsey as we approach. "You do look good," he says to me.

"Thank you!" I reply.

"You're more than welcome."

This banter feels like old times.

February 12, 2017

Out of the blue, Dad exclaims, "You do? Or you don't?"

"I do," I say without a clue.

Dad smiles. "I don't."

Tricked me there, Dad.

February 14, 2017

Mary, one of the newer residents, sits at a corner table in the Commons. Her adult children are gathered around her. It's a family conference. Mary's voice can be heard pleading for them to please bring her home.

"But I don't want to be here!"

Reassuring voices murmur to her that it'll be all right. Despite their mother's pleas, the kids know that all they can do is murmur and reassure. They cannot take their mother home any more than I can take my father home.

Only twelve feet away, Halsey and I visit with Dad at our table, trying to make sense out of nonsense. And amazingly, we can do it! I'm proud of how we've been able to rally around each new normal of Dad's decline, even though each plummet is a gut punch.

All at once, Mary's voice escalates. *"Take me home!"*

The forcefulness causes me to look up and over in their direction.

"Please don't look at me!" Mary calls out to me, pleading.

In unison, all the children snap their heads over their shoulders to see who's intruding on this moment and upsetting their mother even more.

A blanket of embarrassment cloaks me. It wasn't my intention to interrupt their privacy. I quickly avert my eyes.

In a little while, I hear them say their goodbyes. "Go back and lie down, Mom. Put your legs up before dinner. Stay here. Bye, Mom. See you in a little while. See you later. Bye-bye."

A good ten or fifteen minutes pass, then Mary says to a passing staff member, "I haven't seen you in a long time."

"I was on vacation," the staff member says.

"With a walker in a pink bathrobe?" Mary asks.

◆◆◆

I kiss the top of Dad's head as a goodbye.

"I love you," I whisper near his ear.

"I love you too," Dad says in a soft voice.

I look around as I back my way out. I'm startled to realize that only Bob, Shirley, and Dad remain from the original group a little over three years ago.

Some have moved to other facilities.

Others have died.

February 17, 2017

Dad isn't *there* behind his eyes today when we come to visit him.

"Dad, it's Monica," I say.

"I don't think so," he replies.

He does not know me. For the entire visit, he does not know me.

It reminds me of when he asked "What does *Greg* mean?" a few weeks ago. Not even "Who's Greg?" It's a pulling of the rug from underneath your feet.

However, I am encouraged an hour later, as we prepare to leave. I kiss the top of his head, next to that now-always-noticed liver spot.

"Dad, I love you," I say.

"It goes both ways," he says.

Maybe there *is* a place tucked down deep within him that knows who I am.

Chapter Forty-Seven

Iceberg Lettuce

I find an injured butterfly while outside. It's standing upright with beautiful pale-green wings. I can tell something is wrong in the way it stands so straight yet can't spread open and display its iridescent wings to take flight.

I need to help it. But how?

It must need something to eat.

So I carefully cup the fragile butterfly in one hand and walk into the house to see what I can find in the refrigerator.

I spot a bag of already-torn iceberg lettuce. *Do butterflies eat lettuce?* I pluck the bag from the refrigerator and sit myself on the floor, cross-legged. Still holding the butterfly in one hand, I awkwardly tear open an end of the bag with my other hand.

I carefully shake forward a portion of the lettuce, trying to keep the leaves from spilling out of the bag. I just want a few leaves at the edge.

I set the bag in my lap to balance it with my legs, then gently place the disabled butterfly into the opening of the bag, near a piece of lettuce.

Amazingly, he starts to eat!

It feels wonderfully good. I'm providing him with nourishment. Maybe I can nurture the butterfly into health.

As I sit there watching him eat, I feel one of my legs going to sleep. I try to shift slightly, changing my position. No, I need to unfold my leg.

I try to keep the bag balanced and still as I move. But all of a sudden, the bag unexpectedly slips back. The lettuce pieces at the edge—and the butterfly—slide farther into the bag.

Oh no!

I frantically yet tenderly go through the bag, trying to separate each shred of lettuce, hoping to rescue him. Again. But his wings are the same color as the lettuce! I can't distinguish one from the other!

It's a daunting search. Too much sameness. As I search one small section, he could be buried in the heavy rubble of lettuce in another.

He's lost.

Maybe even crushed under the weight of the lettuce.

And then I wake up.

February 19, 2017

Today, we come in the morning. Usually, we come just before dinner, near the sundown hour. We hope that by coming earlier, we'll find Dad more cognizant.

It makes no difference.

Again, Dad does not know me.

February 21, 2017

Again, we come earlier in the day. It's 10:30 a.m.

He does not know us.

And a single clutch at his groin, followed by a wince, has me convinced he has another UTI.

I follow up with the nurses and hospice.

February 23, 2017

Elizabeth, a staff member, calls me at home tonight.

"I just want to let you know that when we came into the Commons tonight, your dad was lying on the floor, sleeping," she reports.

I laugh.

I'm so in tune with Dad that I find nothing but humor in this report. I know that Dad just plain got tired of sitting in his wheelchair. The floor beckoned. He responded. Carpeted or not.

I have no doubt he misses being able to just lie down on the floor and sleep, like he used to for almost twenty years—ever since Mom died. Maybe even before. It makes him feel free. Loose. No boundaries.

I get it.

When the call is done, though, a new thought hits me. Maybe I find more than humor in this report, after all. Suddenly it makes me sad.

Why is Dad the last to be tended to in the evening, to the point that he has to take it upon himself to get out of his wheelchair, lie on the floor, and fall asleep right there in the Commons? He sits in that wheelchair for twelve hours.

Is it because he's not the squeaky wheel? Because he doesn't have *the words* to be a squeaky wheel, even if he wanted the grease? If you're missing words, you're missing assertiveness. And if you just want to blend in, you'd never think to be the squeaky wheel.

Maybe I'm wrestling over nothing. I pause and take a deep breath. I doubt the staff members are neglecting Dad, leaving him last for bed. They probably figured out a long time ago that he's a night owl.

He never went to bed early. He would stay up way past midnight, playing around with our pet hamsters, watching them tumble off their wheel after he'd given them whiskey with an eyedropper. (As I've said before, he himself never drank more than the occasional beer after mowing the lawn on a hot summer day. So how he ever came up with this whiskey-for-the-hamsters antic was beyond all of us.)

The staff, I'm sure, has figured out how to read Dad's cues and needs. Just like I have. When he raises a wooden block with two marbles in it to his mouth, it means he's thirsty. When he scrapes his empty soup bowl with his spoon and doesn't want to give up the bowl, it means he wants more. Specifically, it means he wants more to eat out of the bowl. So you move the food from his plate into his bowl and let him eat it from there. Simple.

You learn how to read your Alzheimer's loved one.

Perhaps I'm just being critical because I'm so aware of Dad's decline. Like the hamsters, he's tumbling cognitively and physically. Cindy confirmed that the UTI has taken Dad to a new normal. And he still does not know me. The name Monica does not spark any memory. Even my teeth can't light the match.

Intellectually, I understand the process. Emotionally, my heart is ripped in two, three—many pieces. I don't know if it can be glued back together. My mind is not communicating with my heart, so it's lost on me. I am a mess.

The dandelion has changed. It's developed into tiny seeds attached to a parachute-like structure. With one pouf, most of the seeds have been sent off to parts unknown. Seeds have floated in all directions.

I can no longer catch them to make a wish.

Chapter Forty-Eight

Rolling Dice

February 25, 2017

We enter the code and come through the Arbor doors. We see Dad sitting at his spot at his table, head sunk down on his chest. Halsey and I sit on either side of him. We are his guardians, his bookends.

The rest of his table is full—which is unusual. The men have gathered, and there is an active conversation going on. Bob on the left; Darrell on the right. Shirley2 sits across from Dad.

Darrell, propped with his head stabilized in his wheelchair, surprises me by speaking. I've never heard him speak before. He has a low, quiet mobster voice. Grainy.

"If you get in at the end, it's sixty-four grand," he says. He nods his head, which is sparsely populated with hair.

Shirley2 has one thing on her mind. "Do you want to go now, honey?" She's clutching at Darrell.

"The last one is your roll," Darrell tells Bob, totally blowing off Shirley2.

"Let's go, hmm?" Shirley2 repeats. She's standing next to his chair, still the annoying gnat.

Darrell looks in Shirley2's direction. "What did you say?" Then back to Bob: "Your roll."

It's becoming obvious that we've dropped into some sort of high-stakes dice-rolling scenario. But there are no dice. No poker chips. No coins. The table is slick and empty. This exchange is purely imaginary, and everyone's on the same page. It's delightful!

"Do you roll dice?" I ask Darrell, wondering if this stems from actual experience or memories.

"I haven't won on anything," Darrell answers.

Shirley2 paws at him. "Where do you want to go, honey? I'll go with you."

I find myself hoping that her real-life husband doesn't happen to come to visit at this moment.

"Four to 3.45 cents," Bob says. "Divided by three." He points to himself, Dad, and Darrell.

Even though Bob is engaged with this play, he's not showing his usual gusto. His mind is just not "as there" as it had once been. Even his appearance seems like a lawn that needs mowing. At least he correctly knows there are three "gamblers" at the table—I'm pretty sure that's one up on Dad.

Stop comparing, I have to remind myself.

Off to the left, Lucy approaches in her walker to join in the mounting excitement. She has short curly hair, a pin-curl look.

(My great-grandma used to have a neighbor lady come and do her hair like this. With her pointer finger against Grandma's scalp, the lady would twirl a small swatch of Grandma's wet hair around her finger, forming a mini donut. The lady would then quickly bobby-pin it tight to the scalp. A whole head of damp donuts.)

Lucy has a wide smile that exposes gums and a big boneyard of teeth. "Don't forget about me!"

"We should have poker chips," I suggest.

"We could have," Bob responds.

Meanwhile, Halsey's rubbing Dad's back.

"You're a sweetheart," Dad says to him.

Bob looks over at them and cocks an eyebrow. Then he says, "I didn't get a chance to get my money." He looks again at Dad and back to Darrell. "Two to one. Times ninety-nine and Chicago. Do you want to take this?"

"OK," Darrell agrees.

"OK," Dad echoes, still with his head down.

"We're up to the third roll," Darrell says.

Shirley2 continues her prattle. "Can we go now? Huh? Can we go now?"

"No," I explain to her, getting caught up in it. "You're on the third roll."

"Oh," she replies. "Can we go on the third roll?"

"Dad, are you in?" I ask, trying to get him involved. I'm enjoying the flurry of this discussion. I wish he were too, but he's not himself, and hasn't been. This UTI hasn't done him any favors.

"Am I in?" Lucy asks.

"Sixty-five grand is not bad," Darrell comments.

"Can we get that much?" Bob questions.

"Of course." Darrell's a high roller.

"It's a critical situation," Bob says.

"Did anybody go out yet?" Darrell checks.

Bob turns to Shirley2. "You don't have anything close to this."

Shirley2 now turns to Darrell. "It's up to you. Are we in?"

"Don't be concerned," Bob continues. "You don't have enough money."

"There's nothing to be concerned about," Shirley2 retorts.

"You'll have to roll again," Darrell says.

Bob nods. "Just watch."

Darrell cups his ear. "Tell me that again?" The overhead vent clicks on, and a few of Darrell's hairs from his comb-over catch a ride.

"This is great!" I pipe in.

Shirley2 frowns. "I don't care for it."

Bob looks at Lucy, who's still standing there with her walker and toothy grin. "How much money do you have?"

"I don't have any money," she replies.

"Do we know what's going on?" Bob asks.

"That makes two of us," Darrell replies.

As excited as I am about the "action" at the table, I'm still concerned about Dad. He's been despondent throughout all this "rolling."

I glance at the time. Dad's been prescribed an antibiotic for the UTI. He needs his first dose at 8:00 p.m.

"If he needs medicine, he should just take it now," I mumble to Halsey.

"That is correct," Bob answers.

Is it just coincidence that Bob made a well-placed comment?

I leave for a few moments. When I return, the two women are gone. Lucy, with her big teeth, and Shirley2, with her constant prattle, have left the room.

Then I see it in Darrell's rheumy blue eyes: a humorous and almost gleeful display of relief. He sees the same look in my eyes. We share a nod of relief.

As we drive home, Halsey comments how Bob seems to be going downhill. I have to agree.

It starts with mild forgetfulness and becomes a slow descent into oblivion. It's pathological warfare. It feels contagious. Do you become what you're surrounded by?

Even I get so involved with the nonsense that I often wonder if I'll be able to make it out intact. I've learned to leave the outside world behind when I enter the code and step into the Arbor. But can I make the transformation back to normal when I enter the code and exit the Arbor? As of now, I feel like I can make the switch between the two worlds. Or am I, too, already descending, and I don't realize it?

Later, I run into Darrell's wife, who has come to the Arbor to visit. I recount the high-roller story to her.

"Your husband is quite the gambler," I say.

A puzzled look gets caught up in her eyebrows. "Darrell never gambled a day in his life."

Chapter Forty-Nine

Showerhead Plaque

March 3, 2017

Dad hasn't been wearing his upper dentures. And only once in a while, the lower dentures sneak in.

Even if the staffers could get those uppers in, I can't imagine the dentures would do any good. Both sets slop around in his mouth.

The lowers have no jawbone to rest on—that bone has been deteriorating for over two years. By now, the lowers are no more than a scatter rug on a freshly waxed kitchen floor. The uppers drop onto his tongue as soon as he opens his mouth.

When eating, a discerning tongue would have a hard time maneuvering food to teeth that won't stand still. Now imagine that with an undiscerning tongue . . .

So, I come with adhesive denture strips this morning. I'm hoping Ben will have luck with them. Dad responds the best to Ben over the other staff members. The lower strips are mint flavored, though, which might be a problem.

I leave the strips in the bathroom, sign in on the visitor log in his room, then eagerly go to see Dad in the Commons.

His wheelchair is positioned away from his table. He's facing the other direction, toward the window, to catch the rays of sun. His eyes are closed. It's 10:20 in the morning.

"Dad," I say, gently touching his shoulder. "Hello! It's Monica."

Nothing.

"You must be tired. Did you have a good night's sleep? A good breakfast?"

Nothing.

"I love you, Dad," as I pat his knee.

His right eyelid lifts a sliver. A window shade ever-so-slightly being peered through. Don't let anyone know that someone's home.

"Hey, Dad. There you are."

The shade drops down.

"You know, Dad—let's pray. I just feel like God wants to be with us at this moment."

And I pray aloud the Lord's Prayer, just as I did over my mom twenty-one years ago as she lay in a coma, breathing her last.

Does Dad hear me? Is he wondering why I'm praying? Does he know how alone I feel? How scared?

I kiss his forehead, then I go home.

March 12, 2017

I'm at a loss.

For days now, I've looked for recognition in his eyes; it's not there. I've looked for him to know my teeth; he doesn't. And yet, dimly, I've seen or imagined flickers that have passed like clouds drifting away. Maybe.

I've kept talking to him—whispering that I love him. What a good man. What a sweet dad. How he could fix anything—broken cars, broken dryers, broken bikes, broken hearts.

I've kept kissing the top of his head, murmuring, "I love you, Dad." I've occasionally gotten a nod.

I've shown him images of Boston terriers on my phone. The pictures alone used to put a spark in him. I've hoped for another nod. For him to say, "Look at that guy." He used to pet the stuffed Boston we gave him. He'd coo to him. Tell him not to "pee-pee" on his lap. That's all changed.

I've brought him fidget toys. He still fiddles with them. He's still a fixer. At least his fingers have memory—even if the connecting dots in his mind are plaqued over.

More and more dots are plaqued over.

I think of our showerhead. The little sprinkling holes are covered with white lime. Occasionally, I scrape off the lime deposits while I'm standing underneath it.

I think of Dad's brain. I want to scrape each of the holes and dots that are closed up. That steal my dad. From me.

My sweet dad has stepped down to this new normal in his journey as an Alzheimer's patient. And even though he doesn't appear to know me, the bottom line is, *I* still know *him*.

I need to help him. To love him. To let him know his family loves him. Forever. As he has so often said—even lately—"I love my family." I need him to feel the love surrounding him, hugging him, keeping him safe and snugged tight in our hearts.

I pray that I can somehow let him know how much he is loved. I pray I can pass the Spirit of God through my touch into his being, so that he can feel the Lord's presence at work within him.

Guard him, O Lord, and let him have peace.

My eyes go to Dad's table as soon as Halsey and I pass through the doors. There he is.

"That's my dad," I say in greeting as we near his table.

Dad nods.

"You love your family, don't you?" I add.

He raises his eyebrows.

◆◆◆

Cindy, our hospice nurse, tells me Dad's receiving MiraLAX and prune juice daily. With Alzheimer's, the body slows down. She's determined that Dad's bowels are backed up.

She tells us not to worry. She'll have him eat lunch. "Since he's eating his napkin," she says, "he must be hungry." And then she'll have him lie down for a rest. She feels that after a nap, the prune juice and MiraLAX will get things moving.

◆◆◆

I start to tell Dad about the duck couple that has been scoping out our yard.

I glanced out our bedroom window earlier this week and saw a drake mallard strutting in front of our landscaping. The male's gleaming green head, gray flanks, and black tail-curl make it the most easily identifiable duck.

He was so out of place in our yard, with continual traffic passing nearby. I welcomed the sight. Then I spotted a hen mallard just off to the side.

As the days passed, the couple scoped out our yard, searching together for the perfect nesting spot. I saw various attempts with mulch mounded around a potential "home." Yet their search continued.

Halsey spotted their final choice behind a yew bush two feet from our entry door. It was secluded and protected from predator activity. Mother hen blended perfectly into the mulch. It was beautiful how she sat still with the mulch around her, her head tucked to the side, and feathers the same color as the mulch.

I did some research on the internet. During the egg-laying phase, a hen will line the nest—a bowl seven to eight inches wide and about one to three inches deep—with nearby grasses, leaves, and twigs. She'll also pull over tall vegetation to conceal herself and her nest. A chameleon—a lovely blend of mulch and feathers. Picture perfect.

The research also said that a hen will lay her eggs at one-to-two-day intervals. The normal clutch is about twelve eggs. During the days she lays her eggs, she'll leave the nest and join the drake to forage for food. After each egg is added, she'll cover the clutch to protect it from predators.

So far, this clutch has seven eggs. That would mean a possible five more to go.

According to the research, once the last egg is laid, a female will start to incubate. She'll sit very tightly, blending into the background. Apart from short breaks to feed and stretch her legs, she will rarely leave the nest. About twenty-eight days later, the eggs will hatch together. This will take about twenty-four hours.

As I share all this with Dad, I realize it's more information than he can probably absorb. It's my tendency to rattle off what I learn, so as to reinforce it into my own memory bank. It doesn't always stick, otherwise.

"Dad, isn't it cool that we have a nest with duck eggs in it? Right as we open our door?" I ask, trying to highlight the basics.

Dad hasn't responded to my story in any manner at all. Instead, he cuts off a bite-size piece from his brownie. But rather than forking that piece, he spears the larger, remaining portion and brings it to his mouth, leaving the smaller morsel on the plate.

Halsey gives Dad a rub.

Dad purrs.

Chapter Fifty

I'm Just a Little Boy Yet

March 14, 2017

I've gone from winks and smiles and "That's my girl" to being invisible.

As Dad picks at his fruit from breakfast, I glance around at the other residents. Gladys is sharing the table with Dad. She's the one who has an extremely difficult time eating, yet she's very proud and turns down my offer to help.

She keeps her head lowered six inches from her bowl. Yet each forkful takes a solid two minutes to make it from the bowl to her mouth.

With a shaking hand, she makes repeated attempts at stabbing a piece of fruit. Eventually she spears a corner of a melon, then tries to balance and guide it to her opened mouth. I find myself cheering when it doesn't slip off the tine and back into the bowl.

She's a baby bird with her beak ready and her head bobbing. When the fruit finally touches her mouth, she slowly maneuvers it past stretched lips and shakily tries to push it in. It's painful to watch.

At least Dad's still able to eat, although his attempts are slowly coming to a halt as well.

I really shouldn't compare them, though. The residents here—they're all so different in their journey through dementia and Alzheimer's.

Mary—the tall, thin resident—has drawn a Frida Kahlo unibrow over her eyes with a dark eyebrow liner. She comes down the hall with her walker. Her head is sunken, her shoulders heavy with her sadness. She spots a staff worker and ashamedly admits to spilling some water in her room.

"Come, Mary," the staffer says kindly. "Let's go take care of it."

Mary quivers some inaudible words. I can hear her voice break, and I can see the anxiety trail of tears.

I look back at Dad. He has picked up Halsey's keys and is trying to eat one.

Someone once told me the difference between dementia and Alzheimer's: with dementia, you forget where you put your keys; with Alzheimer's, you forget what keys are for. I guess this is what they meant.

I'm surprised to see Dad's lower dentures in today—but they slide around in his mouth. His uppers aren't in. I calmly snake the keys away from him. I don't want him to injure his upper gum tissue.

"I'm just a little boy yet," he simpers.

Darn. He understands that I just took something away from him.

I lovingly pat his hand and smile. "I love you, Dad." I know I can't change a thing, but maybe I can bring calm to his storm.

Meanwhile Bob, our Iowa Hawkeyes fan, is resisting a staff worker's attempts at keeping him stationary at the table.

"Bob, stay here. We're going to have lunch soon."

Bob ignores her. A lumbering man, he's hard to restrain. He shakes her off and makes his way out of his chair and out of her grasp. His momentum takes him past our table.

As he passes me, he turns his head in my direction with a defiant grin. He escaped.

I smile back at him.

As he ambles toward his room, I see Barbara with her long white braid coming down the hallway. It's nearing lunchtime. She knows. Most residents follow their inner clock. (Except Bob, who wants to be in his room now. He's the one duck who wanders out of line just as you have the rest of them all gathered.)

As Barbara wheels her chair, she tries to pass through the narrow opening between the piano and a column. She gets wedged.

Halsey and I share a look and get up to leave. Dad glances up at us. I kiss the top of his head.

Even when everything else slips away, including who we are, I think Dad still senses we wear the white hats.

Chapter Fifty-One

The Rest of the Story

March 15, 2017

Dad gums his Fig Newton. He doesn't wear his teeth at all anymore. Oreos are out of the question. There's no point in fighting the battle of trying to convince him he doesn't have his teeth in. And he won't open his mouth to help in the endeavor.

As he works on his Fig Newton and periodically inspects it, I let my eyes see his face through an artist's lens.

There is more to his wrinkled, craggy face. A sense of mirth that started many years before. Each wrinkle is like a ring in a felled tree. Representing his age. His eyes are fogged behind his glasses—the fog that appears over our eyes, over our minds, as we age. His mouth is slack. So he doesn't have his dentures in. No matter. His lips still carry a slight smile—maybe at a passing thought—as he gums his Fig Newton.

He has weathered the years and wears his age with a sense of calm. No longer uptight. He might not know who he is, but he is still here. Instead of a participant, he has become an observer.

He is still Dad.

I scratch his shoulder blade.

He leans into it. "That feels so good."

March 17, 2017

"You are a good-looking, sweet-looking thing," he greets me today.

I find it so hard to get a handle on my emotions. One day, he doesn't know me; the next day, it seems like maybe he does.

Maybe there's no sense in being crushed when he doesn't know me, because relief may come in the next day or two. Maybe everything is fluid.

Just ride with it.

◆ ◆ ◆

"Haven't seen *you* in a long time," Sue, another resident, says to me.

"Whose fault is that?" Darrell answers.

March 19, 2017

Dad is more with us today. He seems happier. He still wrestles with his Alzheimer's, though.

"I can't find out how or why," he says.

I let him know we're on the same page. "We can't either, Dad," I reassure.

Then he swings both arms out to hug me. "Oh, I love you!" he exclaims.

This day is like a homecoming! I want to get up and dance my way around the Commons. Where's the drumroll?

Suddenly, Dad spots Halsey.

"Holy smokes!"

◆◆◆

"God, you have a pretty face," he says to me. "You're looking great."

He takes a sip of coffee. "God, I love it!"

The simple pleasures.

March 23, 2017

It's Thursday, and the residents are playing balloon volleyball in the Commons. They sit in chairs or their wheelchairs in a circle around Laura, who monitors the balloon.

I see Dad in the circle. Slumped in his wheelchair. But at least he's in the circle with the others.

We hang back, just observing.

The first volley is to him. The balloon floats down to him. He thinks it's a gift. He holds it, resting his head on it. (When the volley came to him a couple of weeks ago, he promptly put his head on it and fell asleep. A balloon pillow.) He's soon convinced to give up the balloon and send it across the circle.

Laura volleys the balloon over his way frequently. I'm surprised to see a spark of spirit. Good to see some life.

Meanwhile, I sidle over to tall, thin Mary, who's standing outside the perimeter of the circle.

"Hey, Mary, how are you?"

I'm rewarded with a huge smile. She reaches to give me a hug from her walker, and I can feel her shoulder blades through her sweater.

She's lost some weight. She's a rack of bones, almost as thin as Dad. There's not much to her. Her face is even gaunter than it was a couple of weeks ago. It makes her teeth a prominent feature—coupled with her bold Frida eyebrow.

I've become her best friend. She starts sharing with me how her daughters came to visit, along with her sister, who's eleven months older than her.

"How many kids do you have, Mary?"

I remember seeing some of her family that day they had their "conference." But of course I didn't look long enough to get a good count.

"Seven," Mary replies.

She looks for a reaction. I give her one.

"I knew I'd get that look on your face when I told you! Five girls and three boys. Oh. That's eight."

She wants to get this right, so I ask another way. "How many boys do you have?"

"Two or three."

I prompt her to name the kids, starting with the firstborn, but we're not going to solve this one today.

She sighs. "I am tired out, though."

"Oh, I thought you'd like to play some balloon volleyball with me."

"Are you playing? If you're playing, I'll play."

"Sure. C'mon with me."

We make our way to the circle. I position a chair next to Dad for me, then position an empty chair next to it for Mary.

Shirley2 wants Mary to sit in the chair next to her.

"No. I'm sitting by *her*." Mary nods in my direction.

I pat the chair next to me and have my hand ready to assist as she unsteadily plops down, casting her walker aside.

The game goes well. Laura fends the balloons that don't make the distance across the circle. It's great to see movement and enthusiasm with this group. Some days, they're just fixtures in the dining room with glazed eyes as they sip their coffee or nod off.

Suddenly, Mary pushes her chair back. "I've had enough now."

Then she thinks better.

"Not of *you*," she reassures me.

She gives me another hug.

♦ ♦ ♦

We head back to the table after our balloon fun.

"I like my family," Dad says. "You are a Monica. That's my girl." He looks at me as though I hung the moon.

God has answered my prayer. Dad is back!

♦ ♦ ♦

Shirley (the original, that is) is sitting at our table. Laura passes by and teases her.

"Shirley has a lot of boyfriends."

Shirley has a comeback ready: "If one doesn't work, I'll try another one."

Loud laughter.

Dad puts his finger to his lips. "Shhhh."

Shirley points a finger at me. "*She* has a lot of boyfriends." She then sneaks a peek at Halsey, to catch his reaction. "I like to see a good fight. I never have a chance to have one of my own."

Shirley. Some things never change.

♦ ♦ ♦

"My mother arranged the marriage," Shirley comments. "'This is what you get,' my mom said to me."

And that was that. Shirley says she was twenty years old at the time.

So, this is Shirley's story. This is why she's so infatuated with boyfriend-girlfriend relationships. She probably never dated.

Shirley looks around. "This is a crooked crowd."

♦ ♦ ♦

Steve, the aeronautical engineer, pauses at our table.

Out of curiosity, and because he looks quite young compared to the other residents, I ask, "How old are you, Steve?"

"At what point?" he asks back.

Well, hmm. Good question!

Steve continues on with his pacing. "Where's my wife? I'm worried."

I try to reassure him. "Worry doesn't help. Just have patience."

Pouf ♦ 296

"How much patience do you get?"

I love how his mind works!

Ben joins our conversation. "Do you live north or south of Minneapolis?" he asks Steve.

And Steve—bless him—says, "Depends what direction you're going."

March 30, 2017

I've been seeing a lot of this Steve lately.

"How's it going, Steve?" I ask.

"Finer than frog hair."

◆ ◆ ◆

"At least when I call you 'Dad' today, you look at me," I tell him happily.

I take the opportunity to say this because I'm still so aware of that window of time when he didn't recognize me.

"That's right," he says.

With a wink.

◆ ◆ ◆

I decide to continue with my story of the duck couple.

I tell Dad how I opened our door that morning and was just sickened to spot the remains of a greenish-beige egg on our walkway. Bright yellow-orange yolk spilled from the pecked shell.

I forced myself to glance over at the nest, praying that Mama Duck was still there, protecting the others. The remaining six eggs were recklessly tossed aside, each pecked through with the yolks sucked out.

Mama Duck was nowhere to be found.

Dad doesn't move a muscle but appears to be listening. So I continue.

From my research, I tell him it took her at least seven days to lay these eggs—with an egg a day. She was still in the laying phase, so she needed to leave the nest to forage and to briefly visit with her mate. She left her nest either late last night or very early this morning.

Whenever it happened, it was the wrong time. Preying eyes observed her march and took advantage of her departure.

"Dad, I'm just so sad that the duck lost her eggs to that damn crow."

Dad cocks his head a bit.

A comfortable silence settles in. I decide not to tell Dad the rest of the story.

I don't tell him how I moped around the kitchen after seeing the destruction and how Halsey hugged my tears before looking out the screen door himself.

"That goddamn crow is still out there," Halsey said, spotting his perch. "He's here to finish the business. That's it. I'm getting the gun."

As he shuffled to get the BB gun, the crow retreated.

As I went to put my coffee cup in the sink ten minutes later, I glanced out the window. It was heartbreaking. Mama Duck had returned. I cringed, anticipating her soon-to-come reaction.

She inched her way toward the nest, neck outstretched, eyes targeted. She knew. She saw the devastation of the lone egg on the walkway—a telltale sign of more devastation to come. She froze and stretched her neck forward even more, telescoping in all the unbelievable.

I witnessed the entire saga.

To add insult to injury, that damn crow, the size of a football, laughed overhead on a tree branch. Taunted her as she mourned. Ridiculed her.

She mustered up the strength to waddle over to what remained of the other eggs. She spent a solid ten minutes looking over the tragedy.

All the while, that crow cawed in delight.

Mama Duck's body language told me her heart was ravaged. She slowly retreated about three feet, then paused one last time. With a shake of her tail feathers, she gathered herself and began her crestfallen return to her mate, who was no doubt looking forward to rejoining a flock of males.

Tigger and Puff were at the screen door, watching this all play out too. Even though they're cats, their posture told me they understood that they had just witnessed something terribly sad.

I went outside to clean up the pillage. As I picked up the broken shells and yolk that spilled on the mulch, I found a lone egg in the nest. It was still warm.

Would Mama Duck come back? Did she notice one egg was still there?

Maybe she was coming back to lay more eggs. Or would she now nest elsewhere?

I slumped back into the house and peered through the screen door. Watching. Waiting.

A while later, she returned to reassess the damage and weigh her options.

I tried to reassure her with my whispered words through the screen door. "I know. I know. It's just terrible."

I could see she wasn't comforted by my words.

When I looked out again, she was gone. Not on the driveway. Not on her nest.

An hour later, I got in the car to head for an appointment. She was back again.

It was a different stage of grief now. This was a tirade.

She paced on the driveway in front of the second garage door. As I backed the car out of the first garage door, she started zigzagging in front of me. Her demeanor had changed. She was raging in grief and didn't know which way to turn.

"It wasn't *me*," I pleaded to her from my car seat.

When I returned from my appointment, she was gone. This time for good.

Sitting here now in silence with Dad, I'm sad but also hopeful. I read that when a nest gets destroyed, mallard hens usually start over, typically within a week.

Let's hope that's the case.

Chapter Fifty-Two

The Last Few Days

April 5, 2017

Last week, Cindy told me that Dad is declining with his Alzheimer's. Of course, we've been seeing a lot of decline over the last three and a half years. But this is different. Now he's not eating. Doesn't know anything.

A few days ago, Trent and Sterling came to visit Dad. Dad petted Sterling's head and said, "You've got nice beautiful eyes." Pet, pet. He said it again, "You've got nice beautiful eyes. Poopie, poopie, poop. Poop."

Today I arrive at the Arbor alone. I didn't even tell Halsey I was going. It just felt like it needed to be a private moment.

Cindy greets me outside Dad's room. "Be ready," she says. "Don't panic. He's OK for a month or two. But if he doesn't start eating, we may lose him."

He's nearing the end.

"What are the signs?" I ask.

"He's using no energy," she says. "The desires for everything go down. He wants nothing. He's half in heaven, half on earth."

I slip in to see Dad. His body is mere twigs under the covers. His head is turned, and his small frame is listing away from me.

"Dad?" I whisper. "It's me, Monica. How *are* you?"

The irony hits me. *How do I think he is? He's slipping away from me.*

I sit by his side for four hours. Feeling his silence like a draft. Caressing his face. Telling him what I think I'd like to hear if I were in his place.

"I love you. Forever. And ever. Thank you, Dad. You've been the best dad in the whole world." I coo the words as I stroke his face and around his chin. Crying silently.

I maneuver myself over the bedrail and make myself as skinny as possible so I can lie at his side and cradle him gently. I don't want to break him.

After a while, I move back to a chair. His wheelchair. I feel a connection by sitting in *his* chair.

I invite him to try some baby food in a squeezable pouch, an idea a friend recently suggested when I told her Dad wasn't eating.

"Just a pinch, Dad. For me?" I squeeze a small strip of mango banana puree into his mouth.

It just sits there on his dry tongue. He has no interest. None. In seconds, it trails out of the corner of his mouth and down his chin.

He is not starving, but he will not be eating. Again. Ever.

He is dying. His body knows it; his daughter does not. Or doesn't want to. Another cause for tears. Where are they coming from? My mind knows what's happening. My heart refuses to get on board.

There's a low light in the room. Unobtrusive. A chapel feel. Just a natural glow coming in through his shuttered windows. Some happiness on the other side of the window.

Someone rustles behind me, entering the room. It's Jasmine, the hospice music therapist. She has her guitar slung over her shoulder by a strap. We share a sad smile.

"Your dad's been reacting to the music," she says gently. "He still hears."

I swipe at the tears that insist on coursing down my cheeks.

"Why don't I just strum some chords and sing randomly for him. You can continue to touch his face. They're most sensitive by their temples and around their mouth."

I move my light caresses to those areas.

She starts plucking her guitar strings. Random chords that produce a melancholic, tranquil background. I just want to dissolve forever into the softness of it.

Quietly, she sings, "Your daughter's here. Your daughter is touching you. She loves you."

I feel sobs creeping up from deep within, but I shove them back. Forget about me and my sadness. I need to be here for Dad. Give him all that I have.

I'm eventually able to become one with the music and with Dad. My fingers trace his face. I study his firm countenance and engrave it in my memory.

Honor thy father and mother.

Jasmine continues singing.

An hour goes by in a minute. She says she'll come again tomorrow. I latch on to this.

I will come again.

April 6, 2017

I have Bible study from 10:00 to 11:15. The music therapist will sing again for Dad at noon. Do I dare go to Bible study with Decon Ray? Maybe I should go directly to be with Dad?

I call hospice before my study, and Cindy reassures me.

"Monica, your dad, as you know, is displaying a few signs of dying, but there are a few more signs that haven't shown up yet. You go to your Bible study."

So, I do. I'm half-attentive during the study—looking forward to later, when I will spend that special hour again in the quiet of Dad's room.

Halsey wants to be a part of it as well. We get there in tandem with Jasmine.

Dad is again on his back in his hospital bed, which has been lifted to a slight incline to raise his head. He continues with the death rattle, a breathing that can continue for hours and often means that death is near. Hospice doesn't like it when I refer to it as the death rattle. I didn't know there was anything else to call it.

Jasmine sets up and starts strumming soft chords, as she did yesterday. She asks for suggestions. I suggest she start with "Beer Barrel Polka." From there, she slides into another polka.

I think Dad might be smiling. There's a glint of happiness around his mouth.

Then I suggest "Du, Du Liegst Mir Im Herzen." She rolls right into it and sings in German.

Dad used to play it on his accordion. I can see the memories fleet across his face. We're reliving a different, younger, and happier time.

"How about Patti Page's 'How Much Is That Doggie in the Window?'" I ask.

She breaks into song.

I point—Dad's toes are tapping under his blanket. Slowly, yet with a flourish, he pulls his right arm out from under the covers. He's conducting! All with a slight, gaping, toothless grin.

I see life! I just want to bask in it.

We continue singing for another forty-five minutes. Jasmine winds down with "God Bless America." I'm sad to hear it end.

We agree to meet again after the weekend. Monday at noon. Little mini concerts just for Dad.

Jasmine leaves.

Halsey and I stay at Dad's side. After a bit, he starts showing some restlessness and anxiety.

A staff member comes in to give him a dissolvable morphine tablet. She then dips a mouth swab in some water and moistens his lips. He half-heartedly sucks some of the moisture out. She dips again. One more time he sucks. She pats him on the shoulder.

"Rest, Jerome," she says as she leaves the room. A few moments pass, but we find he's not resting; he's in a fit of anxiety.

"Halsey," I say, "go find Cindy. Quick."

As he gets up and hurries out the door, I turn now to Dad.

"Dad, Dad—it's OK. We're getting help."

He's gasping. I try to maneuver him into more of a sitting position. But eighty pounds is still eighty pounds. It's more than I can handle alone.

I vault the bedrail. I'm on the bed, straddling his chest and lifting under his armpits, pulling upward from the pillow so he can catch his breath. I'm fully aware of the pain he has in his hip.

"I'm trying, Dad. We're getting help. I don't want to hurt you."

I feel frantic inside. And helpless.

"Help. Me," he says.

Two words.

I would do anything for my dad. You name it. But I am simply incapable of fulfilling this one request of his.

"Dad, I'm here. I'll help you," I say, hoping my reassurances still count for something. I pull some more to elevate him while his breathing rattles on.

Finally, *finally*, Cindy arrives. She motions for someone to close the door for privacy and takes a chair on the right of Dad. Halsey and I pull up two chairs to the left of Dad's bed.

"Jerome, we're going to help you," Cindy tells him. "I'm giving you a little more medication."

She then hoists him up in a more upright sitting position and takes his hand in hers. Dad is fixated on the ceiling line, and his rattle continues.

It is then that I know. He does have one foot in heaven and one foot at my side. He needs my help to cross over. This is what he meant. *Help. Me.*

This I can do.

Remembering Jasmine's instructions, I lightly stroke his temple as I chant in his ear, lightly, softly.

"Dad, I love you. Forever and ever. I will always love you. Always."

He's staring off.

"Dad, do you see Mom? Is she beautiful? Is she smiling? She's been waiting for you. Isn't she beautiful, Dad?"

Suddenly, I actually *see* my mom. She's wearing a cheerful dress with a small flower print. She's in her late thirties. She's beckoning to Dad. Not forcefully, but in a reassuring, joyful gesture.

There's a slight whisper of a breeze. I see my brother Stevie in my peripheral, although not as clearly. I sense Grandpa and Grandma—Dad's parents—to Stevie's right.

"Dad, Stevie's with her. Do you see him? He's so happy to see you! He hasn't seen you for so long. He's smiling too. They've missed you so much. And there's Grandma and Grandpa."

Dad leans forward toward them. Then pauses. Hesitates.

"Dad, I'll always be here for you. Always. I love you forever and ever. Forever. See Mom's smile? She's so beautiful. She's missed you. And Jesus will be there to greet you."

Moments tick by with my reassurances of love. That Jesus is waiting.

Radiance comes from Dad's face.

Slowly, but ever so surely, he slips forward in a diaphanous haze, a wisp, into the lighted pathway. The ceiling line has disappeared.

I see him carried up and away. And I know in my heart that I granted his request. I helped him by guiding him on the journey to his eternal home. What a blessing—to know his journey will be to a more beautiful place.

He has left his human shell behind on the hospital bed, like discarded clothing. That is all I see. A shell. His beautiful essence has taken leave of this world, and he is with our Maker. The Creator of it all.

Cindy looks at her watch. It is confirmed. It is done. She gently lays him back down on the bed, his color already leaving his beautiful face, disappearing from the top of his head and draining downward. A mercurial thermometer.

I kiss him one more time on the top of his now pale, waxy, sweet head.

"I love you, Dad. Forever."

◆ ◆ ◆

Halsey and I leave Room 131—Dad's room. I collapse against him. Just for a minute or two—enough time to gather strength to make calls.

I leave a message for my brother to please call me. I reach both my sons. They're on their way with their families. I'm told by the staff there will be a

Procession of Honor as soon as we have all arrived. The staff needs to know when to call the funeral home. I ask for two hours.

Within a couple of hours, both of my sons' families have arrived. I have not heard back from Greg.

The rest of us gather at the far end of the hallway, down from Dad's room. A circle of the remaining ten of us. The same ten that gathered around Dad each Christmas Eve throughout the years. On each grandchild's and great-grandchild's birthday. On our annual boat cruise with brunch on Lake Minnetonka. On Thanksgiving. For holiday-dining gatherings. Any time we could adjust calendars.

Only, this time we are missing one important person. The eleventh of our circle. The absence is glaring. He lies in room 131 down the hall, alone.

We are a solemn group.

Cindy beckons to us from the far end of the hallway, outside Dad's door. Our family moves as one.

"Come and see how nice I have your dad dressed," she says. "I even put his glasses on."

We trail into his room. The great-grandkids avert their eyes as they search for a place to sit. A couple of them are experiencing their first exposure to death. They're uncomfortable, and they leave the room after a few moments—long, awkward moments for them.

Time is suspended as the rest of us stay gathered in the room. One by one, staff members respectfully slip into the tiny quarters to rub shoulders with our family, express their condolences, and grow our circle of support. "Sweet man" resonates as the common attribute.

Yes. Sweet man. My sweet dad.

Eventually, they drape the white pall over his body and wheel the bed into the front lobby, while we process behind it. I see the hearse waiting outside the lobby doors. I look away. I refuse to connect it with Dad at this moment.

One step at a time. Baby steps.

Just then, three outsiders awkwardly enter through the lobby door. They're embarrassed to be interrupting our cocooned ordeal. I find myself feeling sad for them. They reverently step to the side, their chatter replaced by respectful silence.

Staff members utter more comments about how we always had the largest table at holiday-dining events—the largest table of support for a resident.

Dad had his family. His anchor to the world.

Chaplain Jen lovingly enfolds her parting words of prayer around us.

It feels surreal that Dad has just gone, yet it doesn't. We've been losing him bit by little bit since the start of this horrible disease. The dandelion, once vibrant, was disappearing as we watched. One pouf at a time.

Then one final pouf! And gone.

Chapter Fifty-Three

They Are All Gone

To the untrained ear, the words in the Arbor are a cacophonic flurry of chatter. But to those of us who are regular visitors, the words are music. Each resident adds their unique notes, composed of the music in their own mind. Each note is more precious than the note that came before.

Those notes become a song, and the song becomes a symphony. Some days, the room swells with the harmony of it.

My dad was first chair. His untethered words were the sweetest music my ears had ever heard, each nonsensical word an instrumental note lilting on a scale.

The other residents filled out the rest of the orchestra.

But now he's gone.

They are all gone. It's possible that one or two might have been moved to another facility. More likely not, though. Odds are, they are all *gone*.

Irene, with her gray hair scraped back into a ponytail. Irene, who would click her teeth rapidly at you, like a gopher, if you were to greet her by name.

Irene is gone.

Jean, who proudly splayed the fingers of her right hand to show you her newly polished nails . . . while keeping her left hand under the table, because those were the nails she nibbled down to nubs. Her "everyday hand."

Jean is gone.

Bob, the industrial tech teacher and artist who always wore the yellow Iowa Hawkeyes sweatshirt. Bob, who would sit next to Dad to play dominoes and could make the right moves while Dad could only fiddle the pieces and trace the dots.

Bob is gone.

Ann, who was one of Hopkins's first Raspberry Queens. Ann, with her small back hump, who felt pursued by a drunken father who had long ago left this world.

Ann is gone.

Charlie, who served his country for "three years, nine months, three days." Charlie, who was very serious and reserved, and who was offended when I kiddingly suggested he was flirting with me—"I don't do that."

Charlie is gone.

Joyce, who toted a basket in front of her walker, just like how we used to have metal baskets in front of our bicycles to lug our books to school and back. Joyce, whose basket held her most prized postcards and tchotchkes. Joyce, who could cut you down at the knees without a second thought.

Joyce is gone.

Janet, who would be the first to sashay over to see us as soon as we entered the room. Janet, who shared secrets with me, and who would laugh so hard with me that the tears would stream down our faces. Janet, who told me she loved me.

Janet is gone.

Paul's wife, Helen, whom I never heard utter a word. Paul would come every day and lovingly spoon-feed his wife and wipe the corners of her mouth.

Paul's wife is gone.

Ted, the musician who would rap rhythms on tabletops. Ted, who would stare off in space with his poindexter glasses perched cockeyed on his face and smile to himself at a private memory.

Ted is gone.

Ruth from Renville, whose son would periodically bring her a vanilla milkshake. Ruth, who was brought up on a farm and would come alive when the conversation turned to farm stories.

Ruth is gone.

Lorraine, who would wander from table to table, clutching her baby doll to her bosom, cooing words of comfort to it. Lorraine, who bore the ridicule of many of the other residents, with harsh words unveiling the fact that her baby was not real. Lorraine, who held on tight to Dad's hands and wouldn't let go.

Lorraine is gone.

The woman in the corner, whose name I didn't even know. The woman who could be heard every time we visited with her cries of "Help! Help!"

She is gone.

Gwen, the former elementary school teacher, who would rally the residents at the sing-alongs. Gwen, who loved Halsey's singing voice and chastised him for not being a member of our church choir—"Shame on you."

Gwen is gone.

Dode. Little Dode, who knew the words to every childhood song from back in the day. You'd start singing "Daisy, Daisy . . ." and Dode would carry it to the end with you. Every single verse. Dode, who two weeks ago had a huge birthday party with over twenty people. Cupcakes, sweets, and birthday wishes.

Dode is gone.

Lorraine2, the gynecologist who beat up men with her eyes. Lorraine2, who would stab you with her walker if you happened to be male and happened to pass in front of her.

Lorraine2 is gone.

They have all, one by one, picked up their instruments and taken their music to the Master Composer. Snatches of their music still linger with me, though. They occasionally trill through my mind.

And I know that new musicians will take their places within the symphony, and different music will be heard. The first chair will be filled by a member of another family.

But for me, there will never be another first chair who can capture every single song note perfect.

Chapter Fifty-Four

One Month Later

May 6, 2017

I'm back at the memory care unit. I pause in front of the door. After taking a deep breath, I gather myself. I reread the poem. The one posted to the right of the closed door.

Do Not Ask Me to Remember

Do not ask me to remember,
Don't try to make me understand,
Let me rest and know you're with me,
Kiss my cheek and hold my hand.
I'm confused beyond your concept,
I am sad and sick and lost.
All I know is that I need you
To be with me at all cost.
Do not lose your patience with me,
Do not scold or curse or cry.
I can't help the way I'm acting,
Can't be different though I try.
Just remember that I need you,
That the best of me is gone,
Please don't fail to stand beside me,
Love me 'til my life is done.
—Owen Darnell

61982*
Bzzzzzzzz.
Click.

I drag myself to make it through the doors. It's hard to believe that I looked forward to these visits twice a week for over three years. But things are different now.

Laura, the recreation coordinator, meets me with a face questioning my own. It's been a month, but the pain is still etched on my face. She gives me a hug.

Steve, the aeronautical engineer, is still pacing.

Darrell is alone in his wheelchair.

"Darrell. How are you?" I greet him.

"Tired," in his hushed gangster voice. Raspy.

"Do you remember me?" I ask.

He nods. "What are you doing here?"

"Oh, I just thought I'd come by to say hi to my favorite people."

"Am I one of those?" he hungrily asks.

◆ ◆ ◆

It's about the people.

I see Mom raise her eyebrows in affirmation, just as she did twenty-one years ago from her hospital bed.

It's about the people.

Epilogue

APOE e4 Positive

It made sense to find out about my *APOE* status. The *APOE* gene can provide insight about the risk of developing late-onset Alzheimer's. I wanted to get tested so I could use the knowledge to lower my Alzheimer's risk. It involved a simple blood test of apoE protein isoforms. I got it done when I had my blood cholesterol checked.

I made a follow-up appointment to learn the results. Was I *APOE* e4 positive? The e4 isoform is associated with a higher risk of Alzheimer's.

"Well," my doctor responded, "you can't put too much stock in these tests. Just keep up what you're doing. Lots of exercise. Exercise your mind."

Hmm. Pretty much a "yes." Without saying it.

To the internet I went to learn more. Being *APOE* e4 positive doesn't mean you'll develop Alzheimer's. It just means you have an increased risk of developing it. And even then, there are still many ways to mitigate that risk: taking folic acid, avoiding head injuries, limiting saturated fats, eating lots of antioxidants, exercising regularly, and building "cognitive reserve" through mental, physical, and social activity.

"Why would you want to know this?" I was asked after sharing the results.

For some people, such knowledge might promote anxiety. Not so for me. I prefer to armor myself and be proactive. Not obsessively, but enough that I feel like I'm taking charge—even a little bit—of my situation.

Because I am *APOE* e4 positive, and because of what that could mean, there's a continual stream of truths and advice I'd like to pass on to Chad and Trent—before "what's up here doesn't come down, so it can come out."

♦ Make God number one. He is the Creator of it all.

♦ After God, value your family above all else. Nurture the relationship you have with your wife and children, loving each of them with all that you have and are.

- Speak kindly to the family in which you grew up. They will always be your history. You cannot erase the branch you sprouted from. Think kindly of them. Forgive them if necessary. And keep a kind pocket in your heart for them. Always.

- Be sure to water and feed your friendships. You will chance upon people, and you'll have no reason to think they'll be part of your life. But then suddenly they will be. Cherish them. Let them know how valued they are.

- Each day, take a moment to breathe deeply. Walk outside. Disappear from the drama of your day, the senses that have been overstimulated. Breathe. Calm your energies. *Just disappear.*

- Savor the small moments. The grateful look of the homeless man at the end of the Penn exit, to whom you opened your window and passed a bill. Savor his toothless grin and his gray hair fringed over the top of his ears under his ball cap. Hold his smile close to your heart.

- "It's about the people."

- And remember, I love you more!

Acknowledgments

Pouf is not only my book. It belongs to all those who helped me with their encouragement, special skills, and wisdom.

To begin with, all thanks belong to God, who gave me the Assignment. And nudged me, in a very stern way, more than once, to get on with it. All glory goes to Him!

My appreciation and my unending love goes to my husband, Jerry Hall—Halsey. He is my partner and closest friend. He walked the journey with me as we shared my dad's final years at the memory care unit. Every visit, every laugh, every fear, and every tear—Halsey was there. This story wouldn't be without him.

My heartfelt appreciation to my sons, Chad and Trent Kannenberg, and their families for their support and tolerance as I dedicated time to walk this journey with my dad.

To Trent, for the never-ending love you shared with your grandpa.

Thank you to my beta readers, who read *Pouf* in the rough and raw yet still encouraged me to continue: Ann Kalin, Lauren Abel, Ann Aubitz, Trent Kannenberg, Gracie Rayburn, Lefty and Connie McIntyre, and Erin Bernardo. Thank you for believing in me.

My most sincere admiration and appreciation to my editor, Angie Wiechmann, for believing I was better than I am and for joining me in my sometimes-crazy thoughts. You pluck the words right out of my mind. I love you! Thank you for loving me.

To Taylor Blumer, my proofreader. Your attention to detail is amazing! Thank you.

To Ann Aubitz, my publisher, who gave me the necessary shots in the arm to stay on target and who captured my vision to a T for my website and book cover. You nailed it!

To all my friends and supporters who expressed an interest in seeing this book in its published form—thank you! Your interest encouraged me to keep on keeping on.

About the Author

Monica Vierling Hall was born in Shakopee, Minnesota, where she still lives. She has raised two faith-filled and well-accomplished sons. They have passed their faith on to their own families.

Monica wrote *Pouf* as part of her commitment to helping others maintain and enjoy their relationships with loved ones suffering from Alzheimer's and dementia. She hopes families can see that these loved ones are just on a different walk in their lives and that there is incomparable beauty, joy, and laughter found while sharing this walk with them.

This is her first book.

CPSIA information can be obtained
at www.ICGtesting.com
Printed in the USA
LVHW022343030820
662342LV00004B/1467